INSIDE THE
WRITER'S MIND

INSIDE THE WRITER'S MIND

Writing Narrative Journalism

STEPHEN G. BLOOM

Author of **POSTVILLE** *A Clash of Cultures in Heartland America*

Iowa State Press
A Blackwell Publishing Company

Stephen G. Bloom is associate professor and head of the Master's Professional Program at the University of Iowa School of Journalism and Mass Communication. He has been a staff writer for the *Los Angeles Times, The Dallas Morning News,* the *San Jose Mercury News, The Sacramento Bee,* and the *Latin America Daily Post.* He also is a frequent contributor to Salon.com, as well as other on-line magazines. Bloom is the author of the nonfiction book, *Postville: A Clash of Cultures in Heartland America.* (Harcourt, 2000).

©2002 Iowa State Press
A Blackwell Publishing Company
All rights reserved

Iowa State Press
2121 State Avenue, Ames, Iowa 50014

Orders: 1-800-862-6657
Office: 1-515-292-0140
Fax: 1-515-292-3348
Web site: www.iowastatepress.com

Authorization to photocopy items for internal or personal use, or the internal or personal use of specific clients, is granted by Iowa State Press, provided that the base fee of $.10 per copy is paid directly to the Copyright Clearance Center, 222 Rosewood Drive, Danvers, MA 01923. For those organizations that have been granted a photocopy license by CCC, a separate system of payments has been arranged. The fee code for users of the Transactional Reporting Service is 0-8138-1779-X/2002 $.10.

♾ Printed on acid-free paper in the United States of America

Library of Congress Cataloging-in-Publication Data

Bloom, Stephen G.
Inside the writer's mind: Writing narrative journalism / Stephen G. Bloom.—
1st ed.
        p. cm.
ISBN 0-8138-1779-X (alk. paper)
1. Reporters and reporting. 2. Journalism—Authorship. I. Title.
PN4781 .B54 2002
070.4'3—dc21
            2002004212

The last digit is the print number: 9 8 7 6 5 4 3 2 1

CONTENTS

ACKNOWLEDGMENTS

This book is dedicated to Iris and Mikey, who lived through many of these stories, and to Nancy Kruh, my editor at *The Dallas Morning News* who taught me the power of (edited) words. My thanks also go to Kate Corcoran, my colleague at The University of Iowa School of Journalism and Mass Communication, who typed the stories reprinted in this collection, as well as copyedited the new text. Finally, I wish to thank the newspapers, magazines and Internet sites where these articles originally appeared for allowing Iowa State Press to reprint them in book format. Each story is published as it was originally printed, with only stylistic inconsistencies changed and typographic errors corrected.

INTRODUCTION

What exactly is this book in your hands? How is *Inside the Writer's Mind: Writing Narrative Journalism* different from other journalism anthologies? And the most important question: How might this book make you a better writer?

The fact is, this book might not make your writing sing. It might not improve your reporting skills. It might not move you further toward a career as a top-notch journalist or nonfiction writer. *Inside the Writer's Mind: Writing Narrative Journalism* is an eclectic mix of stories culled from more than 2,000 articles written over a span of 30 years for more than two dozen newspapers, magazines and Internet sites. Some of the stories were written on deadline, others over the course of several weeks. Few were assigned by editors, and almost all were the product of enterprise. All demonstrate the tools of the trade of a working journalist. Their common thread is that they are *stories*. And as such, each has a beginning, a middle and an end.

Inside the Writer's Mind: Writing Narrative Journalism allows readers to see how a seasoned writer thinks and reasons. It affords readers a peek at how a journalist conceived specific story ideas and then went about reporting those stories. It propels readers into 30 very different stories—some written for magazines, others for newspapers and the Internet. The book gives readers a look at how each story was written and ultimately transformed to the written page. *Inside the Writer's Mind: Writing Narrative Journalism* provides an epilogue for each story, updating the reader on the impact and fallout that each piece generated. Ultimately, the book is a step-by-step manual on how a professional writer goes about his or her task—from idea conception to story aftermath.

The stories contained in this reader are the product of one writer, a small army of editors, the peculiarities of the publications that printed the stories and the politics of the times when they first appeared. For better or worse, they are a snapshot of American journalism. What makes this book different—and I hope valuable—is that it opens the writer's mind to the reader, so that he or she can catch a glimpse of the sausage maker as well as the sausage-making.

Good writing is storytelling, i.e., turning observation into narrative. I make no distinction between narrative journalism and creative nonfiction. Narrative journalism is what many people who write for newspapers, magazines and Internet sites do; creative nonfiction writing is what is taught in a lot of graduate programs at American universities and appears in long form in literary journals and some magazines.

But realize this: both literary conventions are the same. Both come from the same tradition. If executed well, both impart knowledge to the reader in an effective, efficient and eloquent way. *Inside the Writer's Mind: Writing Narrative Journalism* contains varied examples of nonfiction writing: short and long stories; profiles; investigations; memoirs; news and features, some humorous, some deadly serious; third-person and first-person narratives.

Such variety hasn't always been the case in American journalism. In the classic 1952 film *Deadline USA,* a savvy gossip columnist (played by Jim Backus) defined the difference between a journalist and a reporter: "A journalist makes himself the hero of the story. A reporter is only the witness." That's probably as succinct a definition as any of what 15 years later became known as The New Journalism. In the late '60s, Tom Wolfe, Gay Talese, Norman Mailer, Truman Capote and Hunter Thompson left the reporter's world to become "journalists," heroes of their own stories, published in magazines such as *Rolling Stone, Esquire, Playboy* and (the now-defunct) *Ramparts.* Newspapers, though, wanted their reporters to stay reporters, and the first person was avoided at all costs. Reporters, like me, who tried to slip "I" into their stories were advised to write novels. Journalism students were whacked on the knuckles for thinking in the first person.

No more.

First-person stories are all over American journalism today. One of the reasons is the Internet, which welcomes energetic, irreverent and alternative voices. Internet stories often explore personal experiences, and are not afraid to take a position. Many have attitude, and brazenly shove that attitude into the reader's face. Not wanting to be viewed by the public as stuffy, many conventional magazines and newspapers are following suit—cautiously.

An advisory: first-person narrative isn't an excuse for personal indulgence. No public thumb sucking allowed. Rules for first-rate, first-person stories are the same as for all narrative journalism: the writing must be exceptional. The prose has to offer a compelling story, often told with wit, opinion and edge.

Make no mistake, though. The stories printed herein are not the best of anything. Not by a long shot. In fact, while rereading them, I noticed plenty of flaws. But instead of going back into the pieces and fixing them, I chose to let the errors stay. I alert the reader to many of my blunders—and some of them are pretty glaring—in the accompanying epilogues.

With all this in mind, here are some essentials.

1. Ledes are like Japanese haiku. They have to sing. They have to be eloquent but to the point. They are the store window. If the reader doesn't like the opening to your story, he or she isn't about to venture inside. Craft your ledes. Polish them. Rewrite them. Shorter is better. Each word must be indispensable (that goes for the lede as well as any other part of your story). Not enough has been said about the importance of the period and how close it ought to be to the first word of each sentence.

2. Ideas are king. You will learn how to write if you do it every day, have a good editor (if not, find one) and are committed to making your writing as good as

it can be. But ideas, well, they are something else. Coming up with new, strange, wondrous ideas may very well be intuitive, but it's a process that all writers must master. A fresh idea can turn great writing into exceptional writing. Walk around with a small notebook that you can fit in your pocket, briefcase or backpack. Keep a notebook next to your bed and in your car so you can write down ideas as they come to you. Don't think your memory will be good enough to remember all your ideas. Every place and event is fodder for material. Ideas are currency among writers. When you go shopping, while you're waiting for the bus, write down thoughts that may translate into story ideas. As a writer, ideas ought to flood your brain all the time. You can take a vacation, but you'll always be working. All life experiences are material.

3. The three-second rule. The writer's job is to get the reader to read. This is not easy. The nature of the printed word starts the writer out at a disadvantage. Television, radio and the Internet are much more user-friendly than magazines and newspapers, which display stagnant words on a page. After a graphic, headline, perhaps a subhead, then the writer's story begins. And unless that story jumps out and grabs the reader by the throat within the first three seconds, pulling that reader into the story, then all the effort the writer has put into crafting the story is for naught. The reader chooses to pay out symbolic currency when he or she decides to spend time with the writer's creation. It's like a taxi meter ticking away: every second that goes by with the reader sinking his or her eyes into your story is costing that reader something. For the story to work, its crafting has to be superb. The piece has to be riveting. It has to seduce the reader, and it has to do it fast.

4. Good reporters are information junkies. Read voraciously. Go to movies. Surf the Web. Read nonfiction as well as fiction. But don't be lulled into satisfaction by someone else's story. Probe how the writer tells the tale. Don't be afraid of converting another writer's idea into your own by localizing the angle or the news hook. Figure out how you would tell your story differently.

5. Pay attention to good storytellers, whether they are writers or not, and understand their tricks and methods. The tradition of story telling began before its written counterpart. Learn how skilled practitioners parcel out information, using dialogue, narrative and suspense to spellbind listeners.

6. News is coverage of an event, trend or sentiment that people care about—or should care about.

7. Good writers prefer their own story ideas to those of an editor. Infuse yourself in your ideas. Sell story ideas first to yourself and then to others. Seed

your environment with the strength you feel in your bones for the story you are pursuing. Invest in the story. Don't take no for an answer when one editor turns your idea down. Listen to criticisms and suggestions—then come back with an airtight argument that allays the editor's concerns. Writers learn how to sell story ideas to editors trained to be wary and cynical.

8. Good reporters go where other reporters won't go. Pack journalism is for reporters who are too scared or comfortable to light out on their own. Question similar stories written by multitudes of reporters.

9. Write about victims. Give voice to those without any. Remember, though, that in the legal and journalistic worlds, people can be labeled "victims" only after a perpetrator is convicted of a crime. Similarly, people are not "rapists," "murderers," "drunk drivers" or "scam artists" until adjudicated guilty of those crimes. Always use the word, "alleged," (as in "alleged victim," "alleged robber," "alleged crime ") until a guilty verdict has been rendered.

10. Quotes are essential. They must reflect opinions and ought not be recitations of fact. The first quote normally is the best quote you have, something I call the "killer quote." It's strong and flushed with opinion. It sucks readers into your story. When interviewing a police officer, don't use a quote such as, "The driver's blood alcohol level was .30." Instead, quote the officer when he or she says (perhaps in response to your question), "That guy was the drunkest driver I've seen in my 30 years on the force."

11. Commas and periods always go inside quotes marks. Question marks and exclamation points go inside quote marks if they are part of the quoted matter. If friends tell you differently, tell them they ought to move to Great Britain.

12. When quoting a person, use the verb "say" (in its present or past tense)—not "aver," "maintain," "sneer," "laugh," "quip," "promise," "stress," "declare," "remark, or "utter." "Say" is neutral, and lets the quote speak for itself. Avoid the construction, "according to," either at the beginning or end of a sentence. Use the word "claim" only as a noun (as in what to file with your insurance company when you get into a car accident). When quoting a person posing a question, use the verb "ask."

13. Be aware of sources and their motivations. They are using you as much as you are using them.

14. Good writers always write too long. They relish good editors, but they also

realize that they themselves are their best editors. They go through their stories numerous times, editing out adverbs, cutting to the chase faster each time they reread their stories. There is a place for adverbs in stories, but make sure when you use them they are absolutely, positively essential (as the two adverbs in this sentence are not).

15. Be aware of how you tell a story, selectively parceling out information so that the reader stays constantly engaged. Readers tend to read in chunks with paragraphs being the most common markers. Most readers make decisions on whether they'll continue reading a story at the end of each paragraph. Good writers increase the velocity of the sentences within each paragraph so that the reader feels an increased drama as the paragraph winds up. This forces the reader not to put down the story, but instead to go from paragraph to paragraph. Creating suspense this way is good.

16. Paragraphs generally are separate cells of information, the laying out of a specific element that leads to the overall theme, feeling, conclusion of your story. Since the reader's eye automatically gravitates to white space, you should be hard-pressed to come up with a compelling reason for a long, meandering paragraph.

17. Don't split infinitives. "To think clearly" makes sense; "to clearly think" does not.

18. Fully identify people you write about. Use middle initials. Ask people their ages (and be prepared to give your own, if they ask). Be specific about job titles and affiliations. Don't write, "John Doe of the State Air Resources Board," since the identification doesn't convey whether Doe is the board's janitor, senior engineer or director.

19. Don't place emotions or thoughts inside people's minds. Attribution is fundamental. Avoid: "Mayor Jones believes that Councilman Smith is a 'good-for-nothing dirtbag.'" Better: "In a heated exchange at last night's council meeting, Mayor Jones called Councilman Smith a 'good-for-nothing dirtbag.'" If the mayor never articulates in public his opinion of Councilman Smith, then with some enterprising reporting, perhaps you could write: "Mayor Smith apparently is showing increased impatience with his opponent, Councilman Smith. In private, the Mayor has taken to calling Smith a 'good-for-nothing dirtbag.'"

20. Avoid the passive. Bad: "A home run was hit by Billy." Better: "Billy hit a home run."

21. Avoid using "it" as the first word of a story. In such a context, "it" is a vague reference, as well as a contrivance. Bad: "It was raining hard." Better: "The rain came down like a sonofabitch."

22. Show, don't tell. Avoid summations. Don't write that the transsexual "dressed colorfully." Describe how the transsexual dressed: "...in six-inch stiletto heels, a black bustier with a plunging neckline, and fishnet stockings held up by a red garter belt."

23. The word "presently" does not mean "currently." It means "soon." You probably ought not to use the word "currently" anyway. "Now" works fine.

24. Avoid official jargon. Banish the word, "vehicle." Find out the make and model of the car, motorcycle, tractor, snowmobile or truck.

25. Realize the power of your words. Fully understand that what you write will have an impact. Unlike the ephemera of the spoken word, the written word lasts. Don't shy away from writing what you see, but be aware of possible consequences. This plays itself out in different ways, some large, some small. I once described a woman as "big-boned and handsome." Boy, did I ever hear from her.

26. Understand and acknowledge your own cultural, class, racial or gender biases. Be alert when writing about people and events that conflict with your own values. At The Los Angeles Times, when an editor (who was white) inserted the word "controversial" before the name of Muslim leader Louis Farrakhan, a reporter (who was black) protested, saying, "In my neighborhood, Ronald Reagan is controversial; Louis Farrakhan is not." The reporter was right to protest.

27. Editors are your friends. They subjugate themselves to you. Remember, it's your name atop the story, not your editor's. You might have to educate your editors, but they are the gatekeepers, and ultimately they have a larger picture of your story than you do. Listen to them.

28. Question whether telling a story chronologically is the best approach. In news stories, it seldom is. Your job is to order the significance of events. At the conclusion of a city council meeting, if someone shoots the mayor, that would be your lede, not that the first reading of a no-smoking ordinance passed by a vote of 5-2.

29. Concentrate on the task at hand. I have a fortune-cookie fortune taped to the

top of my computer screen that reads "Stay Focused." You'll know you're cooking the moment all your senses are focused straight ahead. Some writers describe this sensation as the Zen of writing. You feel a part of the computer screen, the keyboard an extension of your fingers. Metaphorically, if a bomb were to explode under your chair, you'd hardly notice it. Practically, when the telephone rings it should startle you out of your sense of concentration. On the old television show "Get Smart" (aired these days on the cable station, TVLand), whenever spy Maxwell Smart and the Chief wanted to engage in a top-secret conversation, the "Cone of Silence," a cheesy-looking plastic cutout, would come down from the ceiling and the two could begin their secret discussion. When your writing is going well, you ought to feel as though the "Cone of Silence" has descended, isolating you from the rest of the world.

30. Learn to juggle multiple tasks. Good reporters know how to work on different elements of many stories at the same time.

31. Pick a place and a time to write. Dedicate your time in that place to writing. Try to do your big-picture thinking somewhere else, so that when you get to your writing place you can concentrate on putting into words what you've already mulled over in your head.

32. Things are different from each other, not different than each other.

33. Accuracy, accuracy, accuracy. That's a given. Names must be spelled correctly. Addresses, ages, eye and hair color, which leg was blown off in the blast—you've got to get it all right. That's basic. Remember, though, there is a vast difference between truth and accuracy. Truth is held to a higher standard. Six million Jews died in World War II. That's accurate, but not true. Your task as a writer ought to be to get at the truth: to dig deeply, to think clearly and with imagination, to examine from different angles what you see and hear and to value what your gut tells you. Only after you do all that, can you make perceptive observations and then synthesize those observations into an approximation of the truth.

34. Never write "brutal murder." All murders are brutal.

35. "Easter Sunday" is redundant.

36. Writing is a process of refining your thoughts and the words you've used to approximate those thoughts. As such, good writers are always rewriting, polishing, redrafting to make their writing as strong as it possibly can be. Every

version of your writing should be a draft. Whatever you write can always be better.

37. Break rules if they limit your ability to tell the story effectively. Convention is important, but not if it gets in the way. Listen to your own voice on how best to convey the essence of your story.

38. Have fun. Writing shouldn't be drudgery. Enjoy the solitary time making sense of your perceptions of the world.

THE ART OF THE INTERVIEW

The black box of all narrative writing is interviewing. Information-gathering—and interviewing is an essential part of that process—is a key to your success as a writer. Some writers are vacuum cleaners, sucking up information voraciously. They enjoy meeting people and listening to them. They know how to ask probing questions. Other writers are painfully shy and avoid excess contact with people. They shine when they are writing, alone in front of a computer screen, crafting phrases, stacking paragraph after paragraph to perfection. You will find your own niche. But whichever it is, you will have to interview people to gather information. Here's how.

- Don't rely on a tape recorder. Inexperienced writers push the record button and forget about everything else. Seasoned writers take notes; they develop a sense of the interview subject's cadence. If the person interviewed talks too fast, then ask him or her to slow down. Interviewing is an enervating activity. It takes skill and practice. If you do it right, you should be sapped when you are finished.

- Always say who you are, your affiliation (the name of the magazine or newspaper you work for, or whether you are a freelance writer or student) and why you are doing the interview.

- Shut up. You're asking questions, not giving answers. Let the person talk. People are uncomfortable with silence. Allowing for it often rewards the interviewer with revealing comments.

- Write out your questions in advance. I use a legal pad and write my questions in longhand and in the order that I want to ask them. I don't want to start with an adversarial question that may chill the interview, so I often leave such questions until after I establish a rapport with the interview subject.

- Look the person in the eye.

- Be involved. Don't slouch. You are asking a stranger to give you a glimpse into his or her mind. Show respect. Show interest.

- Stay in control of the interview. This is your show. Don't let the subject spin you. Stay on track. Understand what you came for and get it.

- Pay attention to detail. Note what the person is wearing, how he or she talks (fast, with hands, stumbles over words, so slow it's pretentious and preachy). Jot down your impressions.

- Not all interviews should be done face-to-face. The telephone and e-mail are wonderful tools for reporters. If all you want is raw information, i.e., basic facts, a phone or an e-mail exchange is more time-efficient for you and the person who's got the information you need.

- The hypothetical question is a trap, but a good one. An example: "Senator, if you decide to run against candidate X, do you think you'd be able to beat her?"

- If a person goes off the record, make sure you understand why. Media-savvy people go on and off the record for their own self-serving reasons. Guard against being used.

- Ask open-ended questions that elicit provocative responses. "Why do you think that?" is often better than "What do you think about that?" Through the reporting you've done before the interview, you should already know the subject's position on most issues. Banish forever: "How do you feel?"

- When interviewing victims or their families, talk honestly and sympathetically. Effective reporters care about the stories they report, as well as the people they interview. If, for example, you are interviewing the parents of a missing child, a sincere admission ought to be, "I hope you find your child, and my story may help."

- Always get home and work phone numbers from the person you are interviewing, so in the crush of deadline you can call back.

- If the source asks to read your story before it is printed, tell him or her absolutely no. Depending on the type of story you are writing, a possible compromise may be to read back the source's quotes to make sure they represent his or her thoughts accurately.

ORDINARY PEOPLE

1

ALWAYS RIGHT AT HOME

Lots of writers write about heroes, but what about antiheroes, the antagonists of everyday dramas? Such stories usually slip between the cracks.

The accompanying story came to me one balmy summer evening when I was driving past a neighborhood baseball diamond in San Jose, California. I had just finished work and it was too pretty an evening to go home. So, on a lark, I parked and took a place in the stands. The Little League game in progress was in the sixth inning, and tensions were running high on both sides. Parents were yelling in support of their kids—that was to be expected. But some were also hurling all kinds of unbelievable insults at the home-plate umpire. When the umpire called a kid out on a third strike, the guy next to me shouted at the umpire, calling him a "burrito." The crowd must have been taken by the unusual epithet, and for several minutes, everyone in the stands started chanting, "Burrito! Burrito! Burrito!" It was a funny moment, of course, unless you were the umpire.

When the game was over, parents converged on the field, congratulating their kids, high-fives all-around. The parents and coaches formed an archway for the players to run through. After lots more hand slapping, as everyone was packing up to go home, I caught a glimpse of the home-plate umpire. He was a solitary figure, slinking off the field without fanfare, without notice. Just at that moment, I caught the umpire putting his two fists together side-by-side horizontally, then twisting his wrists, as though he was breaking an imaginary carrot. What was the guy doing? And for whom was he doing it? I wasn't quite sure, but the gesture prompted me to run over and start interviewing him on the spot.

Always Right at Home

Three times a week for the last 20 years, Clem Holguim has performed a very strange act in the privacy of his own home.

With a Darth Vader-type mask over his face and a puffy pad covering his chest, Holguim crouches in front of a full-length mirror. Then he screams.

Holguim is neither an actor nor masochist, although his profession borrows from the repertoire of each.

What he does in his bedroom—screaming "Strike! Ball! Out! Safe!"—is essential to his moonlighting job: a Little League umpire.

Before you discount such an occupation as trifling, consider the emotion it stirs:

Holguim, 46, has been called a jerk, a blind man, a wife-beater, a Cyclops, an ostrich, a burrito—and those are the printable epithets.

Bottles, bicycle handlebars, baseball gloves have been hurled at him in anger. Few parts of his body haven't been pummeled by errant baseballs and bats. Mouth, feet, shins, thighs, chest, groin—all have been bruised. Five years ago, his jaw was dislocated by a flying bat, and he now wears braces to correct the damage.

To make matters worse, when Holguim is injured during a game, spectators usually cheer.

It's not only injuries that routinely stir fans, it's close plays. After a controversial call two weeks ago, a team of 12-year-old Little Leaguers surrounded Holguim. "It looked like a lynching party," he recalls. An off-duty cop who happened to be in the stands escorted Holguim to his car.

Considering all this, you might think that today—the last day of Little League playoffs that end the season—would be cause for Holguim to celebrate.

On the contrary, it's a day of mourning. "I dread this day every year. I root for extra innings, rain, anything," says Holguim, a barber at Hacienda Barber Shop in San Jose when not umpiring. "I look at baseball as religion."

Holguim, the director of the 32-man umpire association ("We'd take women, but none have applied.") that oversees San Jose Little League games, earns $10 to $25 per game during the regular season. During playoffs, though, because of league budgetary problems, most umpires end up volunteering their services.

"It's hard to get umpires who are willing to work for next to nothing, who are knowledgeable and also calloused," says Holguim, who umpires 130 games a year.

He recalls when his nine-year-old son was up at bat, and he was the plate umpire. Holguim called his son out on a third strike that, to many, looked wide.

His son gave Holguim a "Dad-how-could-you?" look, and then slunk off to the dugout. For the next week, Holguim says, his wife wouldn't talk to him.

She responded, says Holguim, like all the other spectators. "Hating the umpire is something ingrained in people. For every call you make, half the crowd hates you."

Like Holguim, those in the local Little League umpire association are not specifically trained to be umpires, but must attend several local baseball clinics that include quizzes on everything from the infield fly rule to what's the correct call when a ball gets caught in a chain-link fence. The clinics, like the profession, are not something for the casual dabbler.

All umpires accepted into the association must supply their own uniforms—light blue shirt, gray slacks, official umpire shoes, shin guards, a chest protector, face mask. When behind the plate, umpires carry a whisk-broom and hand-held ball/strike indicator. The entire get-up costs about $800 and weighs about 10 pounds.

Unlike players, who are on the field half the game, Holguim is out there the entire time. To build stamina, he works out in a weight room complete with an Arnold Schwarzenegger poster pinned next to the full-length mirror. "It gives me an incentive," says Holguim.

What makes a good umpire, of course, isn't the uniform or the conditioning, but a thrill of the game—a thrill so great it means often enduring pain.

"Even in Little League, you've got to conceal pain. If you don't, the spectators will crucify you," says 22-year-old umpire Ed Nelson, who cracked a rib last year and never bothered to stop play. "Once you're hurt, watch out. You're at the mercy of the crowd."

Little League umpire Dave Yniquez, a 36-year-old roofer, says fans love it when an umpire gets hurt. "They forget you're a person; they look at you as an authority figure and when you're down, they let you have it."

Yniquez's injuries have included two chipped front teeth (now capped) and a nasty line-drive–inflicted bruise on his left thigh that lasted more than a year. Two weeks ago, he was hit squarely in the groin, and was in such pain that he lay writhing on the ground. He had someone lift him by the belt and then gently release him, a practice that helps such an injury, he says.

It didn't elicit any sympathy from the crowd, though. Later in the game, after a close call, a fan in the stands yelled at Yniquez, "*Yo tengo un treinta y ocho*" ("I have a .38").

Umpires say they become stoic about such cruelty, and intensify their concentration about the game when fans get vocal. There are exceptions.

Armando Martinez, an umpire for the last eight years, recalls earlier this season when he was hit in the mouth by a flying bat. His upper lip was split. Blood spurted, dripping onto his blue umpire's shirt.

"I was full of blood, and fans were still cheering." He had had enough. "I said to a couple of people, 'You want some blood, I'll give you some,'" Martinez, 27, said. No one took him up on his offer.

Few insults ever lead to physical violence. But just in case, umpire Yniquez says he parks his car either very near the field, or very far away. Both have advantages and disadvantages.

"You park close by, you can make a quick getaway. But everyone knows which car is yours. You park far away, few know which car to target, but it takes longer to walk to your car in case of an emergency."

Tom Hammill, the editor of *Referee* magazine, affiliated with the National Association of Sporting Officials in Racine, Wis., says he receives six to eight reports a month of violence directed at umpires, but they involve all sports and all levels.

Hammill, 40, recalls umpiring when the mother of a losing team's coach smacked his partner across his face with her purse, and then tried to wrestle Hammill and his partner to the ground.

The woman's husband threatened to kill both umpires. On the way home, Hammill's partner quit umpiring for the rest of the year.

Such fan reaction is, of course, extreme. "We're not idiots. If the abuse were that bad, we wouldn't be doing this," Hammill says.

The thrill of the job, say umpires, is being able to be at the right spot at the right time, getting closer to a critical play than anyone else.

Once there, though, do umpires ever make the wrong calls?

It happens, they say. "Umpires can make errors, just like players," says Rudy Muñoz, a 23-year-old Little League umpire who plans on enrolling in a professional umpiring school this winter in hope of breaking into major league baseball. "When you're starting out, the wrong word can come out of your mouth even though you don't mean it."

"You say 'safe,' and you mean 'out,' " he says. But once out of the umpire's mouth, there's no recanting.

Even in Little League, Muñoz says that's one reason why "selling your call" is important. Good umpires appear demonstratively certain when they make their calls—no matter how uncertain they may be beneath the surface.

"You have to make the call with authority and with a flourish. It keeps the heat off of you and the other umpires," he says.

And like actors, umpires develop their own distinctive styles. Most umpires thrive on close or "bang-bang" plays, as they call them, when they have a chance to demonstrate that style.

To watch Muñoz call a bang-bang play is to see an actor who has meticulously honed his skill, the product of years of practice before a mirror. It is a sight to behold.

As the runner rounds third base, Muñoz looks like a hyperkinetic lizard, hovering around the plate, his eyes bulging, his mouth small, pursed and mean.

As the runner slides into the plate, Muñoz's right finger suddenly arcs down toward the ground in a whirl of motion as though he's nabbing a giant fly. Then he screams, "Out!" which sounds more like an angry belch than a decision.

When calling a batter out on a third strike, Muñoz abruptly pulls his right forearm toward his torso as though it were about to be chopped off by a power saw. At the same time, he lifts his left leg, bends it to a 30-degree angle as though he is about to skip through a flaming hoop, and grunts "Strike three!" as though Muñoz has just been stabbed.

It is that ecstasy of performance that makes an umpire—even a Little League umpire—tolerate the ridicule, the threats, the potential of physical harm.

"You're the center of attention," says Muñoz, who when not umpiring works as a clerk in an Ethan Allen Furniture warehouse in San Jose. "On the field, you have power. Whatever you say, goes. You are the one in charge."

For Holguim, that responsibility is not to be taken lightly. Baseball to him is sacred.

Sometime this evening, when the last out is made, Holguim will put his two fists together. Then he'll twist his wrists, as though breaking an imaginary carrot.

That's his signature, something few fans or players ever see, but the way Holguim has ended the more than 2,600 Little League games he has umpired over the last two decades.

As in the other games, Holguim will then take off his blue umpire's cap, neatly fold it, and carefully stuff it in his back pocket. He will walk off the field and wait for next season to begin.

San Jose Mercury News, July 24, 1987

WRITING THE STORY

I knew I had a live one on the line as soon as I introduced myself to Clem Holguim. Even though he had just finished officiating a neighborhood baseball game between 12-year-olds, it might very well have been Game Seven of the World Series. Holguim breathed baseball. To him, baseball was the single greatest invention of man, next to the computer and the airplane. I gave Holguim my business card, and promised to call the next day.

The next morning, I called and arranged to meet Holguim at the barbershop where he worked. Between customers, I asked him everything I could think of— from how (and where) he practices his calls to the worst injury he had sustained on the job. Through him, I got introductions to four other local Little League umpires, Ed Nelson, Dave Yniquez, Armando Martinez, and Rudy Muñoz.

I opened the piece with a little drama. Originally, the last word in the lede was "bedroom," but supercilious editors changed it to "home." The editors said they thought with the word "bedroom," readers might look at the top of the piece and think Holguim was into some strange sexual gear. As a writer, you have to pick your battles with editors, and this didn't seem like one worth fighting (or winning). My idea in the lede is to plunge the reader into the depths of Clem Holguim's mania for his job. The line about his repertoire borrowing from acting and masochism helps sell that idea.

In the fourth graf, when I finally get to revealing what Holguim does, I try to anticipate the reader's reaction. I want readers to stay with the story, and that's why I string a slew of easy-to-read names that Holgium has been called. I'm banking that "Cyclops," "ostrich" and "burrito" are outrageous enough taunts to prod the reader to continue with the piece. I follow with a similar string of body parts that have been bruised by flying objects. Then it's time for the zinger: Instead of welcoming the end of the season, Holguim dreads it.

In the next section, I dispense basic information: salaries, roster, number of games, training. But the section is a transition to more meaty material. The anecdote that Holguim gives about calling his own son out on strikes has a great kicker —that Holguim's wife was so steamed, she wouldn't talk to him for a week!

I switch to another umpire, Dave Yniquez, whose description of getting hit in the groin by a fastball ought to make anyone groan. In response to my own very sincere question ("Gosh, how do you deal with something like that?"), Yniquez supplied a fascinating answer ("Have someone lift you by the belt and then suddenly drop you."). I have no idea whether this actually works, but the response certainly merits a line in the story.

Outside of calling an umpire a burrito, my second favorite insult came from Yniquez, who recalled someone in the stands yelling in Spanish, "I have a .38." Yniquez neatly summarizes the plight of Little League umpires by explaining the pros and cons of parking your car too close or too far from the playing field.

The quotes from all the umpires were right on the money, but the piece requires more observation of these guys in action. So, after convincing my boss to allow me to spend four or five evenings at the local park to see how these umpires go about their tasks, I realized many of them were magnificent actors, especially when it came to calling close, bang-bang plays. And for that, I chose to write about Rudy Muñoz, who indeed did look like a lizard, his tongue darting in and out of his mouth as he waited to sell his call of "Out!" at home plate.

Despite all the stories and quotes I got from the five umpires I interviewed, I chose to end the piece with how I got into it: Holguim's two-fist, carrot-breaking signature. I followed that with another piece of observation: Holguim solemnly folding his umpire's hat and placing it in his back pocket. It seemed the only way to close.

This was one of those stories that begged for a response—from the umpires I wrote about, the parents, players, baseball lovers, personal injury attorneys, from anyone who read it and had an opinion. But I heard from no one. After a week, I could stand it no longer. I called Clem Holguim at the barbershop and asked him if he had read the piece.

"Yeah, I saw it," he replied.

"Any reaction?" I asked, hating myself for courting favor.

"Not really," Holguim said.

"Nothing?"

"I gotta go. I got two more guys waiting on me, and I got an umpire's meeting in an hour."

ASSIGNMENTS

1) Interview part-time umpires and sporting officials in your area, and write about their gratifying—and most harrowing—experiences.

2) Write a story about the intense competition often played out between parents of teenage athletes. Write about the pressures parents place on their children-athletes and the fierce rivalries, spurred on by parents as much as by players and coaches, that exist between teams.

3) Look at another set of unheralded heroes—crossing guards, appliance repairmen, knife sharpeners, shoe repairmen. Hang out with them. Plan to spend a shift with them. Find out what they get out of their jobs.

2

BUSY SIGNAL

Who hasn't experienced being treated like a flea-infested, pariah dog by the medical establishment?

Writers often say that certain stories "write themselves," and that was the case with "Busy Signal". The piece is a straightforward diary of pain. As though extreme back pain weren't bad enough, "Busy Signal" delves into the numbing insensitivity of physicians, nurses, technicians, attendants and receptionists at one of the nation's top medical centers. The only solace to my misery was that just when yet another insult was about to be hurled my way, I could chalk it up to material for the forthcoming story I was already composing in my head. Right from the beginning, when Frau Farbissina defined severe lower back pain as losing control of your bowels, I knew I had a story so incredible I'd have to work overtime to ensure that readers didn't think I was making the stuff up.

Busy Signal

Back pain is no guarantee your doctor will see you, even at the best clinic.

Four years ago, I'm packing up my stereo, putting it into a cardboard box, back arched, arms outstretched like I'm giving parking directions to a 747, and I think I hear something snap in my lower back.

This is not some muscle you pull while trying out Position 62 of the Kama Sutra. The pain comes from deep within the core of my spinal cord about five inches north of the crack in my buttocks. I drop to the floor, feeling like a deer walloped by a semi going 60 mph.

Still on my back two hours later, I'm finally able to inch my way to grab the phone. The University of Iowa Hospitals and Clinics (UIHC), one of the largest university-owned teaching hospitals in the United States, is about two miles away from where I live. This medical center is no doc-in-the-middle-of-the-corn-fields. It employs 7,000 doctors, nurses and professional staff. *U.S. News & World Report* ranks its department of orthopaedics eighth in the nation.

After getting a busy signal for 15 minutes, I finally reach the orthopaedic clinic. "This is an emergency," I croak. "I must get in to see a doctor. I can't move."

I momentarily imagine the voice on the other end responding, "Poor baby, come in immediately. Back pain is simply horrible. We can give you drugs, shots, lotions, anything to make that terrible ouch go away."

Instead, this is what I get: "Have you lost control of your bowels?" from a woman who sounds like the thin-lipped Frau Farbissina, the evil henchwoman in the Austin Powers movies.

Come again?

"Have you lost control of your bowels?"

Despite the agony in my back, I keep repeating to myself, "Remember this, because no one will ever believe you."

"No," I answer, getting Frau's drift about how far the needle must go on the Pain-O-Meter to merit an appointment. "But if losing control of my bowels is what it takes to see a doctor, I will climb on your desk, squat over your appointment book, and let loose."

Click. I imagine Frau's lips turning upward to form a satisfied smile.

My next call is to a physician friend, suitably sympathetic, who calls in a scrip for Tylenol 3 to the local Walgreen's, although I'm uncertain how I will get there to pick it up.

"Bed rest, that's what you need," my friend prescribes. "Lie flat on your back for the next week. Don't move."

That's what I do, and sure enough, the pain disappears.

Flash forward. At 5 a.m. one Tuesday last April, I awaken and my lower right leg has gone totally numb.

"God, could this be a stroke?" I ask myself, my heart racing like I have won the trifecta. From knee to big toe, you could stick in long, sharp needles and I wouldn't feel a thing.

I tap my wife on the shoulder. She is snoring lightly.

"Am I speaking clearly? Is my speech garbled?"

"Go back to sleep," she says, hugging her buckwheat hull pillow.

"Kaan yu oonderstund da wurds I um saaaayig?"

"Go back to sleep," the wife advises again, this time more sternly.

So, I'm not having a stroke. But my right leg and foot are still numb, and the moment the clock radio goes from 7:59 to 8:00, I call my internist over at University of Iowa Hospitals and Clinics, rated by *U.S. News & World Report* as the nation's sixth best medical center for primary care.

"He's out till tomorrow," secretary Denise says. "But he'll call in for messages, and I'll ask him to call you."

"But this is an emergency, Denise!"

"He's booked until next Wednesday, his clinic day. That's the day he's reserved to see patients."

Where does the hospital get these people? The reject pile of token-takers at the New York City Transit Authority? The motto seems to be, "How *can't* we help you?"

"You can always go to the emergency room," Denise offers cheerfully before hanging up.

Like an idiot, I actually think the doctor will call back, so I sit—actually lie— on the floor by the phone, all the while the pain still radiating from my lower back, shooting down my right leg like I stuck my big toe into a 220-volt electrical socket. The doctor does not call.

I call Denise at 8 the next morning. "Oh, he's in clinic," she says as though I should know better. "But I left a message with him, and he should return your call."

Another day goes by. The doctor does not call. The pain gets worse.

I call Denise. "Doctor is still in clinic," she tells me as though that explains everything.

If they treat me like this, and I'm a tenured professor at this hallowed institution, how do they treat a pig farmer from Sioux City? Then I wonder, how would they treat a University of Iowa tight end with back problems, slated to start in this Saturday's game against Penn State?

Used to be your doctor would see you the same day. That was his responsibility, his oath to serve you, the patient. He (and it almost always was a he) was your private personal manager. You had a relationship with him.

Next time you're at the movies, try shouting, "Is there a doctor in the house?" and see if anyone but a pervert comes to offer you mouth-to-mouth resuscitation. These days it takes papal intervention to set up an appointment with your physician six weeks in advance.

I am desperate. I want to know what's happening to the trusty body that has given me prime service for 47 years. For Christ's sake, I can hardly walk, and my own physician is too busy to see me.

I turn testy. "If the doctor is in the clinic, could you give me his pager number?" I ask Denise in a tone she is unaccustomed to hearing.

I page doctor, and seconds later, hallelujah, praise the Lord, he calls back.

I am in agonizing pain, but I need to *talk* like I'm in agonizing pain, which I do. "The pain is *ex-cru-ci-ating*," I tell doctor, pulling out the word like Atlantic City taffy.

"How fast can you get over here?"

"Any time," I answer breathlessly. Do with me what you will, but do it now.

"I could see you—but only if you can get here in the next 15 minutes."

"OK," I answer, thinking I've scored an audience with John Paul II himself.

I tear over to the hospital complex and whip into a parking spot; all the while my right leg feels like a fully operational cattle prod. I go through the rat's maze of the hospital complex and find the internal medicine clinic. After I wait 10 minutes, a nurse checks me in. First she weighs me (180 lbs.) and then takes my blood pressure (143/83).

"Is your blood pressure always this high? This is something you might want to talk to Doctor about."

I demur from saying, "Your blood pressure would be high if a couple of days ago you thought you were having a stroke, and now you feel pain that possibly rivals childbirth, and you've called 'doctor' three times and each time you've been lied to, and now, miracle of miracles, the Holy Shaman deigns to see you."

Doctor comes into the examination room. He lifts my leg. I respond accordingly, which is to scream, and he says: "These things usually go away. Rest, and if it doesn't get any better in a week, call me. We could give you an MRI and an x-ray, but all that would do is cost you and your insurance company $1,500. And whatever you do, don't see a chiropractor."

I don't want to see a chiropractor. I want to spend the $1,500, but am not given a choice. Within 10 minutes, Doctor is out the door, and I am alone again with my pain—and a prescription for Darvocet.

Exactly seven days later, the agony hasn't gone away, so I call Doctor, and it's back in the ring again with Denise.

"Doctor can't see you today."

"But he told me that if in a week I didn't improve, I was to call and he would see me."

"Doctor is on rounds today. He can't *possibly* see you."

"But I'm still in *ex-cru-ci-ating* pain."

Silence.

This has gone too far. Fortunately, I'm a pack rat; I find the crumpled piece of paper with Doctor's pager number on it, and call him, punching in my telephone number.

Doctor calls back, sounding annoyed. I go into my song but not the dance, and Doctor tells me he'll call one of his friends at orthopaedics, but gives me precise instructions.

"Wait five minutes. Then call this number. If the line is busy at first, call back. They will answer." It sounds like Doctor is setting up an undercover drug buy.

I wait the prescribed time, call orthopaedics, and finally no Denise. A dulcet-toned woman who sounds like Jaclyn Smith in the 1985 made-for-TV movie "Florence Nightingale" tells me to get over right away. She thinks she may be able to squeeze me in.

I race over to the hospital, park, pull my peg leg out, hobble through the maze to orthopaedics, only to meet Jaclyn Smith, who summarily waves me toward a waiting room. All seats are taken, which is just as well, because sitting is too painful, so I stand.

Twenty-five minutes later, another clerk shows me to an examination room. It is now 10:15 a.m., and the pain is shooting from hip to toe. My leg feels floppy, like an electric eel about to impress the kids at the Shedd Aquarium. This isn't altogether bad: I want to be experiencing intense pain when the Holy Shaman arrives so that he can properly diagnose me. The worst thing would be to tell him that the pain comes and goes, and it just went.

So I sit down; this increases the pain. I'm in this tiny room, writhing in agony, waiting more than an hour, flipping through old issues of *Field & Stream*, when a guy in a white coat who looks about 12 years old comes in.

Ah, the medical student, aka the warm-up act.

He pushes and pulls my legs and seems nice enough, jotting notes on my chart. The warm-up act informs me that the Holy Shaman will "be with you shortly."

"Shortly" turns out to be 70 minutes. Back to the *Field & Stream*s. Gore-Tex waders are in, by the way, but expensive.

Finally, the H.S. comes in, and introduces himself as "Dr. Found." I'm tempted to ask if he got lost, but I demur. He is *the doctor,* after all. Found manipulates my limbs, writes something down, pulls at my big toe, then says, "Let's schedule an MRI, x-rays, and a test to see how the nerves in your leg conduct electricity."

At x-ray, I wait 15 minutes before they take their photographs, and after that, I'm afraid I'll be late for the MRI, so I tell the x-ray people that I want to take my x-ray films with me. The secretary looks at me like I've lost my marbles, but after 30 minutes, hands over the x-rays.

I find MRI. I slide inside the MRI tube, which makes me feel like I'm in a straitjacket, but I handle it by repeating a mantra I learned in my transcendental meditation class back in 1972. When I slide out, the technician tells me that the MRI people won't have time to read the MRI because it's too late in the day, but he promises to keep my x-rays and MRI together for the Holy Shaman's mystical circle-reading tomorrow. By 3 tomorrow, x-ray and MRI will be in my file at orthopaedics. "Guaranteed," the technician says with a smile.

Friday, I get the conductivity test, called an electromyogram or EMG. Another warm-up act, about 14 but not wearing an identification tag or white coat, comes into the examination room.

"Who are you?" I ask. "And how do I know you're a doctor?"

"You'll have to trust me," he says, looking like Frau Farbissina's colleague, Mustafa, without the fez.

"What are you going to do?"

Mustafa disappears without answering. He returns with a thick maroon medical textbook. This is not reassuring.

Mustafa starts poking my back with electrical probes, which make my legs jump when he turns the dial on high. "Yeow!" I scream. He is not impressed.

Mustafa leaves, and this time returns with a guy shuffling in Haflinger clogs, who starts pushing the needle into my lower back, each time saying "Aha!" whenever I yell "Yeow!" After 15 minutes of making my limbs twitch, Mustafa tells me, "Wait there," pointing to another room.

After 20 minutes of nursing my burns, I tiptoe into the office area, where Mustafa and Clogman are huddled around a computer. Mustafa looks menacingly at me and points me back to the waiting room. "Sit there," he commands as I slink back to the Naugahyde couch.

I make my way to ortho, and ask about my MRI and x-ray. Jaclyn Smith smiles warmly, but says my MRI and x-ray are nowhere to be found. "We've checked with x-ray and MRI and they say we have them." She shakes her head, tossing her springy hair. "We could always put a trace on them, but that's likely to take a couple of weeks." She smiles.

Within the recesses of my brain I hear the voice of Mrs. Torresee, my fourth-grade elementary school teacher, saying, "Act mature. They might not remember you, but they'll remember your manners."

Out the window with Mrs. Torresee. These are desperate times. I place my palms on Jackie's desk, lean forward as far as my back allows, and say in a low but steady voice, "I want you to listen to me very carefully. I want you to get up slowly from behind your desk. You're going with me to MRI."

"That's right," I say. "I mean what I'm saying. Get up, now!"

Jackie is not alarmed. She deals with back-pain lunatics every day. "Sir," she says calmly, as though she's the one on Darvocet. "I can't leave my post at ortho and go with you. You can understand that." Jackie's eyes squint, showing emotion. She tilts her head and frowns, her pink lips producing a slight pout.

Smooth. If only Jaclyn Smith could act this well.

"Please," I say. "I have been in *ex-cru-ci-ating* pain for three weeks. Can't you please, please help me?" Tears miraculously well up in my eyes.

Mao said all it takes is one person to start a revolution. Before my eyes, Jackie transforms herself into Tania, the hospital guerrilla.

She looks me in the eye, nods her head, and rises from behind her desk. Together, as comrades, we troop down the long corridor to MRI.

Standing in tandem in front of the MRI desk, I say defiantly to the clerk, "Ten minutes ago, I was told that ortho had my MRI. Ortho doesn't have them."

"You must be mistaken, sir," the clerk informs. "Ortho does have your MRI."

At which point, I lay down my royal flush.

"Well, *this* is ortho," I say pointing to Tania, "and ortho doesn't have my MRI."

Tania smiles smugly. "He's right. You never sent it to us."

A stalemate of sorts for a minute or two. The clerk's eyebrows go haywire. She starts to say something, then looks to her right and left. The other clerks have retreated, abandoning her. This could be a postal situation.

The clerk disappears and ducks behind the Great Oz's curtain, into the Holy Shaman's offices. In five minutes, she returns with a large envelope, and ignominiously hands over my MRI.

I look at Tania, wanting to give her a high five, but instead we smile at each other dreamily like in a Correctol TV commercial.

As we're walking back to ortho, the thrill of victory coursing through my veins, I ask Tania when Dr. Found will be able to look at my newly discovered MRI.

Poof! All traces of Tania are now gone. "Oh, he couldn't possibly review them today. His wife just got a new job and he's home looking after the children."

"Could he perhaps look at them Monday?" I venture timidly.

"I wouldn't count on it. He's very busy, especially since his wife got the new job."

Over the weekend, while I'm waiting for Dr. Found's wife to adjust to her new proletariat life, the back pain gets so bad I think that maybe a chiropractor wouldn't be such a bad idea. Could I possibly be in worse pain? But the thought of someone manipulating my back makes me wince. Instead, I dose up on the Darvocet. When I'm not on my back, I pace around the house stiffly, as though I have a pole stuck up my butt, making my posture resemble Al Gore's. To bide my time, I read a book my wife buys, "The Mind-Body Connection," by Dr. John Sarno, a runaway best seller that says my back problem is all in my head.

At 8 Monday morning, Dr. Found does call with the results of the MRI. It shows a "significant" herniated disk between my fourth and fifth vertebrae. He suggests I get an epidural cortisone shot. He says he can get me into the steroid people at 3. "If that doesn't work, we may be thinking of surgery down the road."

Waiting for 3 is like waiting for the Venus space shuttle to launch. The pain has come back with a vengeance. Sitting is impossible. The only thing that doesn't hurt is lying flat on the floor, which I do as I count down to 3.

At the appointed hour, I queue up behind another aching back. When it's my turn, the receptionist is busy talking on the phone. Jackie is nowhere to be found. The check-in lady continues yakking as though I am invisible. The shooting pain has me going through the roof, so I lean against her desk, but this time, I am in no mood to play the hostage game.

Instead, I lie down on the floor in front of her desk.

"Please help me," I mumble from the textured maroon carpet.

But the check-in lady continues gabbing on the phone.

Could this be Frau Farbissina, the woman who four years ago asked if I had lost control of my bowels? Again, I say to myself, "Remember this, because no one will ever believe it."

After a minute or two, while I'm collapsed on the floor, Frau—still on the phone—gets up from her ergonomic chair and peers down her half-glasses at me. She puts the caller on hold and dials the PA system: "Nurse: Stat to front desk." Then she goes back to her phone call, for all I know talking about last night's episode of "ER."

A nurse shows up, bless her heart, and wheels me on a gurney to a sterile-looking cave where a doctor who goes by the name of Tartar sticks a needle in the base of my spine, injecting a steroid into the fluid surrounding my spine.

In another five days, I have another injection. That seems to do the trick.

Five months later, I am following the recommendations of my physician friend. I have given up golf. No raking leaves this fall, and come winter, forget shoveling snow. Too much cross-body movement. I try giving up making the bed, taking out the garbage and emptying the laundry hamper, but so far, the wife has not bought these precautionary measures.

About 43,000 patients a year have the stamina and perseverance to get an appointment at the world-famous ortho clinic, which makes it among the top 10 busiest academic orthopaedic centers in the United States. Back pain is the leading cause of disability for people between the ages of 19 and 45, and eight out of every 10 Americans have severe back pain at least once during their lives.

But what good is a back doctor if you have to lose control of your bowels before he or she will see you? And if you just have *ex-cru-ciating* pain, then the next available appointment isn't for another five weeks.

I guess it comes as no surprise that today when I call to see how long the wait is for a checkup, I get a busy signal, and when I finally get through, I have to leave my name and number on an answering machine. If Frau and her troops haven't already put me on some hit list, then I'm sure my name will be on one soon.

I can hardly wait for the next time my back goes out.

Salon, October 7, 1999

WRITING THE STORY

Telling the story chronologically is the way to go with "Busy Signal", in part, because the tone of the piece has to be conversational. Most people talk using chronological sequencing, e.g., "You're not going to believe this, but here's what happened ...". Then they start at the beginning of the tale. In "Busy Signal", I'm trying to maintain that same sense of storytelling. As any storyteller, I need to parcel out information carefully. Too much at once can ruin the story; not enough will send the reader packing. As code to the reader that the piece will be told without stuffy constraints of formality, I opt immediately (the fourth word in the piece) for a tense change (Four years ago, *"I'm"* packing up my stereo). To heighten the story's colloquial tone, I write in the first two grafs phrases like "parking directions to a 747," "Position 62 of the Kama Sutra," and "five inches north of the crack of my buttocks." The intention is to signal to the reader that the piece will be casual and (I hope) comedic.

The other reason I lead the story chronologically is that the opening anecdote, ending with Frau's comment about my bowels, is simply too good to bury. The quote serves as a recurring theme for the entire story: "How can I *not* help you?" is the mantra of many of the hospital workers in "Busy Signal".

I chose the moniker Frau Farbissina because the night before I started the piece, I saw the Mike Myers movie, "Austin Powers: International Man of Mystery," in which the evil henchwoman is named Frau Farbissina. Using pop-culture names is tricky business and can backfire, but even if the reader isn't familiar with the thin-lipped, celluloid Frau, her alliterative name is weird and Teutonic enough to use. I also introduce other characters who come and go— Denise, Doctor, the Holy Shaman (aka: H.S.), Mustafa (also from Austin Powers), Clogman, the Jaclyn Smith look-alike, Tania, Dr. Found. By threading the bizarre cast of Felliniesque characters through the narrative, I'm banking that their equally bizarre antics will provide enough juice to satisfy readers till the end.

After Frau and her bowel inquiry, I need to work hard so that the reader's mind won't wander. Following the fifteenth paragraph ("Flash forward four years ..."), I introduce dialogue as a calculated way to suck readers further into the story. Dialogue is often easier to write than pure narrative, and short conversation exchanges are easy on the reader's eyes since each comment carries its own short paragraph. The use of gibberish ("Kann yu oonderstund da wurds I um saaaayig?") in the sixth graf after the break, is also designed to draw in readers, based on the sheer novelty of seeing made-up words on the page.

Self-deprecation ("Like an idiot, I actually think the doctor will call back.") and throw-away humor ("These days it takes papal intervention to set up an appointment with your physician six weeks in advance.") helps to create a persona. That's essential in a long story like this. I establish myself as a tour guide through this dungeon of terrors called the Modern American Medical Center. All the reader needs to do is take my hand and we're off to see the Holy Shaman.

The bulk of "Busy Signal" is basic reporting (with plenty of attitude thrown in) of indignity after indignity tossed my way. I report details, but only if such detail adds to the core of the narrative. Extraneous detail detracts from the flow of the story. Every word, description, action must conspire to contribute to the story in a fundamental way. I don't want to slow the reader with unnecessary information. Each paragraph has to continue to captivate. I want to keep the paragraphs short. I need every literary device I can muster to keep the reader engaged for the entire piece. Once you can call the reader yours, you still need to coddle, entertain, and inform in a lively way. You need to continue staging literary pyrotechnics so he/she will stay till the last word.

EPILOGUE

While "Busy Signal" is laced with humor, it ultimately is a tragic story. "Of all the forms of inequality, injustice in health care is the most shocking and inhumane," said Martin Luther King, Jr., 40 years ago. "Busy Signal" is about how minor players in today's convoluted healthcare management mess wield so much power. The litany of petty power plays described in the piece reminds me of the time when I stood at a New York City subway booth, buying a subway token. I heard the No. 3 train roar into the station, saw commuters boarding the train, and instead of speeding up my transaction so I could catch the train, the vendor deliberately slowed her actions. She handed me the token in such a deliberate manner that as soon as I raced through the turnstile, the train doors closed. Her timing had been perfect. Exasperated, I looked back. and then I saw it: a sly, little smile. Another Frau Farbissina wannabe, this one engaged in guerrilla warfare in a New York City subway booth.

People seek power in predictable ways. While the healthcare profession is filled with caring, dedicated workers, like many bureaucracies, its limitations and frustrations often have a profound effect upon the personnel charged with enforcing the rules. The list in this story of healthcare workers who overlooked their primary responsibility—do everything in their power to ensure the well-being of the patient—is extensive. All the players in "Busy Signal" are real. I reported everything the way it happened. But unlike the subway worker, these players are involved in life-and-death issues.

I suppose the irony of "Busy Signal" is that I was treated at all. What would have happened if I had no healthcare insurance?

An additional point worth making is that even after the drones depicted in "Busy Signal" had finished poking and probing my lower back, it's the writer who ultimately gets the last word. I'm the one who gets to write the story, to place blame where it belongs, to call attention to a system that's broken. That's the power to afflict the comfortable and comfort the afflicted. It's the writer's revenge.

As long as the writer's back doesn't go out again.

ASSIGNMENTS

1) Write a first-person account of a frightening medical experience that undermined your health and well-being.

2) Interview local healthcare workers—physicians, nurses, orderlies, technicians—about imposed, cost-control limitations that make their jobs harder to carry out effectively.

3) Follow an uninsured patient who seeks medical care, and write a compelling story of the patient's experience.

3

BIZARRE SLAYING STUMPS
SAN FRANCISCO POLICE

Working in a bureau for a newspaper can be an ideal job. You're away from the mother ship, fewer editors breathing down your back, fewer office politics swirling around your head. But to keep your job, your work has to be indispensable. And therein lies the risk. Out of sight, out of mind. Your work from a bureau, by its very nature, isn't local, and local coverage is the bread and butter of most newspapers. Analysts who study such things say that newspaper readers are provincial. They want to know about test scores at their kid's schools, potholes in neighborhood streets, whether the mayor is getting a divorce or just separating from his wife. In my case, the newspaper I worked for *(The Sacramento Bee)* was 90 miles from the bureau where I worked. I tried to stay on the lookout for local Sacramento angles, but after that I was on my own. I patterned myself as a full-service correspondent, which meant that I covered hard news, breaking news, political analysis, cultural affairs, environmental issues, financial events, even sports and lifestyle. The marching orders I fashioned for myself were these: In 100 years, when a curious reader wants to get a glimpse of what it was like to live in San Francisco in the late twentieth century, he or she should be able to go to the stories I had written. That was the bar to which I held myself.

In keeping with that charge, I occasionally wrote about crime and punishment. To cover a nine-county metropolitan area with a combined population of six million and *not* write about crime would have been irresponsible. I didn't cover daily crime—there was way too much, and who in Sacramento would have been interested? Instead I wrote about what I thought were extraordinary events, which somehow were larger, more important, more telling stories than usual police blotter fare. "Bizarre Slaying Stumps San Francisco Police" is one of those strange stories that begged to be told.

Bizarre Slaying Stumps San Francisco Police

There are suspects, but no solid leads.

SAN FRANCISCO—Robert Young had a penchant for opera. He spoke German, Korean, Latin and Arabic. He spent hours studying antique maps as well as the Talmud. But what the brainy 44-year-old man liked most was delving into legal research.

Last Feb. 8, just as the sun rose on a foggy San Francisco morning, someone shot Young at point-blank range. A witness heard a popping sound and then saw someone wearing a white hat running from the crime scene. Young died en route to San Francisco General Hospital with a small-caliber bullet wound to his chest.

Police say they don't have the evidence to arrest anybody but have twice questioned a South Bay couple, David and Susan Beugen. David Beugen doesn't deny he had a motive for killing Young. In fact, quite frankly, Beugen is ecstatic that Young is dead.

"Thank God, someone got to him," Beugen said in a recent interview. "You bet I'm glad he's dead. Absolutely. It's a happy feeling to know he's gone."

To celebrate Young's death, Beugen bought flowers for his wife on the one-month anniversary of Young's slaying.

For the last eight years, Beugen and Young had been embroiled in a series of legal battles that began when a business deal went sour. So embittered were the two sides that at one time, 52-year-old Susan Beugen tackled Young and bit his left hand. David Beugen, 59, then punched Young in the mouth.

The murder has San Francisco police scratching their heads.

"It's one of the most bizarre cases I've ever had," said Inspector Art Gerrans, who has been a San Francisco cop for 28 years.

The case also has friends and associates of Robert Young angry and bewildered. As in many deaths, the killing opened up a shadow world few people knew about the dead man.

Unknown to his closest friends, Young had run up more than $70,000 in credit card debts in his own name and in an associate's, police said. Also discovered after his death was a Financial District apartment Young apparently rented to entertain young Asian men.

At the time of his death, Young was a paralegal for the Sierra Club Legal Defense Fund. Lawyers who knew him say Young was more knowledgeable about California civil codes than most attorneys.

It was his zeal for legal minutia that earned Young the wrath of the Beugens. David Beugen estimates that he paid $300,000 in attorney fees and spent "hundreds of hours in court" with Young.

Beugen attempted unsuccessfully to get the court to declare Young a litigious nuisance and bar him from filing more suits.

Young, who always acted as his own legal counsel, was so obsessed with getting even with the Beugens that the small San Francisco apartment he shared with two other men was knee-deep in legal documents.

"He barely had enough room for a little mat," said Zaide Kirtley, an attorney who befriended Young. "Gradually, there was hardly any room for him to sleep."

Young's problems with the Beugens began when he and one of his roommates, a Korean-born barber by the name of Hyon Mun, bought from the Beugens two Command Performance hair salons in Reno. On their first meeting, as a symbol of good will, Young gave Susan Beugen a box of chocolates.

But later Young said the Beugens misrepresented the profitability of the businesses. Thus ensued the years of lawsuits and countersuits.

So fed up was the couple with the continual paper parade of lawsuits that in 1986, they tried appealing to the media. Susan Beugen wrote letters to "60 Minutes" and *The Wall Street Journal* about Young's alleged harassment of the couple.

In one letter, Susan Beugen wrote: "There is nothing I can do, short of killing the bastard, to keep him from destroying my family, and I might be justified in doing so."

David Beugen said the threat "was a figure of speech," and that attorneys the couple hired used to say: "You gotta kill this guy. He's not gonna go away."

Beugen admits he's "no angel, but certainly I have nothing to do with murder."

By all accounts, Young was a handsome, disciplined man with a photographic memory who loved German arias.

The Little Rock, Ark., native studied Latin and German at the University of Alberta. In New York City, he became captivated by Orthodox Judaism and attended Yeshiva University.

In the late 1970s, he moved to San Francisco, where he worked both for the U.S. Postal Service and as a legal secretary. He attended law school in the city, but never graduated.

"Robert was precise," said one of his roommates, David White, who also served as a process server for Young's numerous filings against the Beugens. "He was the consummate gentleman. He almost never got angry."

White said the five-foot-eight and 175-pound Young slept only three or four hours a night but "could nap for 14 minutes and be refreshed for the whole day."

Attorney Kirtley said Young was driven by a compulsive need to be thorough. "He couldn't stand how I put staples in papers. He used to take the staples out and put them back in his way. He also had his own way of lining up stamps on envelopes."

For their part, Beugen and his wife have been involved with a handful of businesses, including the beauty salons, factory-discount clothing outlets and an Italian ice cream parlor. Although they live in a $1 million home in the posh San Mateo County enclave of Woodside, the couple filed for bankruptcy in 1986.

Upset by the lawsuits, Susan Beugen called Kirtley and threatened to burn down her red truck and her San Francisco home "with you and your two dogs in it" if she continued assisting Young in the court filings against the Beugens, Kirtley said.

Attorney Thomas Hunt of Sacramento, who represented an advertiser who said he was owed money by the couple, said he advised Young to be careful with the couple.

"They are slick people. This is nothing to be taken lightly," Hunt said he told Young.

Hunt said police had called him in early 1990 and were investigating an alleged murder-for-hire plot in which someone had allegedly paid $10,000 to have Young killed.

Three years earlier, Kirtley said, San Mateo County sheriff's deputies called her and said they were investigating a payment of $4,000 David Beugen allegedly made to a woman as a finder's fee to arrange a gunman to kill Young. No charges were ever filed in either case.

Although Beugen categorically denies allegations linking him to the incidents, on Friday he called Young "the slimiest piece of garbage. ... He sucked blood out of you. He was worse than a murderer."

Now, though, the Beugens hope to make money in the wake of Young's death. They have appeared on two television shows, "Inside Edition" and a local talk show, "People Are Talking."

Beugen said he thinks there are three possibilities in the murder of Young. Authorities said Young's roommate, Mun, had been diagnosed with the HIV virus, and Beugen said he thinks Young staged his own death because he was dying of AIDS "and wanted the police to blame us for the murder."

The coroner did not test for the presence of the HIV virus, although Kirtley maintains that "no way did Robert have AIDS. He didn't carry on relationships with anyone. He had an interest in gay pornography and gay videos. He liked to be around young Asian males, but there were no relationships or contacts."

Another scenario is that someone who frequented Young's Financial District hideaway killed Young or hired a gunman to kill him.

The third possibility is that Young just happened to be in the wrong place at the wrong time, the victim of a random shooting. He was killed one block from a San Francisco public housing project, around the block from where Kirtley lives. He had stopped by Kirtley's house to borrow her red Chevrolet S-10, so he could drive to yet another court proceeding with the Beugens.

Inspector Gerrans has asked the mayor to offer a $10,000 reward for information leading to the arrest of the killer.

"That's going to be our best chance at finding out who did it," he said.

The Sacramento Bee, May 25, 1991

WRITING THE STORY

I got the idea for the story from a small piece I read deep inside *The San Francisco Chronicle* one day. Buried in the piece were the names of several suspects the police had interviewed in a recent murder. The prime suspects figured to be a couple that had been involved in nasty and prolonged litigation with Robert Young. That sounded an alarm in my mind, and I called the couple, Susan and David Beugen.

I was rewarded immediately with their responses to my questions about Young. "Thank God, someone got to him," David Beugen told me. When I asked whether Beugen was glad that Young was murdered, Beugen went as far as to say, "You bet I'm glad he's dead. Absolutely. It's a happy feeling to know he's gone." Beugen volunteered that he bought flowers for his wife on the one-month anniversary of Young's death. Further down in the piece, Beugen bested himself by saying that Young had been "the slimiest piece of garbage … worse than a murderer."

These replies were not typical responses to questions about most dead men, and even if they were, how many people would be as forthcoming with a stranger as Beugen had been with me? If Beugen had killed his archenemy, Robert Young, then these comments were a novel way of deflecting police suspicion that he murdered Young. To bolster the details of Young's life, I accessed public court files, and was able to interview a friend, Zaide Kirtley, who had acted as Young's armchair attorney, as well as one of Young's roommates, David White. Near the end of the piece, David Beugen takes the reader on a wild ride when he speculates on Young's death: that perhaps he staged his own murder out of revenge.

EPILOGUE

The case of Robert Young is still unsolved, and no one has ever been arrested in connection with his murder. Homicide inspector Art Gerrans, the lead San

Francisco detective assigned to the investigation, retired from the police department in 1998.

Two years after I wrote the piece, *The Sacramento Bee* closed its San Francisco bureau. In a budget-cutting move, editors said the bureau was a luxury. Readership surveys showed readers preferred more news from their neighborhoods than from the large metropolitan area 90 miles away.

ASSIGNMENTS

1) Do a story on the cold-case section of the homicide division of the police department in your region. In large metropolitan areas, specific detectives are assigned to such a detail. Find out how many local homicides have gone unsolved in the last 10 years, and which are the oldest or the most prominent. Interview homicide detectives to find out what breaks were needed to crack a recent cold case.

2) On the anniversary of an unsolved murder, revisit the case. Interview family members, suspects, police officers. In your story, report any new developments in the case and specific steps police are taking to solve it.

3) Interview the local medical examiner to find out whether AIDS and HIV tests are routinely administered during autopsies. If such tests are not given routinely, what conditions must exist to warrant testing? Can family members or law enforcement personnel request that these tests be administered? Find out how other counties and states handle these often thorny issues, and compare their policies to those in your area.

4

COUPLE'S FIRST CRUISE: "IT'S TURNING INTO A FELLINI MOVIE"

As a journalist, I am offended when I read puff pieces in newspaper travel sections, and every Sunday, scores of newspapers run what amounts to free advertising for the travel industry. Such stories often are the outcome of junkets that newspapers accept, sending travel editors or writers on free trips in exchange for published articles that promote specific tourist venues. Magazines aren't immune to the charms of a free trip, and every month magazines abound with such valentines. Often, it's freelance writers who contact travel vendors and promise them favorable publicity in exchange for free or discounted vacations. To those in the tourist industry, these published stories are more valuable—not to mention cost efficient—than actual advertising, since such articles carry the semblance of legitimacy and objectivity that editorial copy confers.

No one could possibly confuse "Couple's First Cruise: 'It's Turning into a Fellini Movie'" with such industry-sponsored publicity. Maybe that's why the piece is so unusual. It's a basic, straightforward story about seven miserable days aboard a cruise ship. At its root, the story is a consumer piece. Anyone who selects a cruise ship and pays more than a grand for the privilege of being a passenger for a week ought to know what he/she is getting into. The story works, though, on another level, too. Once teased, readers want to know about the rubbery lamb chop dinner, the pulsating disco above our shabby room, the $20 bribe I gave the purser, and the smelly sewage that oozed into our sink. Everything I write in "Couple's First Cruise: 'It's Turning into a Fellini Movie'" is exactly how it happened.

Couple's First Cruise: "It's Turning into a Fellini Movie"

The burning question is this: Can two hipsters fast approaching middle age enjoy a slow Caribbean cruise?

Can two budget travelers, accustomed to bed-and-breakfast inns, bicycle vagabonding and knapsack lunches, enjoy midnight pasta binges, ballroom dancing and shooting skeet off the rear of a 600-foot-long ocean liner?

Frankly, it wasn't all that difficult getting accustomed to tanned cleavage oozing from bikini tops. My Ping-Pong serve improved. We didn't get seasick. There weren't any phones. We didn't have to haul our baggage. Our pillows were fluffed every night. When I returned home, my co-workers noticed my tan.

But, really. The dining-room food was cold, more caloric than savory. The ship, touted by our travel agent, was more like a Greyhound bus on water than a floating luxury hotel.

Cruise ships, we learned, aren't elegant yachts. The days of opulent luxury sailing on the high seas are largely over. At the bargain price we paid—for the seven-day trip it was $1,100 per person, including round-trip air fare from the West Coast—we knew we wouldn't be hobnobbing with the Caroline-of-Monaco set.

One caveat before I go on: This is one ship, one cruise and one couple's story. What happened to us is not indicative of all cruise ships and all Caribbean cruises.

●   ●   ●

Oh, no! We are ambushed by the ship's photographers as we embark in San Juan. It should have told us something. The swarthy guys armed with black Nikons stalk the ship's decks with one thing in mind: Photo opportunities. Over the next week they catch me swimming, dancing, eating, shaking hands with the captain, pawing at two hatcheck girls in black fishnet stockings.

The passengers all seem to have a wrinkled, tropical look—hot, flushed, tired. Our first dinner is a choice of steak, chicken or fish. To get to the dining room, we line up along the main staircase, anxiously awaiting the promise of sumptuous food and beverage. The maître d', a bald guy with shiny shoes whose name is Guiseppi, is like a corral master, deciding who will go to which feeding stall.

Theme for the first sitting: Shove as much food at the passengers as they can eat. Then get them out fast.

For someone who's been to Denny's, the food preparation and arrangement are disappointing. Anyone who enjoys anything resembling *nouvelle* cuisine must feel let down with the heaps of greasy chicken on trays that we pass around the table. It looks like dinner at Bob's All You Can Eat Smorgie. The fish is served at room temperature. The steak is thin, curled at the edges and well-done.

On cue, Guiseppi exhorts us to leave, to make room for the second herd of ravenous passengers lined up outside the dining room. The first night is at variance with the brochure left in our room: "During every cruise, world-renowned executive chefs are complimented on their superb cuisine."

Surely, things will get better.

Three bands are cooking in full force: a steel drum ensemble in the Lido area, a five-piece combo in the observation lounge, four throbbing electronic disco men and a sultry singer in a fringe skirt doing hip grinds on the rear deck.

We're tired, so we check into our cabin. Bad news. It's directly under the hip grinder. The disco floor is our ceiling. The acoustical tiles don't seem to be doing anything except vibrating to "Proud Mary."

We manage to sleep—until 3:30 a.m., when the music stops and is replaced by what sounds like a rat gnawing its way toward our headboards. In the morning, we discover that our room is next to a dumbwaiter.

I complain to the ship's purser on the phone, asking for a room change. "All sold out, sir. Sorry."

But the purser tacks on an offer. "Why don't you come here and talk to me in person. We'll see what I can do once we arrive in Caracas." So the gambit has been offered. Given a big enough tip, we figure, the purser will change our room.

We proceed to the sun deck and check out the bikinis, the Speedos, the tanning oil, the pina coladas (At $2.40, they're great!). The atmosphere seems tame. The most going on is a secretary from Philadelphia having two guys from Kansas City smear her back with No. 15 Bain de Soleil.

Hot dogs on the Lido deck, a couple of dips in the pool, lots of Danielle Steel, Eric Segal and Jackie Collins, burgundy prosthetic nails, toupees, pinky rings, Ray-Bans. I narrowly lose two out of three Ping-Pong games, despite a surprise serve.

Dinner is less hectic than the night before, but the food leaves us wanting more (not in quantity). Really, I'm not a snob. But tonight's veal scaloppini sauce tastes like sweet brown paste better suited to a Foster's Freeze than to meat. Guiseppi apologizes and says tomorrow will be better.

After the meal, The Great Robert, a magician from Queens, stars in the observation lounge. He muffs two magic tricks, one involving a size 44 D brassiere, but nobody seems to notice.

We arrive in Curaçao on day three and plan to get as far from the madding crowd as possible. We go to an underwater park for snorkeling. Down under, the water is clear and peaceful. But the sun and gulps of salt water make me queasy. I climb back aboard.

Dinner time again. The inferior food we're getting must be a temporary aberration, I figure. I'm willing to give Guiseppi another chance. But what should be cold isn't. The vichyssoise is served room temperature, not chilled. The lamb chops look like deflated whoopee cushions and are as rubbery. The duck is not crispy. I ask for a steak knife.

Back in our room, the disco beat begins at 8 p.m. It sounds like someone's dribbling marbles on our ceiling. We check out the movie selection. It's "Attila the Hun," dubbed into Spanish. We try to sleep.

"And a very good morning to you, ladies and gentlemen." The voice mumbles through the loudspeaker every morning, the greeting followed by a rundown of the ship's activities. Bingo, flower arranging, ice sculpting and parlor horse racing are the biggies. When the microphone isn't being spoken through, it's connected to Muzak that seeps through the speakers all day: "Strangers in the Night," "Feelings," "Puff the Magic Dragon." It's more like mind mush than mind control, with the not-so subliminal message: Aren't we having FUN!

We arrive in Caracas at 9 a.m. without having had much sleep, and take a taxi after haggling with a driver who says his name is Antonio, but we should call him Gordo. The ship docks in La Guaira, and we have until 2:30 to see what we can of a city of 5 million people.

We do our best. We race to a handicraft market, eat a hurried lunch, run through the Museum of Contemporary Art, and then it's time to get back.

I pay a personal visit to the purser and ask about getting out of the marble rock hop that we call home. "I think so," he says, not so enigmatically.

Then he winks at me. I give him a $20 bill, placed squarely in front of me so that no one else can see. He takes it into the palm of his hand.

"Oh, you didn't have to do that," he says, pocketing the double sawbuck, then smiling. "You will be very happy in the new room."

We are. We've been moved to the top deck of the ship, into a cabin with a picture window of the ocean and a full-size bath tub. Just for an extra $20. And it's quiet.

The sleeping accommodations improve, but the food down under does not. The cruise, for us, is turning into a Fellini movie. Passengers plop themselves down and order all seven courses. Some order as many as three entrees. The waiters oblige, placing overflowing dishes in front of determined diners who methodically consume everything.

Passengers actually seem to be gaining weight right before our eyes. Fat seems to be developing on midriffs. The circles under many passengers' eyes seem to be getting deeper. It is as though we are sleepwalkers whose sole function in life is to eat, waddle, then doze off.

We try to stay as active as possible, and in Grenada pay $10 for five minutes of water skiing. I busily snap pictures with our new camera, only to find out later that there was no film in it.

Back on the beach we meet Debbie, a dental hygienist from Denver who is angry. She says she decided to book passage on the cruise, her first, because of all the lush ports the brochure promised we would explore. That's true: six ports in seven days. But precisely because of all the miles we have to cover (almost 1,600), there's no time to do much of anything when we arrive.

Our schedule upon docking is something like this: Race off the ship, walk around in the port area with thousands of passengers from other ships, drop $50 on perfume and liquor to be given away to someone back home, then hurry back before the ship departs for another in-and-out port.

Debbie says something else that is disturbing: The 76-year-old ship's physician wanted to examine her in his cabin last night. Imagine!

Is it all the doctor's fault? No wonder he's bored. Outside of Robert the Magician and "Attila the Hun," there's not too much to do but spend more and more money on slot machines and drinks aboard.

There is, of course, other on-board entertainment:

- Mandy, Mindy and Tammy, an oversized trio of "entertainers" in black lace and high heels, who look like out-of-work lap dancers from the Des Moines gentleman's club, Hogs and Heifers.

- Sexy Coffee and Freddy, a singing team that screams a lot and does a mean version of "Louie, Louie." (For the last five days it was just Sexy Coffee, because Freddy had an appendicitis attack between Martinique and Caracas.)

- Mucho Macho, an Argentine David Brenner who skips rope while slamming down onto the floor what looks like a walnut tied to a string.

- Los Caballeros, a Mexican combo whose members play wooden mouth organs in unison.

All the sedentary pleasure takes a toll on my stomach: I gain six pounds in five days. I've gotta do something about the drooping dough beginning to hang over my Speedo. A visit to the ship's exercise room is in order.

Alas, it's closed from noon until 4 p.m. I return at 4:05 and meet the on-board exercise guru, Wilma. Puffing on a cigarette, she says the stationary bicycles are broken.

Why? No one seems to know. This seems to be typical of the ship. No bowls for cereal in the morning. Plastic utensils on the rear deck. When we are about to disembark in Fort-de-France, Martinique, the line of passengers is 150 long. The reason: photo opportunities. One of the photographers is posing as a drunk French sailor at the foot of the gangplank, and the passengers can't get by him without having their pictures taken. (They're later made available at $4 apiece.)

Other irritants begin cascading. Out of the drain of our sink a murky brown fluid erupts. It looks suspiciously like sewage. It doesn't drain out, and stops up the sink and tub.

Also, the sheets. Ah, the sheets. They are changed only once during our entire trip. I know because after I drop a pen, the mark is on the sheet from then on.

The last port of call is St. Thomas. We are so tired of being corralled and managed that we ask a bartender in town to recommend a restaurant far from the madding cruise. "Go to a place called Famous. It's run by a guy from Jersey named Buddy. He'll set you up real well." We take a rain check.

We pass up all the bargains. All the liquor, the perfume, the Louis Vuitton handbags. The only item we buy on the entire trip is a $1 beaded spice basket in Grenada.

We didn't have a bad time. Cruises generally are exceptional values, and this one would have been, too, if we hadn't run into some exceptional problems. If you go, be careful. Watch what you eat. Take along some reading material. Come with guarded expectations.

The Sacramento Bee, March 8, 1988

WRITING THE STORY

I didn't like the lede when I wrote it, and I'm not sure I like it any more now, 15 years later. This is at least what I was hoping to do: Instead of trying the more standard anecdotal opening, I opt to let the reader know who we are, where we are going, and whether or not such an unlikely vacation for people like us would be a bust. The gambit has been set. I'm banking that the reader will stay along to find out how the drama ends.

Detail, again, is paramount in the piece, and in phrases like midnight pasta binges, ballroom dancing, and shooting skeet from a 600-foot ocean liner alert the reader that the writer is concerned with precise facts, not dreamy sunsets. The third graf lets the reader know that the piece will not be devoid of cheeky observation. The next graf serves as the "nut" of the entire piece—that the particular cruise ship we set sail on is more like a Greyhound bus on the high seas than the love-boat image the cruise industry merrily drills into the public's mind.

The rest of the piece is set in the first person. The story moves faster that way. A few words about how I go about reporting: I am always with notebook in hand. Just about everywhere I went on the cruise, I took notes. If I went swimming, then I left the notebook on my chaise lounge. I brought my notebook with me to the dining room, to the Lido deck, to the magic show with The Great Robert in the observation lounge. If I happened to forget the notebook back in our room, then as soon as I returned, I'd sit down and write in it. That way I was able to preserve the immediacy of what happened. (The first person format helps with that, too.) Writers who think they can reconstruct dialogue, facts, sequence of events when they get home solely from memory often find themselves in for a surprise. At least I can't do it. So I write everything down as it is happening. I still sit in front of my computer and mull over the events and what they mean, but I have a framework of details that starts with facts and observations recorded in a notebook.

I try to drive home this piece with its unconventional tone. I don't pull punches and try to share my perceptions, as they are happening, with the reader. My role here is as a trustworthy tour guide, telling a story that seldom gets told in published travel stories.

I must say that when I handed this piece into the special-sections editor at *The San Jose Mercury News*, she read it and blanched. The story had been slated to run in the semi-annual travel section devoted to cruise stories (and cruise-ship advertisements), but the editor flatly refused to run the story. She killed the piece on the spot. Way too negative, she said. And besides, she said, I had never identified myself as a reporter to the cruise-ship personnel, which nullified the story.

"Do restaurant critics announce to the chef, waiter, and maître d' that they're critics?" I retorted. If they did, they certainly wouldn't receive the same treatment as the average diner, and their reviews would be inaccurate.

I offered to contact the cruise ship and ask for specific comments on everything that I wrote about. No matter. The editor spiked the piece. I left *The Mercury News* shortly thereafter and submitted the same story to another editor at another newspaper, *The Sacramento Bee*, for its Sunday cruise section. This time, the travel editor liked the piece, but wanted to delete the name of the cruise ship and instead had me insert wiggle room in the fifth graf of the piece, a disclaimer that this was one reporter's story and not meant to be representative of all cruise ships. The editor also had me tack on a summary ending to the piece, which seemed to take the shine off the piece. At least the story finally ran.

EPILOGUE

The day after "Couple's First Cruise: 'It's Turning into a Fellini Movie'" was published, all hell broke loose. Travel agents, cruise-line personnel, and would-be cruisers called the newspaper *en masse*. The industry employees couldn't believe the paper would ever run such a negative story, when, as one cruise-line executive told the travel editor, "We pay your salary!" The chief complaint among readers was that by withholding the name of the cruise ship, the article damned all cruise lines. Readers had a right to know which cruise ship I took so they could avoid it.

I knew instinctively that the readers were right. But I had given up on the battle, tired from wrangling with another editor over the fate of an unconventional, honest story. I had wanted the piece to run, but in retrospect, this was a battle I should have fought. The only positive thing I learned from the fallout was that a reporter's job is not to withhold information from the reader. With the exception of mentioning alleged victims' names in certain crime stories, it's the reader who ought to decide how essential specific information is, not the editor or reporter.

ASSIGNMENTS

1) Take a cruise and write a first-person story on the voyage. Make sure your story is bolstered by details of the cruise. Avoid writing about "lively" ports of call, "stunning" vistas, "sumptuous" buffets. Write a realistic story about your experiences aboard the ship—warts and all. If the trip was stupendous, write precisely about why; if the trip was a nightmare, write what happened.

2) Do a consumer piece comparing tour packages to a specific destination. Compare all details, including costs, transportation, lodging, food. Interview people who go on different tour packages to ascertain which accommodations offer the best value and/or the most luxury.

3) Interview ex-employees of a cruise ship. Find out what issues most affected these employees, from salary differentials, to tipping, to living quarters and food, to rules about fraternizing with the public. Your story should examine the world that few passengers see aboard a cruise ship.

4) Write a story for a journalism review, such as *Columbia Journalism Review* or *American Journalism Review*, about the practice of travel editors accepting free trips in exchange for published stories. Find out which newspapers and magazines have rules prohibiting such practices and which do not. Talk to editors and writers about methods used to circumvent such rules.

5

DR. FART SPEAKS

Ever find a story about flatulence in a conventional newspaper or magazine? You might come across something in an arcane medical journal, but it's unlikely you'd find much about farts in any general-circulation publication. That gets at one of the reasons why the Internet has been so successful in carving out a niche as an essential information medium. Internet sites take on taboo, controversial, obscure and narrow subjects that the mainstream press, for fear of losing readers, won't touch. Everyone farts, yet there is a virtual blackout in the establishment press about our own natural gas.

When I broached the subject of doing a piece on farts, the health editor at *Salon* enthusiastically said yes. We quickly agreed how best to do it: Find an authority on flatulence and let him gas rhapsodic. A quick Internet search revealed that Dr. Michael Levitt was our man. After I interviewed Dr. Levitt, I called back the editor with a suggestion for the only headline that would do the story justice. She wholeheartedly agreed.

As I began writing the story, I realized how much fun this was going to be. Merrily typing away, I thought, "What other job would allow me to write about something everyone does but no one wants to talk about without snickering?"

Dr. Fart Speaks

When I told my wife I was going to write a story about farts, she said that if I mentioned her name I was dead meat. Fact is, there is nothing to be ashamed of. Everyone farts. The amount of gas and the volume at which a fart is expelled are another issue. My wife does fart and she farts loudly but, thank God, her farts are mostly odorless. This is not the case with mine.

To understand the nuances of farting, or flatulence, I called upon Dr. Michael D. Levitt, a gastroenterologist and associate chief of staff at the Minneapolis Veterans Affairs Medical Center. Levitt, 64, could well be called Dr. Fart because he is the world's leading authority on flatulence. He has had 275 articles printed on flatulence in medical journals, as either the principal author or the co-author.

In fact, Levitt's career could only happen in America. "In other countries, no way would a scientist study farts. But for reasons I can't completely figure out, farting is considered wrong in America and people are worried about it. Farts have been good to me. I've done very well, thank you."

Levitt works with four assistants out of a small laboratory on the third floor of the V.A. hospital, about a mile west of the Mississippi River. Every day he receives at least one long-distance phone consultation from a worried farter, almost always a man whose wife has prompted her husband to find out why he cuts the cheese so often.

Levitt's job doesn't end when he leaves the hospital at night, either. "Every cocktail party I go to, I always get at least one wife who comes up to me and complains about her husband's farts."

To clear the air (there will be no more puns in this story), Levitt says that his research has shown that on average the normal number of flatulent occurrences a day is 10. There are scores more, but they are all internal explosions and since this gas technically never leaves the body, it can't really be considered flatulence.

Levitt notes that if you have on average more than 22 separate flatulent occurrences a day, then you may want to consider several things: what you eat, how fast you eat it and how much air you swallow when you eat or drink.

In his 40-year career, Levitt has seen only two patients (both men) who farted upward of 140 times a day, but these extraordinary cases were lactose-intolerant individuals and, once dairy products were cut out of their diets, they returned to the normal range of acceptability. "These two were the biggest farters of my career. One of them complained that his sex life had been ruined by his chronic farting," Levitt says.

There are four possible reasons why some people fart more than others: They eat a lot of carbohydrates; they swallow air when they eat; the bacteria in their intestines are more efficient in turning carbohydrates into gas; or, conversely, the bacteria in their intestines don't consume carbohydrates efficiently, and therefore produce gas.

Levitt says an average male fart is made up of about 110 milliliters of gas (almost half a cup), with 80 milliliters for a woman's (a third of a cup). That adds up to a lot of gas—38 ounces during a single day for men, 27 ounces for women. Although some women claim they never fart, Levitt says that's not true. They just fart less because they are smaller.

Gassy food is gassy food for everyone, says Levitt, with a crucial caveat. Some people are able to absorb and tolerate the gas they produce better than others. The single most gas-producing food for most everyone, Levitt says, is—no surprise—baked beans. The musical fruit is made up entirely of simple carbohydrates, which are not absorbed in the intestines. Once inside the intestines, the sludge that was once beans is broken down by bacteria and enzymes, and then ferments. In that process, the thick, gooey substance can produce potent gases that have nowhere to go but down—and out, thank goodness.

Out is important. While Levitt says he has never treated someone who held a fart in too long, there are dangerous side effects (including dizziness and headaches). Your colon becomes bloated, and theoretically, the methane and other lethal gases could add enough toxins to your blood to poison you. Levitt does not recommend holding in farts.

Besides beans, vegetables (especially broccoli, brussels sprouts, cabbage and cauliflower) are also gas producers, as are grains and fiber. (Pumpernickel, the dark-grain bread, means "goblin that breaks wind" in Old German.) In fact, some of the healthiest foods, touted as anodynes for cancer and heart disease, are the foods that produce the most gas.

But what if you don't eat lots of veggies and carbs and you still exceed 10 explosions a day on the fart-o-meter scale that Levitt says is normal? There could be several reasons:

Drinking too many carbonated beverages. The fizz in most carbonated beverages comes from carbon dioxide, which is dissipated by the time it reaches your intestines. But many soft drinks contain fructose, a sugar the intestines have a difficult time absorbing, thereby causing flatus, the medical term for farts (which comes from the Latin meaning "the act of blowing").

Drinking through a straw. If you sip air when you swallow, then the air has to come out some way, often through your butt.

Eating too fast, and eating too much fast food. Chew your food slowly. The act of eating quickly tends to induce the diner to take in air, thereby bloating the colon, as well as turning the air inside deadly.

Chewing gum. When you chew gum, you swallow air, and that means more of the above.

Not enough exercise. Exercising helps the body absorb gases in the colon, thereby dissipating them by the time they reach your anus. If you happen to fart while you are exercising, particularly in a health club, it's usually not so bad because most people wear headsets and listen to music, which tends to obscure the sound. As for smell, workout places often are venues of assorted bodily odors, so run-of-the-mill farts often go undetected, particularly if you don't look suspicious.

Speaking of silent but deadly, Levitt doubts their existence. "Noisy farts can smell just as bad as silent ones," he says. "That's another myth that needs to be put to rest."

Whether silent or musical, all farts are made up of a variety of gases. The majority is made up of nitrogen, oxygen, carbon dioxide, hydrogen and methane—all odorless. As anyone who has been to summer camp knows, methane, even in small amounts, can torch a match. The higher density of methane, the greater the bluish-green flames. The hydrogen in farts can cause a loud popping sound when ignited. Fart smells come in when sulfur gets stirred into the gaseous mix. Hydrogen causes the fart to waft quickly upward.

So, now that we know what's in them, how do we make them go away? Levitt says that over-the-counter items like Bean-O and Gas-Ex rarely work. Bean-O does, though, have a 24-hour toll-free hot line, (800) 257-8650 (no, it doesn't spell out F-A-R-T), and has a nifty collection of promotional materials, including a fanny pack and yellow windbreaker (get it?). Antacids work on some people, but Levitt stresses that for the best results, users should take no more than four tablespoons or tablets a day.

For odor, about the only thing that Levitt says works is a fart cushion made of charcoal, called the Tooter Trapper, invented by a man whose co-workers complained of his farts so much that they demanded he be moved out of the office pool into a separate room with a door. The air filter, which you sit on, does a good job of eliminating fart odors but, of course, treats only the results, not the symptoms, of the noxious-smelling gas, says Levitt.

Forget Glade or Airwick, or even matches, to eradicate fart smells. The thing that works best is opening a window. Lighting a match may camouflage the smell but will not dispel it, says Levitt.

And as for masking the sound, Levitt says that depending on the anatomical peculiarities of a person's anus, sounds can vary when gas is squeezed through such a tight opening. The larger the volume of gas expelled and the greater the pressure exerted, generally the greater the noise, although Levitt says that standing usually tends to minimize the sound over sitting, which can amplify the toot.

Besides food, antibiotics occasionally cause some people to fart more, Levitt says, because the medications can disrupt the natural fauna of the colon, thereby making it more difficult to break down certain foods, and thus leading to more flatus.

Americans are probably the most supercilious about farts. Other cultures are less squeamish about them. The British explorer and linguist Sir Richard Francis

Burton, who first translated the "Kama Sutra" in 1883, contends in one of his many books that a tribe of Arabian Bedouins created a language of arcane codes and warnings through a series of intricately nuanced farts.

Farting came out of the closet in the United States in the breakthrough 1974 film "Blazing Saddles," in which Mel Brooks plays Gov. Le Petomane, who serves up baked beans around the campfire one night and hears the results from a bivouac of cowboys. Actually, Brooks' character was named after Joseph Pujol, known as Le Petroman (which translates to "the Fartiste"), who in 1892 debuted at the Moulin Rouge in Paris with a show that featured Pujol paying a flute, smoking a cigarette, blowing out candles, even singing La Marseillaise from anus air. Pujol extinguished candles from two feet away and became famous for his imitations of thunder, cannons and two yards of calico fabric being ripped. Pujol opened his own theater, the Pompadour, in which he starred for two decades before dying in 1945.

Levitt says Pujol probably was able to aspirate through his anus, that is, suck air in through his butt, and with that air performed his assortment of tricks. So it really wasn't Pujol's farts that amazed his audiences, but merely air that traveled a wee distance, instead of the longer, more arduous trip from mouth to colon to buttocks.

Farts, of course, predate Pujol. Aristophanes' play *The Clouds* contains a reference to farts. In Dante's *Divine Comedy*, flatulent demons in the eighth ring of Hell make "trumpets of their asses." Hieronymus Bosch's "The Garden of Earthly Delights" shows a young woman with red roses shooting out from her derrière. And in 1776, Benjamin Franklin published a book of bawdy essays called "Fart Proudly."

Franklin wasn't the only one who knew that farts are funny. For a host of complex cultural reasons, farts render 10-year-old boys silly, not to mention more than a few grown men who still get amused for some reason by anal gas. It's a strange thing, though, farts. Take, for example, the expression "old fart." It's a term of insult when spoken in the third person, but one of pride when spoken about oneself.

And for those of you who must have an Internet fart connection, there are plenty of places. My personal favorite is farts.com, which offers an audio sampling of scores of farts, and allows viewers to rate the flatulence on several criteria, including verisimilitude, pitch, duration and volume.

Salon, February 24, 2000

WRITING THE STORY

By the time I interviewed Dr. Levitt, I had already spent several days piecing together as much information as possible on flatulence. The Internet was helpful, as was the database Nexis, which I use while reporting most stories. As usual, I wrote out my questions in advance of the Levitt interview. I wanted to make sure that I didn't forget any areas of interest. How many times in my lifetime would I get to talk to the world's foremost authority on farts? One question on my list: "Are there certain ethnic groups that fart more?"

Dr. Levitt paused. He wanted to go off the record—a condition to which I seldom agree with almost all sources. Usually, a good reporter is able to convince the source to go on the record with the comment, but Dr. Levitt was resolute. He wouldn't budge. So, I ceded to his demand. He lowered his voice. He said in almost a whisper that indeed, because of peculiarities of diet, particular ethnic groups *might* fart more than others.

Of the almost-daily phone consultations he does with worried male farters whose wives prompt them to call, he said, "Eighty percent are from one specific ethnic group."

This was news, and damn it, I had allowed the physician to go off the record.

"Which group is that?" I asked, hot on an exclusive story.

"Are we still off the record?" Dr. Levitt inquired cautiously, still whispering.

I tried to wiggle, but Dr. Levitt had me pinned. After I assured him yes, Dr. Levitt dropped his bombshell. He spoke so softly that I had to press the phone receiver hard against my ear to hear.

Years after the interview, I am still not at liberty to reveal Dr. Levitt's prescient observation, but I can share its context. After a suitable pause in our conversation, Dr. Levitt warned, "Now, don't jump to conclusions. That [deleted] call me much more often may be based on cultural taboos against farting, on what the [deleted] farters eat, or that to their wives farts are especially boorish behavior. It also may be based on their willingness to pay for a phone consultation."

Such a good quote, and I couldn't use it. I had let Dr. Levitt slip through my fingers.

EPILOGUE

Interestingly, "Dr. Fart Speaks" is probably the single story of mine that has been most often syndicated, excerpted and written about. I'm not exactly sure what that says about my other stories or what it says about farting and the media's sparse coverage of flatulence. Perhaps I was breaking new ground with the piece. "Dr. Fart Speaks" was cited as "one of the best, most innovative stories ever carried in *Salon*." It has been republished so many times in serious medical venues that I've lost count, which underscores how timid the conventional press is.

Readers might imagine that I paid mightily for the lede, and I did. My wife was not amused. When I told her that my next story was going to be about wives who snore, she said no way. I have honored her request.

ASSIGNMENTS

1) Write about a bodily function, e.g., burping, itching, body odor, halitosis, odorous feet, and find out when the condition requires medical intervention. Talk to physicians and patients about coping with such maladies, as well as the treatments available.

2) Interview "professional patients" who are used as trainers to help medical students gain familiarity and comfort when examining real patients. Medical schools routinely hire so-called "professional patients." Find out who such patients are and why they opt for such unusual moonlighting jobs.

3) Take a widely used modern product of convenience, e.g., snow blowers, leaf blowers, garbage disposals, and write a history of where the product came from, who invented it, where it is most popular, how society has grown to believe it is essential.

6

DEATH OF AN
AMERICAN DREAM

One August morning, while slurping my morning ration of Grape-Nuts, a tiny Associated Press story buried inside *The Dallas Morning News* caught my eye. The article told of a 53-year-old husband and his 50-year-old wife found shot to death in a car on San Antonio's south side. Police found a rifle in the car and suspected that the deaths had been the result of a murder-suicide.

When I got to work that morning, I called the San Antonio coroner's office and learned the couple's names: Tony and Kay Garza. Investigators had found clothes, bedding, an electric fan, and dog food in the car's backseat. In the glove compartment, they found bankruptcy papers, and inside Tony Garza's pants pocket, they found 54 cents.

"Did you find a suicide note?" I asked the coroner.

"Wait a minute," he said.

On the other end of the line, I heard the slapping of footsteps on what I imagined was a clean linoleum floor.

"Here it is," he said. "You ready?"

"I have gone as far as I can with our lives. My wife, Kay, and I are hard-working people that have been reduced to beggars almost. We came to San Antonio to work, not to die. But Reagan economics has nothing trickling down to us. I almost cry every time I compare Reagan to Hoover."

That was all I needed. This was a story that got under my skin and resolutely stayed there. I convinced my editor to send me to Columbus to interview Kay and Tony's friends and former employers. One week later, I drove down to San Antonio to talk to anyone who knew about the murder-suicide.

Death of an American Dream

Collapse of couple's economic hopes leads to murder-suicide in San Antonio

At 9 that Friday morning, the temperature already was hot—87 degrees. The man and woman got into their 1973 Impala, rolled down all four windows and drove to a deserted street on San Antonio's industrial south side.

Once on Roosevelt Avenue, the man parked, went to the sedan's mud-smudged trunk and pulled out a hunting rifle.

Back inside, he pointed the gun at the woman's temple and squeezed the trigger. Her body crumpled onto the worn vinyl of the front seat.

Next, he jammed the butt of the rifle into his thigh and aimed the barrel at his forehead. He looked straight ahead and fired again.

In the man's pants pocket were 54 cents and some wrinkled pieces of paper. On the paper, he had written in a scrawl:

"I have gone as far as I can with our lives. My wife, Kay, and I are hard-working people that have been reduced to beggars almost. We came to San Antonio to work, not to die. But Reagan economics has nothing trickling down to us. I almost cry every time I compare Reagan to Hoover."

Kay and Tony Garza had friends and family who cared deeply about them. After 23 years of marriage, Kay, who was 50, and Tony, 53, were still very much in love. More than anything else, their work was their life.

Accounts of the murder-suicide Aug. 13 grabbed front-page headlines across the country. The Garzas' act was an American tragedy, an account of two ambitious, successful people who could not survive the collapse of their dreams.

Five years ago, the Garzas owned a $175,000 custom-designed home located on five wooded acres in a Columbus, Ohio, suburb. Garza was chief aerial plotter for a respected mapping firm in Ohio. His wife was one of the most gifted mapping technicians in the Midwest.

Five years later, what they had left was in the back seat of their car. Their belongings were in boxes—clothes, a tool chest, bedding, an electric fan, dog food. Bankruptcy papers were in the glove compartment. The 54 cents in Garza's pocket was all the money the couple had.

The Garzas' failure can be blamed not only on their inability to sustain their own business, but also on an economy that now is squeezing thousands out of work. After they lost their business, the couple fled to the Sun Belt, the one U.S.

region touted as having employment opportunities. But even Texas held no promise for them.

Police detective Morris White was routinely cruising San Antonio's south side when he spotted the Garzas in their car.

Inside, Garza's husky, 250-pound body was grotesquely slumped over his wife, a petite woman who weighed no more than 100 pounds. The gun—a 15-year-old, .44-caliber rifle—lay on top of both of them.

White called for an ambulance and backup police units. When emergency medics arrived, they pronounced Garza dead at the scene. Kay Garza died en route to the hospital.

By the next day, the San Antonio medical examiner had determined the Garzas were not under the influence of either drugs or alcohol. The examinations found no evidence of a struggle between the couple before the rifle was fired.

"It appears that these people knew exactly what they were doing," assistant medical examiner Linda Norton said. "There was no surprise. They planned out the whole thing."

Most of the 200 people who attended the double funeral in Tony's hometown of Brackettville, Texas, had never met the Garzas. News of the murder-suicide and of the suicide note that blamed Reaganomics drew the curious from as far as 100 miles away.

After the 45-minute church ceremony, scores of onlookers formed a six-block-long funeral procession, inching down a gravel road to the city's Catholic cemetery, a desolate piece of land dotted with mesquite and poplar trees.

Tony's parents also are buried in the cemetery. He had bought their headstones after his father died in 1972. That was the last time he had been to Brackettville.

The town of 1,676 is located 120 miles west of San Antonio, 30 miles north of the Mexico border. Brackettville's landmarks are three filling stations, a Western Auto store, two churches and Frontier Village, a tourist attraction that Hollywood camera crews occasionally have used in filming movies, including "The Alamo".

Brackettville doesn't have a movie theater, but it once did. Thirty-five years ago, Tony Garza, as a teen-ager, worked at the theater as an usher and sold popcorn.

Tony grew up in the dusty insulation of the small Texas town. His father, who had left Monterey, Mexico, for Brackettville when he was 10 years old, was superintendent of the town's one-man Waterworks Department for 65 years. The family spoke Spanish at home, but the four children, along with their parents, integrated themselves into American life.

"The thing about Tony was that he was the brain of the family," his brother-in-law, Chris Gomez, said. Gomez grew up in Brackettville, married Tony's sister Jane and now works as a telephone lineman in the town.

"Tony was the oldest," Gomez said. "Everyone looked up to him. He became a professional and made lots of money."

The summer after Tony graduated from high school, his mind was made up. He enlisted.

"You reach 18 or 19, and the (military) service is the only ticket out," Gomez said. "You make the move right after high school, or you forget about it."

Tony picked the Air Force and, as the advertisements promise, he learned a profession: map scribing, the exacting task of turning aerial photographs into topographical charts.

Tony and Kay

Tony was a sergeant by the time he was discharged in 1958. He took his first civilian job in Pittsburgh. During the winter, he placed an ad in a local newspaper, looking for someone to write lyrics for original sheet music a friend had given him. Kay Gruber answered the ad. The daughter of a Pittsburgh steel worker, she was a petite, energetic young woman with a penchant for eclectic clothes and heavy makeup. She considered herself a musician and an artist, and enjoyed composing songs and painting still lifes.

Kay and Tony agreed to meet at a restaurant to talk about a songwriting partnership. Within a month, they began dating.

They were opposites attracted to each other. Tony was steady, heavy-set, with an intense look to his eyes. Kay was fragile and so high-strung that, friends said, she often never finished a sentence. Kay chain-smoked filterless Pall Malls and often wore white go-go boots, halter tops and pedal pushers.

Within a year, Tony and Kay were married in a small ceremony on April 4, 1959. He was 30, she was 27.

That summer, Tony scoured the want ads in the *Pittsburgh Post-Gazette* every day. At the time, the Midwest was the region where jobs were most abundant.

Tony answered an ad for a scriber with a small firm in a Toledo, Ohio, suburb. He was hired immediately. The couple moved, but within two years, the man who had hired Tony, Wesley Norris, relocated to Columbus. Norris asked Tony to take a position with the new firm, Berger Associates, a well-known consulting company.

Once again, Tony and Kay moved. They rented a tiny duplex in Columbus, but like millions of newlyweds, they had one goal: to buy their own home.

But the dream went further than that. "Tony and Kay's dream—the thing that consumed them—was not just owning their own place," said Norris, who still lives in Columbus. "They wanted their very own retreat."

They also wanted children, but Kay was unable to conceive. She went to two specialists in Columbus and even took fertility pills for a while, but after Kay reached 35, the Garzas decided the time had passed for them to become parents.

Eventually, they lavished their affection on two Chihuahuas. Their first was named Charlie; after he died, they bought Humphrey. They pampered their dogs, often going to a local delicatessen to buy them roast beef slices.

The luxury was one of the few they allowed themselves. "They were always pinching pennies, stashing everything away in the bank, and it was all for one thing—that home of theirs," Norris said.

Tony never ate lunch out. He drove a Dodge Demon, which he bought at a year-end closing sale, until its flooring rusted through. Only then, in 1978, did he buy the used, dark-blue Impala.

By 1968, Tony and Kay were able to afford five wooded acres in Galena, 30 miles north of Columbus. They bought the property for $1,000 an acre. The land now fetches $10,000 per acre.

They hired an architect to design the house, and co-workers remember how Tony showed off the blueprints. Kay worked with an interior decorator and bought designer furniture. By 1972, the house was completed—cathedral ceilings, huge plate-glass windows looking out to the lake, an oak ceiling beam that stretched the length of the house.

Always somewhat shy, the Garzas opened up to their neighbors Casetta and Paul Dunch, who became their closest friends in the Columbus area. "They were love birds, the happiest people you'd ever want to meet," Casetta Dunch said.

Kay took a special liking to the Dunch's teenaged daughter, Donna, and often gave her presents—an oil painting, an old mink stole. Three or four times, the two families had Thanksgiving dinner together. On weekends, they did yard work together.

In his spare time, Tony taught Kay his craft. Within three years, she had become proficient enough at map scribing to start what quickly turned into a burgeoning business run out of their home.

Tony directed the cottage industry from his office. After he got home, they worked together, often putting in 12- to 15-hour days. They were so busy, and they were making so much extra money, that they seldom had time to cook. They made a list of fancy restaurants downtown and tried almost all of them.

The Garzas finally had arrived. They were firmly entrenched in a comfortable, upwardly mobile suburban life. They were happy.

But a snag developed. Kay's business was doing so well that it soon began taking accounts away from Tony's boss. "It really steamed me up," Norris said. "Tony would be on the phone with Kay three or four times a day, advising her on how to drum up business. There's only a certain amount of business floating around and they were hurting me. I thought, 'This has got to stop.'"

In August 1977, Norris presented Tony with an ultimatum: Disband Kay's business or quit.

Tony considered his options. His salary of $15,184 was mediocre, especially after 18 years with the same company. If he quit, Kay and he could form their own map company. They could apply for lucrative U.S. Geological Survey contracts, abundant during the Carter administration years. And they would get special advantages because Tony was a Mexican-American; they would be eligible for a special assistance program sponsored by the Small Business Administration.

Tony told Norris to hire another map plotter.

A new partnership

Within a year, the Garzas had formed their business partnership, calling the new company Aerial Scribing and Mapping. They rented a 3,500-square-foot office building. Tony and Kay eventually hired a staff of seven map plotters.

Tony's professional reputation soared. In 1980, he was elected vice president of the Eastern Great Lakes region of the American Society of Photogrammetry.

The Garzas' business began to flourish. They got their first break Sept. 28, 1979, when the U.S. Geological Survey awarded them an $86,580 contract. They were to receive an average of $2,400 for each of 37 maps, payable as they finished each one. The terms of the contract were ideal, they figured; it would regularly supply them with funds to expand the business.

Two months later, the SBA granted the Garzas a $21,580 loan at bargain rates, only 9 percent interest, payable within 10 years. By the next October, they had been approved for another U.S. Geological Survey contract—this one totaling $130,000.

The business falters

By later 1979, the Garzas began to experience minor business problems.

One of their first employees, Jim Carey, who worked for the Garzas from September 1979 to January 1980, said: "Tony had a good dream, but the dream got in the way of reality. They didn't know the first thing about running a business."

The expensive equipment they bought was outdated in the rapidly changing computerized field of map-making. When the Garzas got paid, they celebrated during working hours, often showing up at the office at 10 a.m., leaving for a three-hour lunch at noon, and then going home at 6 p.m. Other days, they worked 15 straight hours.

To pay their employees, they needed a reserve of money—something they never were able to accrue. They often couldn't pay their employees on time, and sometimes, they didn't pay them at all. Cash flow was the problem, not lack of business, Tony assured his workers. But they didn't listen. Kay and Tony went through dozens of scribers until word about their business practices spread throughout the local industry. After that, the Garzas no longer could find employees.

Finally, Kay and Tony were left to do the tedious mapping work by themselves, often falling asleep exhausted in their office. The work was too much for two people.

When the U.S. Geological Survey threatened to terminate their contract because of tardiness, Tony resorted to handwritten pleas. In one letter, he wrote: "I am asking for your help. I will tell you that I will put in over 250 hours a month on your contract. The only problem we are faced with is the present payment is very low, and with inflation, it has made it into an impossible situation."

Indeed, in order to get government contracts, the Garzas bid the federal contracts low—ridiculously low, in the minds of most professionals.

"There was no way they ever could have made any money bidding that low," Wesley Norris said. "It was crazy."

Another map plotter, Payfur Durupinar, who, like Tony, had quit Berger Associates to start his own firm, asked to split some of the U.S. Geological Survey work that the Garzas were so drastically behind on. Tony refused.

"He was very, very meticulous about his business," Durupinar said. "Instead of spending one hour on a project, he'd take five hours. And in this business, if you spend too much time on something, you lose your shirt."

By the spring of 1981, Tony had lost more than his shirt. A Columbus savings and loan was seeking to foreclose on the Garzas' house. Their mapping business was a shambles.

The once-prosperous, upper-middle-class couple was on the verge of bankruptcy.

Pleas for loans

Kay and Tony were desperate. Their business was on the verge of bankruptcy; their lake home was about to be repossessed. Everything they had painstakingly built was falling apart.

In an attempt to cut back on expenses, the Garzas rented out their home and moved into their mapping office. But they could get only $400 a month rent for the expensive home because of the 30-mile commute to Columbus.

The Garzas needed income quickly. They had applied to participate in the Small Business Administration's assistance program for minority contractors. But when the SBA failed to find work for them, they believed the federal agency was stalling. They sought help from U.S. Sen. John Glenn's office in Columbus.

Joan Weld, Glenn's administrative aide, thought the Garzas' complaint was legitimate. In May 1981, Weld arranged a meeting at Glenn's office between the Garzas and district SBA administrator Walter Fronstin to iron out the couple's grievances. Fronstin left the meeting, pledging he would help the Garzas secure the work they were seeking.

"There were some serious efforts to find something for them," current district administrator Frank Ray said later, "but nothing came through."

Meanwhile, the Garzas were unable to complete their two federal contracts on time and were forced to default on them. Their income dwindled even more.

Kay and Tony resorted to calling their relatives, pleading for loans. Tony's brother and sister sent them a check, as did one of Kay's sisters.

Most of the loans were for less than $200, and Kay and Tony quickly spent them on living expenses. The Garzas then turned to former business associates. Tony asked his old boss, Wesley Norris, for a $6,000 loan, and even offered him a 25-percent return on his investment, but Norris refused.

Their neighbors in Galena, the Dunches, lent them some money. On four separate occasions, Tony asked John Ray, who taught scribing at Ohio State, for a loan. Ray turned him down, even though he says now that he had complete faith in the Garzas' scribing ability. Kay, he said, was "one of the best I'd ever seen."

28-cent hamburgers

With the savings and loan about to foreclose on their house, the Garzas turned to an attorney—just in time. The lawyer, Douglas Coyner, took their case the day before the sheriff's department was about to auction off the Garzas' belongings. Coyner was able to postpone the sale.

Meanwhile, the couple brought their grievances to John Meekins, an investigative reporter for the *Columbus Dispatch*, and tried to interest him in writing an exposé on how they, and other minority contractors, had been mistreated by the SBA. Meekins also found the Garzas' claims to be valid, and he wrote a story. But the night before it was set to run Kay called and told him to spike it. They were afraid it would eliminate them forever from future federal contract bidding.

"The SBA strung them along, kept hyping up their hopes, and nothing ever came through," Meekins said.

Meekins remembers the Garzas well. "By the time I met Tony and Kay, they were going downhill fast. Kay was a mental case. She was odd, with her crazy-looking makeup, her painted-on eyebrows. Tony was still very steady, but you could see he looked beat."

They survived on pasta and 28-cent White Castle hamburgers. Once Meekins took Kay and Tony to a restaurant, and he remembers their "scarfing down the beef stew like wolves." When they visited Coyner's office, Kay would reach into her purse, pull out an inch-long Pall Mall butt, light it and take one or two hard drags before stubbing it out.

In November 1981, Coyner filed bankruptcy papers on the Garzas' behalf. Among those listed as creditors at the U.S. Bankruptcy Court in Columbus were former employees, the Internal Revenue Service and mapping equipment manufacturers.

Their total debt was $278,494.

"Monday Blue"

There seemed to be no solution to the Garzas' avalanche of debts and deepening depression. But Kay had an idea. She drew on her musical background to compose three country-western ballads. She thought she could sell the music to a Nashville producer.

Over Casetta Dunch's breakfast table, Kay talked like a giggling teen-ager about what she would do once the songs were listed in *Billboard*. Dunch said: "She used to tell me, 'You'll see, someday I'll be famous. I'll be on easy street, and everything will be all right again.'"

The Garzas hired local performers to sing the ballads, and in September 1981, Kay and Tony brought the demo tapes to a Columbus talent agency.

There they met Bob Husted, who thought the songs perhaps could be marketed.

"I remember the first time they came to see me," Husted said. "He used to look at her, and you could see how proud he was of her.

"The songs weren't bad. I've heard worse. I just happened to like the couple. They seemed down on their luck. They weren't kids with the whole world in front of them."

Husted said he'd take the demos with him on his next trip to Nashville, in October. "I told them not to expect much, that it was a one-in-a-million shot."

One of the songs, "Monday Blue," expressed a feeling of abandonment, of falling further and further:

You left me all alone and crying.
I think my heart will break in two.
It hurts so much, I think I'm dying.
Everything is Monday Blue.

The break never came. "I went to Nashville and played the tapes for some people, but nothing clicked," Husted said. "It wasn't what they were looking for that year."

By April 1982, the Garzas had slipped into endless rounds of humiliating financial disclosures. Their days were filled with meetings with their bankruptcy lawyer, creditors, SBA officials. Their only steady income came from the $400-a-month rent for the big Galena house.

During that time, Kate Oklok, who works at Sen. Glenn's office, remembers that the Garzas occasionally dropped into Glenn's office. "You'd notice that their clothes would be looking worse and worse each time, the holes wouldn't be mended, a white blouse would have a stain on it.

"But they were incredibly tenacious, optimistic people. Once they realized they were going to lose the house, they wanted to save an acre of the property, so when they got back on their feet again, they'd have something."

But their most pressing problem was getting enough money to feed themselves. They ruled out food stamps, telling a friend they didn't want a government handout. "They were damn near starving at the time," said Coyner, their lawyer.

Finally, last April and May, they picked up jobs collecting signatures for a political petition seeking the sale of alcoholic beverages on Sundays in two Ohio counties. They were paid $4 an hour.

Their employer, political consultant Roland Sunker, first sent Kay and Tony door-to-door in Columbus. They later canvassed neighborhoods in Troy, Ohio, where Sunker put them up in a motel.

Tony kept calling Sunker, asking for loans to be paid against their future hourly wages. But on Easter, Sunker fired them.

"I was getting tired of getting taken for a ride," he said. "I said, 'No more advances. That's it. Goodbye.'"

The Galena house was no longer theirs, and they hadn't paid the rent on their office for nine months. After a garage sale of the furniture from their home, they quietly slipped out of town in mid-May, leaving the landlady with the task of cleaning the office. "The place was a mess, things lying all over—papers, rags, newspapers strewn everywhere," she said.

The Garzas, with their dog, Humphrey, drove to Charlotte, N.C. They had heard the job market was supposed to be better in Charlotte, the northernmost point of the much-touted Sun Belt.

They checked into the Kings Inn Motel. The rent was $77 a week, and except for once, they paid on time.

The Garzas spent their time looking for jobs, and they continued to work on the map quadrants they hoped the U.S. Geological Survey would accept, even though their contract had been canceled months before.

When Kay and Tony checked out July 2, they gave the maids their black-and-white television, a set of sheets and towels, even their drafting table. The maids couldn't believe it.

"They said something about going to Texas, where he was from," said Becky Martin, the motel manager. "I guess they just didn't want to take all that stuff along with them."

With all the construction work in Texas, there had to be a need for map scribers, and Tony still had relatives living there.

They packed up again and headed for San Antonio. It was only 120 miles from Brackettville, where Tony had grown up, where his sister and brother-in-law, Jane and Chris Gomez, still lived.

When they arrived in San Antonio, Kay and Tony checked into a Motel 6. The room cost only $19.74; they decided to use it as a home base while they looked for work.

From a pay phone on the highway, Tony called his sister Jane and told her he and Kay would be out in two weekends, on Aug. 14. Then he called Elisandro Lozano, a favorite uncle who lived in San Antonio.

"What are you doing in that motel? You've got a home here," the 76-year-old Lozano told Tony. "You drive over here tonight, OK?" Tony and Kay arrived at Lozano's two-bedroom cottage in south San Antonio that night. His wife ran out and hugged them both.

After the Garzas sat down in the couple's small living room, Tony got to the point. He and Kay were broke. They had lost their home and their business in Ohio, and they needed money.

Lozano told them he could lend them $1,000, but Tony said he didn't need that much, that $200 would be enough to tide them over.

The next day, the four of them drove to the Lozanos' bank to withdraw the money.

The Garzas settled in at the Lozanos' tiny cottage. Every day, after reading the want ads, Kay and Tony, along with their tiny Chihuahua, would get into the Impala and leave before sunrise. All morning, they made rounds looking for work.

They'd come back at noon for lunch and leave again, returning at 7 p.m., when the breezes would start billowing in from the Gulf, dropping the temperature of the summer days.

Whether it was the heat, the close living quarters or the rejections they got every day, Kay complained of abdominal pain. Her stomach was constantly in knots. On Aug. 8, she went to see a physician, who told Kay her problem was nerves. She was prescribed a relaxant to take four times a day.

After dinner Aug. 11, Tony and his uncle sat on the back stoop. The breeze was blowing through the four full pecan trees that Lozano had planted in the backyard in 1952. They talked in the soft, muted tones of the Spanish spoken in northern Mexico, where Lozano was born.

"Do you remember the Depression and President Hoover, *Tio*? We're headed for the same times now," Tony said quietly.

"Tony, Tony, look, you wait a while. Come September, something will come through. Just wait," his uncle said. "Take it easy."

The next day, at dinner time, Kay and Tony both were smiling when they returned to the Lozano house.

"You found something. Oh, I'm so glad," Mrs. Lozano said.

"You know, we even got turned down to be dishwashers today," Kay said deadpan, but Tony kept grinning.

"Then why are you smiling?" Lozano asked.

"We went to the food stamp resource place," Tony said, "and they say we're eligible, that we can start buying our own food with the stamps. All we have to do is go back tomorrow to pick them up."

But Lozano wasn't pleased. "Look, these food stamp people, they're going to give you the runaround. They're going to tell you to come back tomorrow, and then it will be the next day, and the next day. The hell with them."

That night, Kay called one of her sisters and pleaded for a loan. The sister said no.

"People have to stand on their own in this world," the sister said. "You just don't ask anyone else for money. I've helped you and helped you, and if I keep doing it, you'll pull me down with you."

The next morning, Kay and Tony left at 5:30 so they would be the first in line when the food stamp office opened at 8. They left the dog behind.

Lozano planned to have lunch ready for Kay and Tony when they returned at noon. He was running late, and he finished cooking by 12:20, but still they hadn't shown up. He had made his favorite dish—chicken, rice and pinto beans.

By 1:30, Kay and Tony still hadn't arrived. Lozano put the food back in the oven, lay down on the living-room couch and dozed off. When he woke around 5 p.m., Kay and Tony still hadn't returned. Lozano turned on the news on his old television. The announcer was reading a bulletin.

Police reported that the bodies of a man and woman had been found in a parked car, victims of an apparent murder-suicide. The man shot his wife and then turned the gun on himself. The car, the announcer said, had Ohio license plates.

Lozano yelled for his wife. "*Ven aqui!*"

She had been taking a shower and had a bath towel wrapped around her. She hurried into the living room, dripping water onto the carpet.

"That's Tony and Kay," he shouted in Spanish.

"Oh, no! Don't believe it, don't believe it. It's not them."

But there, on the TV screen, was a picture of the Garzas' beat-up Impala and the bodies slumped over each other in the front seat.

With the TV blaring in the background, the Lozanos held each other. They started to cry. There wasn't anything else they could do.

The aftermath

That same afternoon, Wesley Norris, Tony's old boss in Columbus, received a long-distance call from an executive at a San Antonio mapping company.

"He was calling to get a reference on Tony for a job," Norris said. "I told him Tony was a terrific map scriber."

Two weeks after the Garzas' funeral, Lozano received a call from the Texas State Department of Human Resources. "Some lady asked if she could speak to Kay," Lozano said. "I said, 'You've gotta be kidding.'" She told me the food stamps were finally ready and asked why Kay and Tony hadn't picked them up.

"I got news for you, honey," Lozano told her. "Kay and Tony killed themselves two weeks ago."

Back in Brackettville, Jane and Chris Gomez, Tony's sister and brother-in-law, say they want to get Tony's suicide note that blamed the Reagan economy. The note is still at the medical examiner's office in San Antonio.

"We want the note so that all the members of the family can read it," Gomez said. "Once we do that, then we'll burn it."

The Dallas Morning News, October 24, 1982

WRITING THE STORY

I intuitively knew that the best way to tell Kay and Tony's story would be to start with their deaths. A husband and wife's murder-suicide is shocking. That their bodies were found in a parked car on a city street made the grisly discovery even more newsworthy. I wanted to set the scene for the reader, to recreate Kay and Tony's last moments of despair. That alone would have been a strong enough opening, but the kicker here was the suicide note. I wanted to get that into the story before the jump, since it transformed Kay and Tony's twin deaths into a political act, placing blame on the economy and on former President Ronald Reagan. There was a natural second kicker to the story, and I knew I had to get that high, too: Five years before their luck had turned, Kay and Tony had been solid members of the upper middle class. They were respected, well-to-do professionals, living in a custom-built home on five acres of land. The scope of their riches-to-rags story had all the elements of a Greek tragedy. My job was to compress these facts into the first 10 paragraphs of the story so the reader would want to read a page and a half of dense copy.

To recreate the crime scene, I called the Bexar County Coroner's Office and the San Antonio Police Department. From each, I was able to get copies of the Garzas' death certificates and a police report of the murder-suicide. In Texas, as in most states, death certificates are public records, and as long as there is no ongoing investigation, police reports are open to public inspection. From the police report, I got the name of the detective who discovered the bodies. From the coroner's report, I got the name of the next of kin, Chris Gomez. From both documents, I was able to paint the scene: the 1973 Impala, Roosevelt Avenue, the hunting rifle, the location of the bodies. I also got Kay and Tony's ages. To get the temperature of San Antonio on August 13, I called the National Weather Service, which supplied me with temperatures that day hour by hour. While in San Antonio, to further set the scene, I drove to Roosevelt Street. On the telephone with a deputy coroner, I got a chilling quote, and as soon as I heard it, I knew it also had to go as high as possible: "It appears that these people knew exactly what they were doing. There was no surprise. They planned out the whole thing."

From Chris Gomez, I learned the names of six people who had known Kay and Tony. After interviewing them over the phone, they told me others to interview. Their responses gave me a basic framework to sketch out Kay and Tony's lives. After I arrived in Columbus, Ohio, I went to the county administration building and looked up the assessed value and size of the Garza property. I discovered whom Tony had worked for and interviewed his former employer. With each additional interview, the thread of those who knew the Garzas got longer. I drove to Kay and Tony's old neighborhood and knocked on neighbors' doors and was lucky to find Casetta Dunch at home. Through several sympathetic government employees at the Small Business Administration and U.S. Geological Survey, I was given access to loan documents the Garzas had completed. When they were turned down, Kay and Tony had gone to a reporter for the *Columbus Dispatch,* John Meekins, who shared his insights on the couple's downward spiral.

At this point, about three weeks into my reporting, I was obsessed with the story. It's all I thought or dreamed about. I wanted to learn everything about Kay and Tony, and in my quest, one of their friends recalled that Kay had called her from a motel in Charlotte, N.C., on the way from Columbus to San Antonio. The friend didn't remember the name of the motel but recalled that "it sounded like a British name, something like Knights or Queens." In the Yellow Pages, I found the Knight's Inn and, after eight or nine attempts, finally was able to talk to the motel manager and two of the maids at the motel, and again I was rewarded with specific personal observations of Kay and Tony.

The two most memorable interviews were to come. One was from Kay's sister, who flatly told me she refused to give Kay a loan a few days before the murder-suicide. She said she had no regrets about turning down her sister. The other was from Tony's uncle, who described learning about the deaths while watching local TV news.

The story originally came in at over 240 column inches, and my editor told me there was no way *The Dallas Morning News* was going to print that much. I boiled down the piece by almost 90 inches, and while doing so, kept searching for just the right ending. As I was honing the final draft one afternoon, the phone rang, and it was Tony's uncle. He had forgotten to tell me something: that the Texas State Department of Human Resources had finally approved Kay and Tony's food-stamp application—two weeks after the couple had killed themselves. The detail proved to be a poignant coda to two people's lives, which, without the intervention of a reporter, would have ended without notice or sorrow.

EPILOGUE

The Dallas Morning News stripped the story across the top of page 1A on a Sunday under the headline, "Death of an American Dream." Immediately, the article caused a firestorm of reaction, provoking more than 100 letters to the editor, more than any other article *The Dallas Morning News* had printed in decades. But instead of an outpouring of sympathy for Kay and Tony, almost to a one, the letters placed blame on the Garzas for not having the gumption and guts to make it. Many letter-writers recalled how they had weathered the Depression. Many resented linking the Garzas' deaths with the economic policies of then-President Ronald Reagan. The sentiment expressed over and over was that Tony and Kay were weak, that they were failures.

"I'm sincerely sorry those two people felt compelled to kill themselves. My compassion ends there. What a misguided notion that 'Reagan economics' was involved in the downfall of their dream. ... I'm sick, sick, sick of Reagan's being castigated for every problem conceivable."

Another letter: "Your 'Death of an American Dream' was disgusting. In the first place, it had nothing to do with 'Reaganomics.' There are people in this world who would have traded their lives for the ones these two people gave up so fast. How dare you publish this garbage?"

Two decades later, I still remember sitting in the hot Texas sun at Kay and Tony's grave in Brackettville, wondering what had made them give up hope. In my odyssey to learn who they were, I had become Kay and Tony's storyteller, the sole chronicler of two ordinary people whose lives had unraveled and spun out of control. Then, as today, I realized that given different circumstances, Kay and Tony could have been any of us.

The callous response to Kay and Tony's deaths presaged a national judgment—a hardening of feelings, a mushrooming lack of sympathy for those less fortunate. That sentiment attracted more converts as an increasing number of Americans in the late 1980s and early 1990s lost their homes and were turned out onto the streets. It continues today as tens of thousands of workers are downsized out of jobs.

ASSIGNMENTS

1) Read the obituaries in your local newspaper and clip at least three death notices of people who seem worthier of a longer, more nuanced story. Explain what you would do to examine their lives more fully.

2) Write a story about a couple that has been together for more than five decades. Focus on how they resolved conflict, financial hardship, personal tragedy. Make sure the piece isn't a valentine but a thoughtful story that explores the strengths and weaknesses of the two people as seen through those who know them.

3) Contact the county coroner's office, review death certificates, and write a profile of someone who died recently. Interview relatives, friends, and business associates to report accurately on the person. Don't write an homage to the dead person but an honest account of who the person was and what lead to his/her death.

7

NAME-DROPPERS ALTER ILL-SUITED IDENTITIES

While covering the court beat for *The Los Angeles Times,* many of the crimes I wrote about were small scale atrocities, and reporting them took a personal toll. After a year on the beat, I strayed a little—as much for my own sanity, I hoped, as for readers'. One afternoon over coffee, a court clerk suggested that I check out "name-change court." It sounded more like a television show than a real-life courtroom, but tucked away in a trailer behind the county building was a courtroom that twice weekly opened its doors to petitioners who wanted to change their names.

Name-change court was a very different kind of courtroom. Unlike other court venues, where there are winners and losers, name-change court had only winners. No conflict resolution, no wheeling and dealing in the hallways among Armani-dressed attorneys, no plea-bargain negotiations between worn-down public defenders and seen-it-all deputy district attorneys. As Commissioner Christine B. Hickman told me, "Everyone leaves name-change court happy."

Name-Droppers Alter Ill-Suited Identities

After 19-year-old Debra Jean Jones got a divorce, she cut her hair, lost 50 pounds and moved into a new apartment. But nothing seemed to pull her out of her doldrums.

Then she seized upon something dramatic: She would change her name.

After a five-minute court appearance, plain Debbie Jones turned into exotic Cybal Fabreona Del Vecchio. Now 27, Studio City resident Del Vecchio says it was "... like getting a face lift, but cheaper and more fun."

Unlike plastic surgery, though, the possibilities are limitless.

"You can call yourself whatever you like," says Los Angeles County Commissioner Christine B. Hickman, who presided over the Los Angeles name-change court until late July. "That's the way it should be. It's really no one's business what you call yourself. The court really can't step in and tell you what is proper and what isn't."

Every week, dozens of people change their names in Los Angeles County Superior courthouses. Many are divorced women wanting their birth names back, children seeking to adopt stepfathers' names, aspiring actors looking for catchy monikers. Some are transsexuals desiring names to accompany new genders. Others are homosexual couples petitioning for identical surnames.

But the majority of those who seek new names do so simply because they don't like the ones they were given at birth.

A case in point is William Wilson Bobo, a 27-year-old insurance worker from Van Nuys, who decided he had heard enough jokes about his surname. The final straw came soon after he learned what his name meant in another culture.

"I married a Colombian woman, and she informed me that the word *bobo* in Colombia is slang for idiot," he said. "She got tired of being married to Mr. Idiot."

So in early July, William Wilson Bobo became Beau Wilson Williams. Upon leaving Los Angeles Superior Court, Williams smiled and kissed his wife.

"This is something I've wanted to do since I was 15," he said. "Growing up with a name like Bobo leads you to a lot of playful harassment. I used to respond when kids called me Bozo or Boo-boo."

Unlike other courtrooms, in which there are winners and losers, in name-change court, Hickman says, "Everyone leaves happy. People have a look of relief when they get out of this court. It's a burden lifted."

Indeed, for many, a name change has a cathartic effect—a severing of ties from an unpleasant past and a hope for the future's promise.

That is how Sydne Desiree Holder, a 26-year-old North Hollywood woman, said she felt when her change was granted last month.

Before she was Sydne, she was Sabrina, named after the title of a 1954 film starring Audrey Hepburn and Humphrey Bogart. Holder has hated the name Sabrina for as long as she can remember.

"You think of a delicate, prissy little creature when you hear it," Holder said, avoiding even a mention of her former name. "I have almost a pathological hatred for the name. It's just not me anymore."

While no records are kept on the number of name changes granted, Hickman says about 100 petitions are approved monthly in the downtown Los Angeles court. In the Van Nuys Courthouse, the number is about 15 a month, says Superior Court Judge Diane Wayne, who supervises name changes there.

The cost for the process is $164: $99 to file a petition with the county clerk, $60 to publish four consecutive weekly notices in a legal newspaper and $5 to file the decree with the secretary of state in Sacramento. The services of an attorney are not needed.

"There's really nothing to it," Hickman said. Petitioners must make one court appearance, which usually lasts no longer than 10 minutes.

In California, as in all other states, as long as the proposed change is not intended to defraud creditors, a person can legally pick any name he or she wants.

Apparently, the only exception is when a petitioner seeks to change his name to a number, as in the case of a Minneapolis teacher who, in 1978, petitioned to change his name to 1069. A Superior Court judge refused to grant the change, a decision upheld by the U.S. Supreme Court in 1980.

Some of those who make the change also make the news, often because of the unusual nature of the switch. Among those are:

- Ellen Cooperman, a 31-year-old New York feminist, who legally changed her name to Ellen Cooperperson in 1973.

- Robert Earl Lee, a Navy captain from Maryland, who changed his appellation to Roberto Eduardo Leon in hopes that he would be eligible for affirmative-action employment programs.

- Frederick Koch, father of Vermont Olympic silver-medalist skier Bill Koch, who changed his name in November to Coke-Is-It. He said he was tired of hearing his name mispronounced "Kotch" or "Cook."

- Enrique Silberg of Marin County, who in April became Ubiquitous Perpetuity God. (Four years earlier, Terrill Clark Williams of Fresno legally changed his name to God, and in 1983 Gary Dion Hanson of Arieta changed his name to Weyoume Supra IV Lord.)

- Winfred Eugene Holley, a 63-year-old, white-bearded West Los Angeles resident, who became Santa Claus in 1983.

- Hawaii resident Valentine Kekahiolanikapukanehunamoiukakuialonoikaouiaulani Kanehailu, 27, who could no longer put up with people constantly asking him to spell his name. He legally shortened it to Valentine Likolehau Likolehau Neuhaus.

For most, however, the name change occurs with little notice.

Some petitioners seek to match moniker to profession. Los Angeles artist Amy Goldberg changed her name in early July to Amy Color. In 1983, a professional clown in Los Angeles made his name "Are You Kidding."

Others just don't feel comfortable with their names.

Thomas Murry, a Newbury Park resident who made headlines as one of 17 hostages held in Beirut in July, changed his name three years ago from Warren Elwood Murry. "He got to be 55 and had fussed about his name for 35 years, so I said, 'If you don't like it, change it,' and that's what he did," said his wife, Jeanne.

Valery Karlberg, an 18-year-old Encino college student, petitioned in July to go from Valery to Victoria. One of her reasons, she said, was that during a Ouija Board session she found out that she had lived in Africa 200 years ago; the name V-I-C-T-O-R-I-A was spelled out when she asked what she had been called.

Del Vecchio, once Debra Jean Jones, says she was misnamed from birth. "Debbie Jean didn't have enough pizzazz for me," Del Vecchio said. She admired the name Sybal but thought it was too mundane. So she changed the spelling and then adopted her maternal grandparents' name, along with a long-lost relative's surname.

"I had a low self-esteem when I was Debbie Jean," she said. "With the new name, I thought more men would be attracted to me. I wanted to start all over, to get away from everything."

Now, as Cybal Fabreona Del Vecchio, she says the name change has had an almost Walter Mitty-esque effect on her life.

Getting reservations in Hollywood and Beverly Hills restaurants, Del Vecchio says, now is much easier. "People think I'm important. As soon as I give the maître d' my name, I get a seat. I also seem to be able to make quicker appointments when I have to see a doctor."

Her desire was to exchange a fairly common name for a colorful one that sounded ethnic. But for other name-change petitioners, the problem is just the opposite: They feel their names sound too foreign.

A Los Angeles Vietnamese-born family with a name impossible to pronounce for most Americans—Nguyen Ngoc Hoang Hong—last month was granted a change to Wilson.

"Wilson! Wilson! Wilson!" the three children shouted joyously, jumping up and down as Hickman granted the name change. The parents embraced and shed tears after the rite of passage.

Some people, such as the former William Bobo, seek to shed names that carry a double-entendre or produce negative reactions.

Los Angeles resident Sandra Ann Fear was fed up with jokes about her surname, so she became Sandra Ann Joy.

Elizabeth Ann Banghard of Studio City petitioned in July to become Elyssa Ann Harte.

Harte, a 33-year-old hypnotherapist, said her old name used to "raise a lot eyebrows." To avoid embarrassment, she often skipped mentioning her surname or spoke the name so rapidly that she slurred it. "I'd do anything I could to avoid dwelling on my last name," she said.

Harte developed her new name based on numerology, as well as its melodious sound, she said. "I've thought about it for a long time; now I've made it legal."

But, says Van Nuys Superior Court Judge Joel Rudof, in spite of how many people do it, there isn't any legal reason to change a name.

"All you have to do is start calling yourself something, begin filling out forms with your new name on them, and *voila!,* you're a new person," he said. "Using a name other than what's on your birth certificate is your option; it's not illegal."

But name changes, whether legally registered or done informally, clearly do not appeal to everyone.

Superior Court Commissioner Bertrand Mouron, pronounced "moron," who replaced Hickman last month as presiding name-change court commissioner, says that for years he has been plagued with insults.

"I used to be teased, and some days I had rough times as a child," he said. "But I never was bothered enough to ever consider changing my name."

In fact, Mouron said, he can't understand why people get so upset over a name.

"I don't see a reason for most of the people who come into court and want to change their names.

"I've been called a moron all my life and I'm proud of it." he said.

Los Angeles Times, August 4, 1985

WRITING THE STORY

This is a story that wrote itself. I led with Debbie Jones because to me her yarn was the most outrageous. She also was willing to pose for a photo, which I knew would help sell her story to readers. I played on Debbie's transformation to Cybal Fabreona Del Vecchio, a name that sounded liked it belonged to an Italian countess.

But as I continued to report the story, it got better and better. Bill Bobo's account of being referred to as Mr. Idiot helped the story, as did the list of other name-change petitioners. Bulleted paragraphs about Ellen Cooperperson, Roberto Leon, Santa Claus, and others came from a database search. My personal favorite was Valentine Kekahiolanikapukanehunamokiukakuialonoiaulanai. As though his new name were going to be easier to spell! Throughout the story, I threaded basic information about costs, regulations, and procedures.

To me, the best part of the story was the tagline at the end. When I found out that one of the name-change court commissioners was Bertrand Mouron, I didn't think twice about the name. Then the light bulb went off in my head, and I laughed aloud. The court reporter looked my way and put her index finger to her lips to shush me. "Mouron," pronounced "moron"? That sealed the ending of the story. I walked up to Commissioner Mouron during a break and asked him point-blank about his name. He didn't pull any punches.

EPILOGUE

I buried the most dramatic of all the name-change petitioners, Nguyen Ngoc Hoang Hong. Instead of focusing on the Vietnamese-born family that traded its name for Wilson, I opted to frame my story around petitioners like Debbie Jones and William Bobo. Their name changes were humorous and made for great copy.

But ultimately, the Nguyen family's story was more newsworthy. Their name change was like a religious ceremony. It was a moment of shedding past identities and adopting new ones. I remember that day when Nguyen Ngoc Hoang Hong was dressed in a white shirt, black pants, and skinny gray tie. His wife sat ramrod straight, wearing a flower-patterned dress that looked freshly pressed. The children, in their Sunday best, stared straight ahead, mesmerized.

When Nguyen's name was called, he rose stiffly. The judge read several paragraphs of legalese that sounded as foreign to me as they surely sounded to Nguyen and his wife. Then the judge slammed his oak gavel. The sound, like a thunderous clap, resonated throughout the courtroom.

The new Mrs. Wilson kissed her husband. She pulled from her purse a handkerchief and dabbed tears from Nguyen's eyes first and then from her own. Despite the children's euphoria, the couple remained seated on the court bench, hugging each other in a long embrace.

Until the newly invented Wilson family received its American name, their lives here had not yet been officially ordained. The Nguyens had not fully become a part of this new land of promise and opportunity. Receiving the name Wilson, as American a name as it gets, was essential to establishing the Nguyen family as proud new Americans.

What makes this story particularly interesting is its collective aftermath. Today millions of Americans—some newly arrived, others long-standing residents—have no desire to cast off original names and nationalities or to shed their cultural viscera. Many Americans whose ancestors received new names at immigrant ports generations ago are now restoring their families' original names. Today, millions of Americans seek to retain to an extreme degree their individual heritages, and part of keeping that history alive is preserving original birth names. I wonder if today Mr. Nguyen would still chose to become Mr. Wilson.

ASSIGNMENTS

1) Find out which local court handles petitioners who seek to have their names changed. Go there and interview petitioners.

2) Attend a U.S. naturalization ceremony, at which petitioners take oaths to be U.S. citizens. Interview new citizens, and find out why they sought to become Americans.

3) Interview people from another culture who seek to retain their traditions, customs and language, vigorously declining to assimilate into mainstream America. Focus your story on why.

.

8

PORTRAIT OF A RAPIST

Violence has always intrigued me as a journalist because it reflects aberrant behavior, the flip side of acceptable, socially condoned actions. I wanted to write a story that would get at the violence of personal crimes, and for a variety of reasons (mostly because of its frightening prevalence), I chose to write about rape.

Journalists have written compelling first-person accounts detailing rape experiences. Victims have talked to the press and vividly described the aftermath and recovery process of such crimes. Crime and court stories appear daily that detail rape from a police or legal point of view. But I wanted something more, something different. I wanted to write a piece that would get inside the mind of the rapist. Who commits rape? Why? What factors lead to the rapist's actions?

I proposed to my editor an interview with a convicted rapist. Let me go right to the source, I pitched. Enough of the interviews with criminologists, psychologists, psychiatrists, cops, prosecutors, defense attorneys; none tells the story from the criminal's mind. My editor was intrigued, and together we cooked up four other pieces that would look at other (more standard) issues surrounding rape. My piece, though, was the lighting rod. It would attract readers, we thought, because of its novelty, as well as what it promised: a glimpse into the workings of a rapist's mind.

Once I got the go-ahead, I went to the clips and found scores of stories about alleged rapes and subsequent trials. When I found clips on Duane P. Corwin, I knew I had something. Corwin had been convicted of raping a 19-year-old woman less than two weeks before she was to be married.

I immediately wrote Corwin a letter and within two weeks got back a hand-scrawled reply.

"You wanna talk to me, fine." Corwin wrote. "I got nothing to hide."

So, early one spring morning, I drove the 110 miles from Dallas to the Coffield Unit of the Texas Department of Corrections in Tennessee Colony where Corwin was an inmate.

Portrait of a Rapist

TENNESEE COLONY, Texas—Duane P. Corwin, 25, is a convicted rapist.

Three years ago, he and an accomplice forced a 19-year-old woman off an Irving, Texas, road, hauled her into nearby woods and took turns raping her. A 7-inch knife was held to the woman's head throughout the two-hour ordeal.

They then drove the woman south to Dallas, where they joined two friends at a home near Bachman Lake. Again the woman was repeatedly raped, this time by four men.

She was released at about 3 a.m., six hours after she had first been abducted. The four men dumped her from a speeding car on a deserted North Dallas street. A passing motorist saw her lying on the street and took her to Parkland Memorial Hospital, where she was treated for trauma and lacerations.

At the ensuing trial, forensic medical experts, witnesses and police officers presented overwhelming testimony against Corwin and his associate, William Peters, also 25. "The evidence was very substantial and did in fact prove guilt beyond any reasonable doubt," recalls the presiding judge, State District Judge John Ovard.

The district attorney asked for the maximum sentence of 99 years and got it. Entered into evidence was the fact that the rape took place 13 days before the victim's wedding.

On Feb. 22, 1981, Corwin and Peters began serving terms at Coffield Unit of the Texas Department of Corrections, a maximum-security prison, 110 miles southeast of Dallas.

Each will be eligible for parole after a third of the term is over, in the year 2000. The two other men involved in the rape pleaded guilty. One was sentenced to 10 years and will be eligible for parole in 1984; the other was sentenced to 20 years and will be eligible for parole in 1987.

Corwin is a husky man with blond hair who came to Dallas from Michigan in 1979. He dropped out of an Ann Arbor high school when he was 16. He can neither read nor write anything but rudimentary words. He speaks haltingly.

Following are excerpts from an interview with Corwin, conducted last week inside the Coffield prison unit:

Q: Talk about your background, about your growing up in Michigan.

A: I went up to 10th grade in high school. My father worked for the Ford Motor Co. in Ypsilanti. It was a pretty happy time of my life until I got in trouble with the law, mostly a lot of burglary when I was a kid.

Q: When were you first arrested?

A: When I was 8 or 9 years old. My brother and I busted into a clothing shop in Ypsilanti, stole some clothes and about $600 in cash. But we got a flat tire and was caught by the police. My brother went to juvenile (court) and they sent me home. From when I was 9 to 14 or 15, I burglarized I guess about 50 houses by myself or with friends. Then I got busted with an armed robbery charge. That got me locked up for two years.

Q: What happened when you got out?

A: I got married when I was 18. Me and my wife stayed together for about two years. But when I got locked up the last time, she just faded out there. It was hard getting a job back up in Michigan. So I made some calls down here. I had a friend in Dallas who got me a job lined up, working with forklifts, bulldozers, that kind of stuff. I came down on New Year's Day 1979.

Q: Describe what happened on the day of the rape.

A: After I finished work, a partner come up to see me. We drank a little bit— beer and Jack Daniels. We smoked a couple of joints. We went over to his house and played a few games of pool. Another guy come over and he tells us about a guy he knows in Irving that has some drugs and stuff there. We just got together and figured we was going to take it from them.

We sat around 'til it got almost dark. Then we drive over there, wait about 15-20 minutes until two people come walking out of this red brick building. It's this guy and his broad. They walk over to his car. He kisses her goodbye and puts a little bag inside. She gets in and takes off.

Now we was going over there to take some of the drugs from the guy. Instead, we see he puts a bag in the car and the chick starts driving away.

We had to know what was in the bag. So we follow her for five or six miles. Finally we pull her off the road.

Q: Then what happened?

A: My partner fired a gun. She said, "What do you want?" My partner grabbed her and throwed her out of the car. We grabbed the bag and it didn't have what we was looking for. Then we drove down the road in my car and pulled off to the side. My partner had to use the restroom, so he went off into the bushes. We walked her off to the woods and then we searched her, drank a couple of beers and fooled around. Then we go to Dallas and take her to a friend's house and put her in the house there.

Two other guys come over to the house then. At 1 (a.m.) we drop her off on the far side of town. That's about it.

Q: Why did you hold the woman against her will?

A: We couldn't let her go at the time. She could have called her boyfriend. She wasn't hurt, man! We held her for a couple minutes, well, maybe it was a few hours, and did what we had to do. We didn't want her to just drive off and not know where she was going.

Q: Before this incident, had you ever been involved in any incidents of rape?

A: Not personally. I've been to a few parties and they had an old broad in the back some place. I know of one incident. There was a juvenile broad. She was having a gang bang, so to speak, with a bunch of people. When she decided she didn't want no more, they just kept on going. So I guess you could say they committed rape there, but no one ever was arrested. I really didn't get involved in that.

Q: How do you feel about women?

A: You can't just run up to them and grab hold of them. You'd have to talk to them and get them halfway drunk first. That's the best I could tell you. I ain't around women too much in this place. I sure wish there were some here.

Q: How do you feel about your 99-year sentence?

A: I don't think it's going to stick. I don't believe it's right. No one should have no 99 years. I won't live that long—not for no year 2000 (when Corwin is up for parole). That's uncalled for.

I thought it was funny in the courtroom. I still think it's a joke. Even if I done the crime and killed the person, I don't think the time should be 99 years. Murder should be the No. 1 crime. A case where nobody was hurt, something like this, I don't see a person spending the rest of their life behind bars for it. A person be here for six months, and then he'd learn his lesson for what he done.

I figure it all depends on what they've done—if they run out and grab a broad that's drunk one night or whether they linger out there in the bushes. If they do that, they should put them away until they get straight.

Q: Are there certain women who are likely targets for rape?

A: I imagine half the world's thinking that about now. Through the years, dresses are getting shorter, everything's growing different out there now. I hear they have purple hair nowadays. Probably a broad that runs around freely with herself, showing everybody what she's got, puts herself in a position to get raped. She ain't going to put herself in that position unless she wants to. If I wanted a woman bad enough, I'd just go down there to "hookersville." For $25, you got what you want without all the trouble. Anyway, I had a wife, so there was no need for that.

Q: Were you and your wife happily married?

A: Yeah, most of the time we was. We separated a couple of times, but we got back together. We have a daughter, 6 going on 7. I don't know where my wife's at now. The kid's with my parents in Michigan.

Q: What's the reaction other inmates here have to rapists?

A: If somebody's in here for rape, they ask how old the girl was. If she's young, they look on it kinda bad. If she's more or less of age, and you tell them some of the circumstances and say she wanted it, then they let it go.

Q: Of the inmates who have been convicted of rape here, how many of them deny it?

A: Some of them do, but usually you catch them in a lie. Somewhere along the line, something just don't look right.

Q: Is there anything you'd like to say to the Irving woman you abducted and raped?

A: I really don't have nothing to say. The best thing she could do is go to court and tell them she made the whole thing up. I'm not ever going to forget her.

April 4, 1983

WRITING THE STORY

All during the two-hour drive to the prison, I thought of the upcoming interview with Corwin. I had researched as much as I could on the case. I had interviewed both the prosecutor and the defense attorney who represented Corwin. I had interviewed the judge who sentenced Corwin. I had written out on a yellow legal pad all the questions I intended to ask Corwin. I had arranged the questions—easier, warm-up, less intimidating questions at first, then harder, more pointed questions later. Still, I wasn't prepared when I was ushered into a long room in the bowels of the prison and was face-to-face with Corwin. A thick glass wall separated us. We talked through a telephone intercom, and as I almost always do, I took notes in a notebook, avoiding the use of a tape recorder.

Corwin didn't look the part of a rapist, I thought at first, but what does a rapist look like? He was a large man with sandy hair and an easy smile. In the beginning, the conversation was slow and halting.

"What in the world could you possibly want with me?" Corwin asked.

Point-blank I told him. "I want to find out what happened the day of the crime."

Corwin hemmed a little, but as the interview proceeded, he was surprisingly forthright, and, I believe, honest.

Just when I was about to leave, Corwin asked me about the world outside the prison walls. I saw a sense of longing in his eyes. He was a broken young man who had been institutionalized. He asked me excitedly about food, music and television shows.

I said good-bye and walked through a maze of electronically controlled sliding iron-bar doors into the Texas sun. Corwin's account was straightforward and, at the same time, graphic, violent and brutal. On the drive back to Dallas, I came to think that this was one piece that didn't require a standard journalistic convention. Corwin's raw, corrosive words and thoughts were compelling enough. To place them inside a conventional story would rob them of their immediacy and of their power.

I opted to open the piece in an intentionally flat manner. The lede is one of the least dramatic openers I've ever written, but it has its own intrinsic power. After simply laying out the facts, I allow Corwin to tell his story, with no intrusion from the reporter. The best way was with a simple question-and-answer format.

EPILOGUE

The section editors of the paper loved the idea to allow Corwin to tell his story in his own words. The managing editor of the paper did not. At 11 p.m., the managing editor spiked the story, and it never was printed. "Too upsetting to readers," he told me the next morning.

Today, Corwin is serving his sentence at the Lockhart State Prison, 32 miles south of Austin, Texas. While still serving a 99-year sentence, he was scheduled for a parole review in July 2002.

ASSIGNMENTS

1) Interview inmates at a state prison serving a sentence for violent crimes. Ask them to explain their actions and to reflect on their crimes and punishment.

2) Talk to the victim of a violent crime in your area several years after the crime took place. Delve into the crime and its aftermath, detailing the sense of loss the victim may still feel. Write about how the crime forever changed the victim's life, as well as prospects for his or her recovery. Can a victim ever recover from such trauma?

3) Do a ride-along with a police officer in your community. Preferably, spend an entire shift with the officer on a weekend night, when crime is often at its highest. Write an account of your experience.

9

THE LITTLE MAN

An ode to a past era, this story is both tribute and tirade. It's a paean to an age that no longer exists. Old-fashioned shoe stores, pharmacies, hardware stores and barbershops are precious relics of the past. With their demise, many things disappear, including wonderful language. I can't go into a shoe store today without thinking, and usually invoking to all personnel present, the lingo of my youth: Alberts, Bennies, Charlies, Davids and Eddies, shorthand for A, B, C, D, and E widths. L.Y. meant shoes left over from Last Year; Double L.Y. meant shoes from two years earlier. Shoedogs today don't even know they're shoedogs! Instead, they're "clerks," or worse, "sales associates." Sales to Murray and the other shoedogs in "The Little Man" is an art form, a huckster's world of fast-talking con men and customers primed to be duped. Blurring the lines between past and present, Murray and Harold expose their motives and ambitions, butted against dreams and obligations.

The Little Man

The old man never got into a fight with anyone. Giving lip was out of the question. My mother, his customers, the landlord, the IRS, cops terrified him. Once we got stopped for speeding on the Garden State Parkway on the way to Florida, and my father started stuttering like Porky Pig. He shook worse than an epileptic.

But in his own environment, my father was king. The old man was a shoedog. His domain was a little shoe store in an industrial town 15 miles northwest of Newark, New Jersey. That's where I spent my summers, slaving away in the stockroom. My father's stock in trade were pumps, slides, sling-backs, wedgies, ripple-soled bluchers, bucks (dirty and white), penny loafers, steel-toe work boots. Much to my disappointment, this was a family shoe store. No five-inch black stilettos, no see-through vinyl "Hi there, sailor" shoes, no white boudoir slippers with purple puffs in the entire place.

The old man never let me sell. He was too scared I'd put the kibosh on any and all potential sales. So like a pariah child with blotches on his face, I was banished to the stockroom. My lot was not to explore the outer limits of foot odor, peds, shoetrees. I was never to know the sensation of caressing the soft, fleshy instep of a 23-year-old vixen in a miniskirt as she slipped on a pair of Life Stride high heels.

The old man's store was called Townley Shoes, not named after some aristocrat who went by the moniker, Townley, but because my father thought Townley would connote "friendly" to the working stiffs whose corn-callused feet he shoved into shoe after shoe, year after year.

Platooned full-time to the stockroom, for weeks on end I shifted towering walls jammed with shoeboxes so that every 7B was positioned immediately after every 7A. The old man had an insane, pathological hatred of shoeboxes on the floor.

"Can't sell 'em if you don't know where they are," he used to scream. "Get your hands out of your pockets, and get those boxes in the wall, now!!!!!"

Whenever a customer entered the store, the old man turned my way, and discreetly nodded toward the back room with a slight arch of his furry brow. That was my cue to vaporize into the black hole of the stockroom. The old man's approach to teaching the fine craft of shoedogging was not trial-by-fire. It was a painfully slow apprenticeship. In the beginning, the pup watches from a distance, observing the journeyman dog hard-sell customers into buying shoes they neither need nor can fit into. Gradually, the junior dog is allowed to wait on customers. Kids under 12 who want sneakers are the only customers allowed in the apprentice's purview.

There also were oral exams to pass. In shoedog lingo, L.Y. is short for "last year's" stock. Alberts are A-widths, Bennies are B's, Charlies are C's, Davids are D's, and Eddies are E's. Cookies or jimmies are felt or cork liners that make big shoes smaller. Ups are customers. Thirty-four is the same as a T.O., which stands for turnover, or passing an up from one dog to another to ensure a sale. A D.I.S. (always pronounced as three separate letters) is short for "discount," usually 10 percent extended to nuns, priests, cops or firemen. An 86 is when an up walks out without buying. That, of course, was the absolute worst, the end-of-the-road, the nightmare of every shoedog. Too many 86s and you were out of a job, bub. If you can't sell her shoes, for Christ's sake, push some slippers for the shleppy husband.

The old man didn't just happen to fall into the profession. When he was a boy, he worked summers selling shoes in *his* old man's store. My father figured that fixing feet would be better than shodding them, so like the kid who becomes a doctor to go one step further than his pharmacist father, the old man graduated from the Ohio College of Chiropody. For 10 years, he was a chiropodist in a small walk-up office above The Leslie Dress Shop on the corner of Main and Day in downtown Orange, New Jersey.

Alas, there was no money in shaving bunions and padding hammertoes. So my father took out a $10,000 loan from the Fidelity Union Bank on the corner, and opened a tiny women's shoe store with Leonard, a 68-year-old dog with thick tortoise-shell glasses who drank three Manhattans for lunch every day. Leonard died of a heart attack while jamming a jimmy into a 5½-Bennie, peau de soie mid-sized heel.

My father sold his share of the store and moved to Cranford, where he became commander and chief of his own musty emporium. However ignominious hawking shoes might be, the old man owned the stinking store, which was the singular dream of tens of thousands of shoedogs across the land. But in his new incarnation as sole owner, the old man became slave to the customer. Each customer had to be handled just right, coddled and coaxed to lay down the greenbacks. For God's sake, no 86s, please! The old man trusted no one else to sell, and only under extreme duress did he ever let anyone else wait on an up. "Can't trust the help. They steal behind your back! They rob you blind!"

In the early 1960s with the advent of discount shopping malls, customers were beginning to flock to places like Thom McCann and Kinney Shoes. Those highway chain stores were absolute abominations to my father. If he ever saw a customer carrying a bag from one of these places, he would wait for the heretic to leave Townley and then tear into a rage, his eyes bulging, his stutter coming on in full force.

"Those d-d-d-d-damn highway thieves! They, they undercut your markup. They, they sell seconds for 20 percent off. They'll cause my ru-ru-ruination!!!!!" The problem was that the highway stores often did sell the exact same shoes my father sold, and for 20 percent less. The chains bought in such large quantities that they could undersell small merchants. Occasionally, they sold seconds—

imperfect pairs of shoes with nicks in the leather, scuffed soles, or faded uppers—but the old man sold them too without telling customers.

To match Thom McCann or Kinney's allure, the old man had a plan. He went after children, playing on parents' fears that if their children were misfit, they'd be pigeon-toed for life. He used to give away either balloons for the Christmas season, or pencil boxes during back-to-school months. Hauled out of the stockroom, my semi-annual job was to inflate red, pink and blue balloons with a little foot pump, tie the balloon with green string, and present the thing to the squealing kid. If the kid was under eight, the old man had me tie the balloon onto the kid's wrist so the mother wouldn't troop back to the store demanding another.

In the fall, I'd reach down in a carton, and give away one (and only one!) pencil box to every kid who bought a pair of shoes. None for brothers or sisters at home, none for cousins, aunts, uncles, friends. You had to buy to get the damned pencil box.

Customers were gold. They were hardly ever right, but they were always customers, the old man's lifeblood. He had a plastered, freeze-frame smile for all of them. Each of the old man's sales had a pitch, a personalized twist that allowed for no exit. Why these working stiffs didn't catch on to his shtik was beyond me. Maybe they were so exhausted with punching out die-cut widgets all day long that they resigned themselves to buy whatever the old man brought out—as long as it was "on sale!"

"My wife has a pair of these exact same shoes, and she just loves them!" he told old ladies. "And today only, they're 10 percent off!"

"They make your foot look so dainty, and my, this style is so smart!" he told fat ladies as they munched on sugary ladyfingers bought from Eppler's Bakery down the block. "And they're on special!"

"I just opened up a new crate of these mid-sized heels. They're the latest in fashion!" he told young mothers. "And what a value!"

"They're sharp, and priced so reasonably today!" he told anyone under 18.

Back in the stockroom, in my chino pants with cuffs that rested just above my ankles, white socks, and a plaid short-sleeved shirt my mother ironed each evening, I passed the time immersed in my own inner sanctum. I found a stash of dog-eared "Gentlemens" magazines secreted between the wall of Wright Arch Preservers and PF Flyers, and carried on a summer-long love affair with Miss June, Dorothy Ann Fox. She stood erect, full and wanting in strappy black high heels. No open-toed taupe Cobbies for Miss June.

Usually for lunch the old man sent me for takeout to Joe's Deli for ham-and-cheese, or pastrami ("Tell Joe to cut out the damned fat!") sandwiches and sugary ice tea. My father made room for the chow on a pea-green card table set up in the back of the store. He pushed aside errant cork cookies, his mushed pork pie hat, Buster Brown shoe catalogues, and an ashtray full of used Stimudents he used to pick his teeth with.

Except for September school opening and Christmas, business was always bad. We seldom broke the ice before noon. At around 2:30 p.m., with about $75 in the cash register drawer, the old man and I used to take a break at Morgenstern's, a fetid and sticky soda fountain run by 75-year-old Claudia Morgenstern.

By the time I knew her, Claudia looked like a washed-up floozy who had been a rumrunner's moll in the 1920s. Her favorite outfit was a form-fitting Japanese red chenille blouse and matching pedal pushers. She wore purple mascara and cakey rouge, and curled her eyelashes. "What happened to all the men who know how to treat a lady?" Claudia seemed to say with her watery, almond-shaped eyes and long lashes that once fluttered. She ran out of time waiting, and married an arthritic constipated loser by the name of Irwin who was addicted to Haley's M-O.

The soda fountain Claudia ran stunk from years of accumulated grease. A gooey gunk had settled on everything. You had to pry apart the plastic-sheathed menus that had mimeographed sheets inside. Claudia hated the restaurant. She hated Irwin. She hated making Cokes. She hated us.

"What didja think of that ice breaker I had? Two double L.Y. Charlies I stuffed with cookies," my father said, slurping his Coke through a paper straw. "Put 'em on her, and she thought the Red Sea parted. And she was almost an 86!!! If I didn't own this place, the boss would give *me* a raise!"

The old man wanted me to share his enthusiasm, but I had no stomach for shoes, the customers, or the mating dance between the two.

"Why'd you tell her the pair was on sale? Where'd you pick up that one?"

The old man shook his head. "Steve, that's *salesmanship*. That's the beauty of it. They give you money and they don't really know why." You'd think the old man was running General Motors.

I don't really know what motivated the old man. He didn't talk about anything higher in life than shoedogging. Oh, maybe a joke once in a while he picked up from one of his salesmen, but that was about it. He fell asleep in the beige Lazy-Boy whenever he watched sports. And although my mother tried to interest him in bridge, he preferred going over the day's receipts every night. He kept meticulous sales records in a book called "Beat Yesterday." If the old man loved to tickle feet, it was something he never shared with me. If he was a leather freak, he never let it out of the closet. He was as much a working slug as the factory drones whose stubby triple-Eddie feet he knew intimately. He lumbered along, day in, day out, year after year, shoving on shoe after shoe, smiling all the while.

Could it have been the heady sense of providing a community service to generations of northern New Jersey families, from cradle to grave, shodding the entire herd? Hardly. With two kids to feed, pushing shoes was his only option after shaving bunions. I suppose the power was some of what turned him on, the slieght-of-hand illusion of being a kind of a con man, able to bamboozle another stiff into buying an 11-Benny loafer when what the sucker really needed was a 10½ triple Eddie. The money really wasn't there. On good days, he took in a 150 to 200 bucks. Bad days, three or four customers showed up, not including Charley, the whacko usher at the movie house across the street.

Charley, who wore a tuxedo to work, could talk your ear off about nothing. He looked more like a mortician, actually more like a corpse. He was my first experience with a nut. Everything was somehow connected, and everyone was out to get him. He jabbered about Kennedy, about the mob, about Jimmy Hoffa, about the damn Catholics. He liked the old man, maybe because my father never paid any attention to him. I was invisible to Charley, just a *pisher* with acne. The old man used to go about his business, paying bills, sizing up what was left on the Burlington Sock rack, totally ignoring Charley. And when the old man went to the head, Charley would follow him and continue talking a blue streak while my father took a whiz. My father would zip up, and Charley'd still be pontificating about Nixon, Helen Gahagan Douglas, James Hagerty, the Ford Motor Company, or the Federal Bureau of Land Reclamation. By 12:30 every day, Charley pulled out his white gloves, combed back his Vitalis-slicked coal-colored hair, and headed to the movies for *Pillow Talk* or *The Guns of Navarone*.

Each spring and summer when the Jersey humidity could suffocate WWF champion Gorilla Monsoon, my father's back used to drive him up the wall. With all the bending, lifting and stooping, he had to resort to Doan's Pills, BenGay, and all the other liniments. He went to an osteopath, then a chiropractor, and still his back felt like someone had whacked it with a monkey wrench.

So one day the old man took me to a place called Heich Prosthetic Devices in Elizabeth to buy a girdle for himself. Above the store window was the store insignia, a silhouette of a dapper man wearing a derby, who had a silver hook for a hand. Lightening bolts flashed toward the hook, which glowed in purple neon. This was the place that could remedy any condition no matter how deformed you were.

The store scared the bejesus out of me. Up until then, my exposure to physical abnormalities had been women midget wrestlers on TV. Since this was before the era of plastic, there was display after display of scary wooden hands and, like the gleaming device on the store's sign, metal hooks. Each mannequin looked like an armed Venus de Milo with brown knit slacks and a yellow polyester bowling shirt. The big ones wore pink muu-muus, under which metal braces flashed. Porta-potties were everywhere for incontinent retirees and customers who could wait no longer. Gargantuan bras hung from the walls and ceiling, designed to fit gals with 60-triple-E cups. As a normal kid, I dreamt of shapely breasts, but these were more like Georgia watermelons than cantaloupes. The lord giveth and giveth, I figured.

The old man bellied up to the counter, tended by a pen-protector guy with an enormous tan hearing aid and a limp in his right leg. My father mumbled something. Like an undertaker, the sales clerk nodded knowingly, discreetly. He disappeared into the stockroom of horrors and came back with a stiff, flesh-colored contraption. It was a medieval apparatus with laces, straps and three metal slats that ran up the corset's back. The Marquis de Sade would have had an orgasm fingering the thing.

Silently, the three of us went into a dressing room. My father dropped his pants. Atop his faded, blue-striped boxer shorts, he buckled the bone cruncher around his screaming lumbar. The clerk tightened the laces, then yanked each of the straps. The old man winced and sucked in his gut.

He endured in silent submission. Each morning, the old man cocked his head like Nipper the RCA dog, and then pulled on the corset's tabs until he was blue in the face. Lumbering out the house every day, he looked like Fred Gwynne on "The Munsters".

Summers were slow. Factory slugs piled their wives and children into beat-up, dented Chevrolets the Gypsies, at traffic lights, didn't even offer to pound out. The whole lot headed to Florida for two-week vacations. Business picked up in September for school-opening days and the pencil boxes, and in December for Christmas presents of Daniel Green slippers and white go-go boots, which were then all the rage. With the increased business, the old man ran his annual sale to get rid of as many L.Y.s as possible, and customers trickled into the store. Then he had no choice. He had to hire someone to hawk.

Over the 10 years I worked summers and Christmases at Townley, the old man had an eclectic assortment of temporary shoedogs, slobs who bit their fingernails, rail-thin racetrack junkies, and other assorted sociopaths.

Manny picked his nose constantly when he thought no one was looking. He went to Joe's one day for lunch and never came back.

Buddy, who looked like Art Linkletter on downers, turned out to be a hypochondriac. Most dogs read the *Newark Star-Ledger* sport section, some of them read the back pages of the *The Daily News*. Buddy must have been the only dog in the world who brought to work the *Physician's Desk Reference*. He was engrossed in the book, and between stock work and ups, Buddy buried his greasy mop in the thick tome the way fundamentalists disappear into the Bible. He complained about his sacroiliac, his varicose veins, his wobbly Herbert Hoover knees, but most of all about his migraine headaches.

"Can't take 'em any longer!!!" Buddy moaned every day. "Someday I'm gonna take a gun and POW!" he said, cocking his thumb and index finger against his forehead.

The poor guy said he never slept more than two hours a night, and his face looked it. His eye sockets were the color of the violets my mother grew in her kitchen window. His jowls looked like sagging twin punching bags.

One morning, Buddy downed 35 aspirins from a bottle of Bayer the old man kept in the back for housewives with PMS. Buddy came out of the crapper rubber-legged. He didn't look like he was going to make it, and blacked out in the middle of the showroom, conked out cold for 35 minutes between the purses and sock racks. Two ladies ran out screaming. A contingent of Boy Scouts on their way to camp circled Buddy's body with a macabre fascination.

"Is he dead? Is he dead?" one tall kid with size-9 Davids kept asking.

"He's probably drunk!" replied the wife of a Pabst brewery worker in for his annual Red Wings.

Two shocked white-haired ladies looking at the Cobbie display, buttoned up their Richard Nixon cloth coats and hurried out.

The old man was fit to be tied. He called for an ambulance, but the rescue squad took its time about showing up. There were customers in the store who wanted to buy, but you couldn't transact business over a man's body.

The old man took center stage. "Don't let this man bother you," he said over the clamor. "This is a temporary condition. P-P-P-P-P-roceed normally, p-p-p-p-please!"

They eventually carted off Buddy, pumped his stomach, and released him from Elizabeth General in a couple of days, but the old man wouldn't have him back. "You take half a bottle of aspirin and then want your old job back? No way, Buddy. Can't take a chance on you again." Poor Buddy was left groveling as the old man shoved him out the door.

One promising dog was a phys. ed. teacher at the local high school who moonlighted after school hours. My father brought Seitzer in with the hope that he would be able to work out a deal with the football coach to get the team account, but all Seitzer did was take long lunch breaks and talk about his glory days as a tackle at Seton Hall University. Seitzer was history when the old man caught him giving a D.I.S. to his next-door neighbor.

Mel was a favorite of mine. He adored Elvis Presley. I think he went into the shoe business because of a desire to sell suede shoes. At 47 and less than five feet two inches, Mel still lived with his mother in a two-bedroom walk-up downtown. It was a good relationship, my father and Mel. Mel resembled an elf, and jumped when the old man ordered him to take an up. He had mutton chops down to the dimple in his chin, and used to comb his hair for hours in front of the full-length mirror near the cash register.

Alas, Mel's days at Townley were over when the old man broke open the lock to the bathroom after Mel was on the can for 50 minutes. With his boxers around his ankles, Mel was bug-eyed looking at the stash of *Playboy* magazines.

"G-G-G-G-G-G-Get the hell out of here!" the old man screamed. Mel zipped up, and hurriedly hobbled out through the back door, grabbing his zip sweater and black Ace comb. That was the last we ever saw of him.

Harry "The Tiger" Kekel worked for the old man a year before he came out of a closet of another sort. Short, squat Harry was built like a fire hydrant mangy dogs loved to sprinkle. He and the old man got along famously. They talked for hours about insteps, toe cleavage, steel shanks. In his late twenties, Harry lived alone. He never got married, he said, because the right girl never came his way.

Then one day, Harry fell in love. The once drab, monochromatic-dressed Harry started to show up for work in bell-bottoms, pink neckties, sprigs of lilies in his wide lapels. Harry started humming Broadway show tunes. Dressed in his new get-up, he had a swagger to his walk. He grew a handlebar mustache, which he twirled with sticky wax from a tube all day long. Harry told the old man he was going to leave the shoe business to open up an antique store in Hartford with a "friend."

"Whadsamadda with you, Harry?" the old man asked. "You wanna give up this great job? You leave me in the lurch for Christmas? And what for? To open up an antique store with some *faygeleh?*

"I guess that's what you could call me too, Harold," Harry said quietly.

The old man's eyes widened to saucers. You could just as well have told him that Judy Garland was Barry Goldwater in drag. My father looked my way toward the stockroom, rather protectively, and lowered his voice. "For G-G-God's sake! You mean you've been working the last year with me and you're q-q-queer!"

Harry was as calm as a Texas armadillo laying in the sun. "Yeah, Harold, it's true. That's just who I am."

The old man kept shaking his head. I was taking all of this in from my perch in the stockroom. I was as incredulous as my father. "Harry, a homo?" I kept on thinking. "I've eaten lunch with him, sat at the counter of Morgenstern's with him. I even used to show him Miss June's foldout. He salivated over her lusty, curvaceous body as much as Buddy and I did."

Harry worked the rest of the week and then left to open the antique store. On his last day, he bid the old man and me good-bye. I think the both of us were scared to death that Harry was going to kiss us. By that time we had gotten accustomed to the idea that Harry was a homosexual, whatever that actually was. We couldn't imagine it, but we were glad we couldn't.

"Harry," my father asked him, needling. "Who's this business partner, this mystery man, of yours?"

I forget who Harry said—Ralph, Joe, Frank—but I remember that Harry smiled kind of sweetly and purred, "He calls me Tiger."

The old man looked at me. I was too embarrassed to look at Harry. There was an uneasy silence. Then the three of us, Harry, the old man and I, broke up laughing.

For a while, no other dog could fill Harry's shoes. The old man couldn't get along with anyone else. It was as though Harry had jilted my father. The old man walked in a trance. He moped around the store, padding around like a lame dog with pinched paws.

Christmas days were around the corner, and the old man had no choice. He had to call on the one-and-only Murray Schwartzkopf, retired shoedog extraordinaire.

Murray was as proud of his forty-seven years in the shoe business as any four-star general is of the theaters of war he commandeered. Murray had his own war stories, whether they were tales of valor about showgirls too poor to pay for their tap shoes so Murray took payment in trade, or yarns of woe about bosses so cheap they would make Jack Benny seem like Michael Anthony on the television show "The Millionaire."

But what Murray could do was sell. If people were flies, they'd come in and beg him to sell them flypaper. Murray's crowning achievement was selling a pair of heels to actress Fay Wray in 1928, when he worked for a son-of-a-bitch miser in a small joint around the corner from the Roxy Theatre. "Some gams that broad had," Murray said reverently about Miss Wray, whose dainty pads, he recalled, were size-6 double Alberts.

Murray himself wasn't too much bigger than Fay, and the old man derisively called him "the little man." Murray was five-feet five-inches, weighed 128 pounds, and wore 7-Albert gray Hush Puppies. He was bald and had two hearing aids, neither of which did much to improve his hearing. Murray had a bum left arm (he mumbled something about a World War I injury), which required that he hold his arm bent at the elbow, perpetually crooked.

"This bum arm of mine," Murray used to curse as he fumbled yet another stack of shoeboxes, tumbling onto a customer's lap.

He came cheap, though. The old man paid Murray under the table, and it's a good thing. Because if anyone saw how little the poor bastard got they'd speak up in righteous indignation. Like the Hush Puppies on his skinny feet, Murray was a sad dog, a Jewish version of Grampa Joad. The old man paid him $1.25 an hour, half what he paid Manny, Harry, Mel, Buddy and Seitzer. Murray got no commission, no vacation, no benefits except for one pair of shoes priced wholesale each year.

Murray's solace was his cigarettes. Like a limber old genie, Murray seemed to appear and disappear with each poof of exhaled blue smoke from his beloved Kents, staring into space, one skinny leg folded over the other at the knee, waiting for the eternal up. But since there were so few ups, Murray had time to ease me into the arcane ways of the shoedog.

"Gonna see a man about a horse," was the little man's way of saying he was about to disappear into the men's room. To this day, I don't understand who the man is, why it's a horse he's got to see, and how the two ever fit into a bathroom together.

To the little man, the working stiffs from the breweries and the few remaining steel mills in Union County were all "Mac."

"Whaddaya want, Mac?" Murray barked in his best blue-collar timbre. " 'nother pair of the usual?"

The usual meant steel-tipped Red Wing boots that weighed 16 pounds each. Besides useful at work, they came in handy at home, able to scare the shit out of

Mac's wife or six children should any of them ever think of getting out of line.

When kids came into the store, if they had Alberts for feet, Murray told them to eat mashed potatoes standing up. If they wore triple Eddies, Murray advised them to stand on their heads so the fat would run from their feet, down their legs, through their arms, out to their fingertips.

The little man had his shtik down, with apologies to Abbott and Costello. He was right out of vaudeville. Whenever a boy came in with his mother, Murray greeted the kid by pumping his hand so hard he almost pulled the little guy's arm out of its socket.

"How ya doin', how ya doin', George?"

The kid looked sheepish. "My name's not George."

"Well, you sure look like George. You sure you're not George?"

"My name's Bobby."

"No way! You're not Bobby. Bobby just left. You look like George!"

"My name's Bobby."

"O.K. Have it your way. Now, whaddaya want, George?"

If the mumbo jumbo perplexed the kid, it goosed the mother good. She was the important one. If the mother was young and had a figure, Murray sometimes played a game on her, too. After he wrapped up the kid, he'd talk the mother into trying on a pair of pumps.

"We've got some lovely new styles, ma'am. I know they'd look wonderful on you."

Pause, then with perfect timing, "No obligation, of course. You just sit down here," he'd say, patting the green vinyl seat cushion. "You just relax." It was a hard offer to refuse.

Then, just as Murray was slipping the heels on the woman's feet, he'd somehow slide his index finger on the soft underbelly of her foot, momentarily pressing a tiny spot under her arch. It happened too fast to protest.

"Oh!" "Ahhhhhh!"

"That feels just right!"

"Yes, yes, slip 'em on! Slip 'em on. "Give it to me!!!!!!!"

Murray had found the G-spot of feet. Nary a smile would come from the little man as the mother squirmed in Townley's straight-back chair, doing everything in her power not to slide down the footstool onto Murray's soft, shriveled noodle. Of course, there was never any implication of sex. No way. This was cold, hard business. Put her on the chopping block and get her to buy. Murray's sad, hush-puppy eyes seemed to say, "Don't hold back. You are putty in my hands, lady. I can drive you to ecstasy. But buy the frigging shoes!"

"Gets 'em every time," the little man casually told me after he wrapped up a sale, pulling on a Kent, fading in and out of view in a plume of azure smoke.

When Murray and I did inventory, the scourge of all shoedogs, the little man called out the sizes and I wrote down on an order pad what was left in the walls.

Murray used shorthand to alert me when he went from one line of shoes to another.

"30!"

"End it!"

"Kill it!"

"Dead!"

"Wilson!"

"Wilson?" I asked.

"He's dead, ain't he?"

I was glad for Murray's company. Buddy, Mel and Harry all had been too weird for me, and Seitzer was too much of a jock. That we got along didn't bother the old man, who thought we kept each other out of trouble. While my father minded the store, the two of us took our afternoon Coke break at Morgenstern's.

Away from my father, Murray stretched out. With a butt hanging from his mouth, he looked like a strung-out version of Montgomery Clift. He still smiled whenever a woman (under 40) walked by (which wasn't very often in Morgenstern's). I half hoped that one of Murray's G-spotted mothers would pursue him, and waylay him on Morgenstern's sticky counter.

Murray ordered black coffee and a grilled Velveeta sandwich with the crusts cut off. Something about his dentures not being able to handle Claudia's week-old bread. I stayed with a cherry Coke, a chaser to Morgenstern's week-old bear claws.

"Steve, let me tell you the story of Newark during the war," the little man started out, raising his voice just enough so Claudia could overhear. Sitting on the grimy soda fountain stools, he put his hand on my shoulder, and pulled me in close. He pronounced my name, "Steeeeeve," stretching and drawing it out like saltwater taffy. I believe the little man reveled in the company of someone who'd listen to him. He had two sons, one an accountant in Tarzana and the other a collections lawyer in Albany. They sent him Chanukah cards, but that was about it. Maybe I was the kind of son he never had, or once had and lost. "Ya open up a vein for your kids, feeding 'em and clothing 'em, then one day they get up and never come back. A card once a year. Christ almighty!"

Despite the bittersweet reverie, Claudia thought Murray was disgusting. For his part, Murray thought Claudia gave it away to the Coke syrup salesman. "This town was wide open in the '20s," Murray said, daintily biting into his gooey orange sandwich. "My buddies and I used to go to burlesque shows on Broad Street, where the cocktail waitresses were all working girls. You know, strippers."

Murray took another bite. I licked my lips. Visions of grainy, black-and-white skin flicks of bloomer-clad girls disrobing in private boudoirs danced in my head.

Murray set down the greasy sandwich and held out his right hand. With one finger at a time, he ticked off their names. "I remember Rosie," up went his thumb. "Emma," he counted with his index finger. Then "Ursula, Mildred and Doris," sticking out his middle and ring fingers and then his pinky.

"But Eva, I could never forget," the little man said, dreamily gazing upward toward Morgenstern's brown ceiling. "They used to call her Eva because she was like Eva Peron. 'Do-with-me-what-you-will' little Eva. She'd grab you by the belt buckle, Steve, pull you into the stockroom between the Bass Weejuns and the Miss America prom pumps. *Je-sus Christo!*"

The old man never talked to me like that! Let 'er rip, Murray!

"Hot as a pistol. Eva could melt anything. Including your heart."

"C'mon, Murray!" I said, shaking my head.

He waved me off. "I used to pick her up at the stage door, then stop by the Drift Inn. Federico'd be there, ready with the set-ups. Then it was back to my room for the real show. Caliente, my friend, *moo-ey* caliente."

"I see you picked up a little Spanish," I teased.

"The language ain't important. You're not doing much talking."

Murray paused, looking around for Claudia.

"A little service, barkeep!" Murray intoned. "A refill for Steverino and me! Chop! Chop!"

Claudia looked like she was gong to smack Murray. She wearily put down the *Star-Ledger* crossword puzzle, and rose from her stool at the end of the soda counter, *kvetching* about her arthritis and rheumatism, Irwin and, under her breath, Murray.

She poured Murray some acid coffee, and squirted more cherry syrup into my Coke.

Murray lit a Kent, and drew on it. He defied the laws of physics. Murray kept the smoke deep in his lungs for minutes on end, talking, gesturing all the while. Where'd the smoke go, anyway? The guy swallowed it like he belonged in a carnival act with the bearded lady.

"So let me get this right," I say. "You meet this stripper, Ava, and you end up in bed with her?"

"'Eva!' and 'stripper' hardly does justice to her," Murray said, exhaling. "Eva was an *ar-tiste*."

I wasn't sure if Murray was putting me on or what. I figured this was an act of contrition, his own way to reconcile where his life once was and where it had gone. Murray's bum arm seemed to twitch.

"She used to dance behind fans, and she'd wear a tight little two-piece number that came off just fine. I remember she had a wonderful pair of marabou mules with little French ticklers at the toebox. No Mary Janes for Eva! She'd kick them off, and then it was down to business. Around the world, baby!"

That was all the indignity Claudia was going to take. She rolled up her *Star-Ledger* into a bat and came after us.

"You dirty, old man!!!!! Get the hell outta here! Now!"

Murray and I ran out, half elated, half embarrassed. We were like two boys Charley caught sneaking into a Saturday matinee. We giggled and loped back to the store giddy.

Just as we walked in, the old man glanced at his Longines watch. He was not pleased. "You guys forget we gotta business to run? This place looks like a shit house with all the shoes on the floor." Blah, blah, blah. Murray and I went to the stockroom to size up galoshes and rubbers.

When Christmas rolled around that year the big sellers were those godawful furry slippers for girls. They looked like either cotton candy or pink-dyed dead wolverines.

The Christmas season went better than expected. We got so busy on a couple of days that the old man let me try my hand at a couple of ups. They bought from me too, a pair of black wing tips, two pairs of Keds, some Florsheim blucher oxfords. I sold a nurse a pair of 7½ double-Alberts, but when it came to pressing her G-spot, I got scared.

On the night of December 24, the old man gave out Christmas bonuses to the help—Murray and me. He'd put a bill in an envelope and send us on our way. I opened mine, a measly 10 bucks. At least I could complain to my mother.

Murray was another story. He opened his envelope. Twenty bucks. This was a serious underpayment, a shot to the little man's solar plexus, a kick to his groin. The little man had worked a total of 10 weeks at Townley this year, and 20 bucks didn't even buy him four cartons of Kents.

You could tell Murray was smoldering. He didn't look up. He muttered something as he walked back to the stockroom. I heard the snap of his lighter, then his inhaling a Kent. From behind the wall, blue smoke wafted to the showroom.

The old man and I looked at each other, not knowing what to expect. Was Murray going to get a pocket derringer and shoot the old man dead on the spot? What the old man figured was that he might have to shell out more money. That this might cost him.

"Pop, you gotta give the little man more," I said, lowering my voice. "Twenty dollars is an insult."

"Mind your own business," he shot back. "You know nothing about this. If you minded the store, we'd go broke!"

I slunk back to the sock rack and started fondling the seamless hose. I flipped through a Florsheim catalogue. Lots of grown-up shiny shoes with buckles and tassels that I could never imagine ever wearing. I secretly hoped Murray would march back from the stockroom with fire in his eyes. I envisioned the little man's black glasses smoldering, his twin hearing aids spewing sparks.

Nothing happened for another 10 minutes. There was an eerie silence in the store as motorists outside honked their horns and shouted to each other in a dash to get home for Christmas Eve dinner.

Another 10 minutes passed. Finally, Murray sauntered back into the showroom.

This was the moment of truth, the point of no return, the moment when the toreador is above the bull, poised to plunge the sword. The little man, the shaman who possessed the secret of the feet-al G-spot, was tired of being treated like a *shmendrick.* Revenge, sweet revenge, was heavy in the radiator-warmed December air.

Murray looked up at the old man. No telling what he would do. His eyes were bloodshot, and the circles under looked like week-old cookies. "Thanks so much, Harold," Murray said without emotion. "I appreciate the gift."

The old man was taken aback. He forced an awkward smile. Murray went to the front of the store, and looked out to the street through the plate glass of the display windows. He took out another Kent and drew on it. Maybe he was thinking about Eva, about Claudia, about all the Georges he had sold sneakers to, about the slew of Macs and their Red Wing steel-toe work shoes. Within seconds, he disappeared in a vapor of smoke.

Oyster Bay Review, September 1997

WRITING THE STORY

"The Little Man" certainly opens a window to my past. The story banged around inside my head for years and finally reached paper while I was working in the San Francisco Bureau of *The Sacramento Bee.* In the late afternoons, after finishing my reporting or filing a daily story, waiting for callbacks from editors, I'd look out from the bureau's offices on the third floor of the Fox Plaza Building, trying to summon forth images of when I was a teenager working in my father's shoe store three decades earlier. How did I get *here*? I used to think, reflecting on the apparent disconnect between my life as a youngster then and as a journalist now. The more I noodled this metamorphosis, though, the more natural I realized the transformation was. As a writer, I knew that some day I'd have to give meaning to that experience long ago, working the stockroom of Townley Shoes.

The mechanics of reporting "The Little Man" involved writing down as much detail as possible in my reporter's notebook. Once I had sold myself on the story, then for weeks I mentally transported myself to Townley Shoes. Every day, I'd fill pages of my notebook, recalling details and elements of my life in the store. I knew the story had to turn on Murray, a character of dubious repute to my father, but of heroic dimension to me. There is a long—perhaps too long— buildup to introducing Murray in "The Little Man," but, frankly, I was having so much fun writing about all the other salesmen and assorted characters in that world that I may have gotten waylaid finally getting to Murray.

The story is set out in naturally progressing episodes: an introduction to me and my father, the world of shoetalk, the history of Townley, the store's context in the fast-changing world of retailing, selling cons, the sidetrip to the girdle store, the multitude of shoedogs, introduction to Murray and his antics, my bonding with Murray, and the climax—Christmas Eve. I'm conscious of telling the story methodically, enjoying each episode, carefully laying out just as much information as I need to nudge the reader into the self-contained world I've recreated.

I must say, though, that my favorite part of the story is Murray's rendition of the G-spot of feet. No doubt, the man had a gift.

EPILOGUE

The story is a memory piece, and as such, its strength lies in how successful I am in whisking the reader off to the past. There is much information-packing in the story, lots of road signs to signal to the reader that this is going to be a trip filled with minute detail and description. The fancy word for that is verisimilitude, which translates to recreation of what actually happened. That's what sells a story, i.e., when readers get transported to another space and time—and aren't suspicious about the artifice of the ride.

In terms of characters, Murray died seven years after I wrote the piece. My father followed, as did Claudia Morgenstern, Charley the movie-house usher, and salesmen Manny, Buddy, Seitzer, Mel and Harry. Sadly, I'm the only one left to pass on memories of Townley Shoes and the galaxy it inhabited.

The old man, of course, turned out to be right about the highway stores. But it wasn't just highway stores that proved to be his undoing. Chain stores in every permutation soon were to rule the land of shoes and practically every other sellable good in America. And what ever happened to shoedogs? You can find them here and there, old men with wonderful stories, but they, too, have just about all died.

ASSIGNMENTS

1) Write about a part-time or summer job you once held (or hold now). Introduce to the reader key players—co-workers, bosses, customers—as well as your duties on the job. String together stories at the workplace, creating in the reader's mind a compelling narrative about your job within the context of working in America.

2) Write about an unexpected and unlikely friendship you've forged, using convincing dialogue and precise detail that anchor the overall meaning of the piece. Make sure your story is told in narrative form. "Show, don't tell" the significance of the new relationship.

3) Write about the arcane language of "shoptalk." Every profession has its own lingo meant to inform insiders and exclude outsiders. Such language can be fast, funny and useful. A waiter could say to the short-order cook, "The customer would like you to make and wrap up a bacon, lettuce and tomato sandwich on whole-wheat toast, but do not, as you usually do, put on any mayonnaise." But isn't "B.L.T down on wheat to go, hold the mayo," better? Make sure your piece introduces the reader to a world of specific shoptalk, one that you are familiar with or one that you investigate.

EXTRAORDINARY PEOPLE

10

DOC OF AGES

Early in my career, I worked as a reporter for the *Latin American Daily Post,* a start-up newspaper pitched to American executives and other English speakers in Rio de Janeiro. A knock-off of the *International Herald Tribune*, the *Daily Post* ran AP wire copy, carried two-day-old box scores of major league baseball games, and published the *New York Times* crossword puzzle a week late next to recycled Charles Goren bridge columns. The *Daily Post* had a tiny staff of five reporters. But the job was as good an introduction to newspapering as any. Actually, it was a whole lot better.

In addition to my day job at the *Daily Post*, the (now-defunct) Field News Service hired me to write features from Brazil. I certainly had plenty to write about. Everything around me was new, and I had the enviable job of writing about whatever struck my fancy. French writer Alexis deTocqueville said that you cannot truly understand your own country until you live somewhere else. "Doc of Ages" and several other stories I wrote from Brazil show that in spades. Most weren't about political or economic shifts in the world's fifth largest nation (I did those pieces, too), but were everyday cultural observations. Material for such stories bombarded me everywhere I went—on the street, on the bus, at the grocery store, at the barbershop, even at the beach (although my editors didn't much buy that one).

The first months in any new place present bountiful opportunities for a journalist. Cultural issues that you might later summarily chalk up to mere regional characteristics are all around you. Pay attention to your instincts; such observations often turn into wonderful stories.

Soon after I arrived in Rio de Janeiro, I couldn't help but notice how many mirrors there were. They were everywhere. In most cities, mirrors are located in enclosed areas (like elevators) to make minimal spaces appear larger, but never had I seen so many mirrors as I saw in Rio. They were in restaurants and apartment foyers, yes, but also in butcher shops and government buildings. You couldn't get away from seeing images of yourself everywhere you went. I came to believe that the plethora of mirrors had something to do with the city's overwhelming premium on youth and beauty. Mirrors were a cultural decree to look attractive, young and buff. They were a conspiratorial reminder that the aging process stopped for no one.

But how to get at this phenomenon and write about it?

Rio's tropical weather surely contributed to an ample display of skin. The beach-nature of the city allowed for locals to wear little on and off the sand. This omnipresent mandate of physical beauty, though, seemed to be more a contagious cultural phenomenon than a by-product of weather or geography. Sure, the girls from Ipanema were beautiful and youthful, but so were their mothers *and* their grandmothers.

That's where I found the beginning of my story. Just because Rio de Janeiro is located below the equator doesn't mean gravity's pull on the body stops for Brazilians in their forties, fifties and sixties.

I searched Brazilian newspaper libraries, scanned display advertisements in upscale society magazines, flipped through the Rio de Janeiro Yellow Pages, called Brazilian physicians and the local medical society. The demand for beauty and youth was so great in certain circles that some physicians told me that Rio could very well be the plastic-surgery capital of the world. When a local plastic surgeon told me that relatively few Rio women over 45, who were either middle or upper class, didn't undergo the scalpel for cosmetic reasons, I knew I was on to something.

Journalists like superlatives: the biggest, oldest, largest, smallest, richest. For this short piece, I opted to tell the story of Rio's most famous plastic surgeon.

Doc of Ages

Plastic surgeon Ivo Pitanguy is on the cutting edge of Brazil's cult of beauty

RIO DE JANEIRO, Brazil—Dr. Ivo Pitanguy has been called the Michelangelo of plastic surgery. He has chiseled countless pounds of fat from cellulite-saturated thighs, molded thousands of drooping buttocks into firm derrieres and stretched yards of flabby facial flesh as tight as Saran Wrap.

Pitanguy has poised scalpel on the skin of more than 30,000 patients, including presidents and their wives, princes and princesses, movie stars and jet-setters.

The 58-year-old Pitanguy (pronounced PEE-tong-gee) doesn't discourage claims he has operated on Marisa Berenson, Jacqueline Onassis, Ursula Andress, Sophia Loren and Raquel Welch.

"They even say I've done Ronald Reagan," a smiling Pitanguy says. "But I could never reveal that. If I say I haven't, people don't believe me, and it would be against medical ethics to say I have."

One of his patients, Princess Farah Diba of Iran, gave Pitanguy a 1,700-year-old Persian rug as a token of her appreciation. Another, actress Gina Lollobrigida, painted a portrait of the doctor, which hangs in his study.

Much of the plastic surgeon's life resembles a scene from a James Bond movie. Long-legged and tanned women lounge in bikinis at poolside on his private island, located 60 miles south of Rio. Servants in starched white uniforms carry heaping bowls of tropical fruit on their heads. A group of Pitanguy's friends, dressed in black karate robes, face the calm south Atlantic and silently go through their routines.

Pitanguy's famous private hospital is located on a quiet side street in the Rio section of Botofogo, five blocks from the beach and less than a mile from Sugar Loaf Mountain.

The Lincoln Continental used to shuttle publicity-shy patients to and from Rio's Galeao International Airport is parked out front. The gray car has tinted windows to shield patients from the public.

The clinic's nurses and receptionists are living witnesses to beauty. All have small perky noses, almond-shaped eyes, deeply tanned skin and shapely torsos. Their white smocks bear the inscription I.V. (the surgeon's initials).

If Brazil is plastic surgery's world headquarters, then Rio is its nerve center.

"Beaches are the reason," says Luzia, Pitanguy's frizzy-haired personal secretary. "Everyone can see everything. People become alarmed when they see their body getting older. They want to resist that aging process."

Indeed, Rio residents who frequent the fashionable beaches in Ipanema or Leblon wear nothing more than swathes of string. So many mirrors adorn Rio apartment lobbies, restaurants and elevators that there is no getting away from the constant reminder that the aging process stops for no one.

It is an unusual Rio society woman older than 45 who has not undergone some form of plastic surgery.

When Pitanguy performed surgery four years ago on Brazilian President Joao Figueiredo and his wife, Dulce, it barely raised eyebrows. The Brazilian president had the bags under his eyes removed; his wife had such a tight face-lift that many now say she looks literally statuesque.

There are 23 private rooms in the Pitanguy hospital, and as would befit a man whose clinic bears his name, the clinic shuts down when the surgeon is out of town—which is often.

Pitanguy, who prefers to be called "the professor," says only he operates on patients at his hospital, even though 30 doctors are enrolled in the clinic's three-year post-graduate course.

The plastic surgeon maintains homes throughout the world. Besides the secluded island, there is the wooded hillside estate in Rio, the mountain retreat in nearby Petropolis, the skiing villa in Gstaad, Switzerland, and the Avenue Montaigne apartment in Paris. Spread out among the houses are paintings by Picasso, Chagall, Miró and Dali, as well as several Henry Moore sculptures.

To reach his penthouse office, visitors must walk by a cage filled with more than 50 varieties of exotic birds. Currently, his favorite comes from the Amazon rain forest and only eats meat. Pitanguy gladly obliges a guest by feeding the chirping black-and-white bird freshly ground steak.

The son of a surgeon from the interior Brazilian state of Minas Gerais, Pitanguy was so eager to become a doctor that he falsified his medical school application, adding four years to his age. He interned at a Rio public hospital, then studied plastic surgery in the United States, France and Great Britain.

He speaks English with a slight Portuguese accent and is apt to go off into one of the six languages he speaks fluently when searching for a word to express himself.

Pitanguy, who is wearing a blue scrub suit and white clogs, says he prides himself on being a "humanist," an "intellectual" whose concerns are "broad and complex."

"People have created a spirit of not hiding, and with that (comes the concept) that plastic surgery is not sinful, that its benefits are both psychological and social," he says.

"We make the patient feel more at peace with himself. If you are a Jew or a black, you don't want to have an excess of ethnic characteristics. We take the disharmony out."

Pitanguy has a reputation for hobnobbing with heavyweights of the international cafe society. When actress Candice Bergen was in town several years ago during Rio's Carnival, journalists recall that Pitanguy assiduously clung to her side for days, proudly showing her the city. Members of Miss Bergen's entourage resorted to calling Pitanguy "Ivo-Stick," for a glue with the same name sold in England.

Pitanguy makes no excuse for what he calls "the many passions of my life." Past passions have included breeding weimaraners and Great Danes, birds, goats, fish, pigs and oysters. Currently, his avocations include tennis, spear fishing, karate, scuba diving and skiing.

Another passion is classical music. Often while he molds and shapes the contours of a patient's body, Pitanguy listens to symphonic music—Strauss is one of his favorites—piped into the operating room.

He says he won't operate on just anyone.

"You should do plastic surgery to be well with yourself. Not to get a job or to get married. But when you feel better about yourself, you are better for society.

"Once I had a woman in her 60s, and I did several lifts on her. Then two years later, she felt so young that she adopted a child. Next I operated on her husband because she wanted him to feel as young as she did."

About half of his patients are Brazilians, Pitanguy says. When travel and lodging expenses are figured into the total, his fees are about the same as a comparable U.S. surgeon. Pitanguy says he has a sliding scale to accommodate those who cannot afford his services. In addition to his private practice, he is a professor at the Catholic Pontifical University of Rio, and once a week operates at a free clinic for reconstructive surgery.

Pitanguy says he likes to consider himself much more than a plastic surgeon.

"I have a constant interest in the destiny of the world. I am not a materialist. I am not a good businessman. I have spiritual values. My son goes to a private school in Switzerland. The idea was to introduce him to basic values."

His island, called Porcos, the Portuguese word for pigs, is where Pitanguy does much of his contemplation.

"It's my retreat. I try to go there every weekend. Usually I will not work on Friday so that I can prepare myself for the weekend. The point of the island is to keep in constant contact with nature. The island gives me an idea of freedom and creativity."

He says the island reminds him of one of his patients.

"When the sun sets, the island looks like a silhouette of a woman—or a mermaid lying peacefully on the water. When the tides come in gracefully, I have the impression she is breathing. It was a savage island before. I was its plastic surgeon. As a woman, I molded it."

The Dallas Morning News, June 3, 1984

WRITING THE STORY

I initiated the piece on Ivo Pitanguy by writing to him, formally asking for an interview. Luzia, Pitanguy's frizzy-haired, quadralingual personal secretary, immediately replied, and after going back and forth about when Pitanguy would be available, we finally were able to set up an hour-long appointment.

I am an information junkie, and before lunging into this interview (essentially a conversation with a stranger), I read dozens of stories about Pitanguy, some that had appeared in the Brazilian press, several in U.S. magazines and newspapers. I also read articles Pitanguy had written for medical journals. I spent an afternoon crafting specific questions for Pitanguy, and wrote them out in longhand. When I met Pitanguy, I was familiar with much that had been written about him, as well as what Pitanguy had written himself.

Once inside Pitanguy's clinic, as Luzia handed me a *cafezinho* (a demitasse of espresso), I sat mesmerized. The place seemed plucked from a futuristic movie set. While waiting for Pitanguy to emerge from an operating room, I scribbled down observations about the clinic and Pitanguy's personnel. Everything—from the walls to the counters to the chairs—was stark, modernistic white, and everyone employed at the clinic was drop-dead gorgeous.

My job, as usual, was to suck the reader into the story as fast as possible, and with Pitanguy as the subject, that wasn't difficult. In the lede, I opted to play with the gobs of fat Pitanguy carves away every day from his patients, which results in skin "as tight as Saran Wrap." I liked ending the lede with the name of the household plastic product since it's a two-word (uppercase) trademark; somehow its novelty helps pull the reader through a long sentence.

Next, I segued into the sheer number of patients Pitanguy had sliced and molded. Since this was a celebrity profile, I included in the second graf patients who were royalty and movie stars. In the fourth graf, I introduced the first direct quote from Pitanguy, and it's a tour de force of media savvy engineered by him. The good doctor raised the *possibility* that he *might* have operated on Ronald Reagan (who was president at the time), but backed off, cutely citing doctor-patient privilege. Here was a man who knew how to play the press, and I fully went along for the ride.

After dropping more details into the story (Pitanguy's clinic at the foot of Sugar Loaf Mountain, the private airport limo with tinted windows), I wanted to widen my focus to place Pitanguy into a larger cultural phenomenon. Details of his private island, his homes in Gstaad and Paris, the Picasso, Chagall, Miró and Dali paintings on the wall thus came next.

Pitanguy held ultimate power in his hands: the ability to give not just beauty, but the illusion of youth, to anyone with enough money to pay for it. As such, Pitanguy floated around like God, and his tag-line quote at the end of the piece amply demonstrated that.

EPILOGUE

In this short piece, I tried to do more than report on the life of a physician whose specialty was plastic surgery. Pitanguy was (and still is) a cultural phenomenon; I tried to place him within the context of the society he serves. In many ways, Pitanguy was a Brazilian version of Hugh Hefner. His clinic had all the trappings of the Playboy Mansion, and while Pitanguy didn't walk around in pajamas, his crisp white, monogrammed uniform was custom designed to serve his own purposes. The challenge in "Doc of Ages" was to frame Pitanguy—his opulent surroundings, his role to his well-heeled youth-centric patients. At the center of the portrait, though, is how Pitanguy defined himself. His direct quotes, more than anything else, revealed his own remarkable notion of himself.

ASSIGNMENTS

1) As a newcomer to a city or region, write out a list of conventions or habits that strikes you as different from what you are accustomed to. Discuss the list with colleagues. Determine how you could proceed to write about these cultural differences in an illuminating way.

2) Determine how pervasive cosmetic plastic surgery is in your area. Find out which procedures are the most popular. Follow one patient from his/her decision to undergo surgery to the outcome.

3) Interview a controversial, high-profile leader in your community. In your story, using self-serving quotes from the local celebrity, focus on why the person has achieved his/her reputation.

11

THE JOY OF DR. RUTH

Ruth Westheimer, aka Dr. Ruth, is an undeniable American icon, and when I heard she was coming to San Francisco, I pleaded with my editor to let me cover her. Ever since I nearly mowed her down outside a Broadway theater in New York years ago, Dr. Ruth had fascinated me. What exactly is it about Ruth Westheimer that captivates so many millions of Americans? Is it her pint size? Her Jewish/German accent? The explicit sexual language coming from a grandmother who looks more at home cooking chicken soup than talking about group sex?

I wasn't sure, and that's what I hoped to find out. Ruth Westheimer had an empire of product endorsements, radio and television shows, advice columns, books, magazine articles, even board and computer sex games. Not to mention a budding acting career in films and television. She was everywhere. America was in love with her.

I contacted Westheimer's publicist and was immediately told that Dr. Ruth would be happy to spend time with me—an hour—sandwiched between an address to 500 women and an appearance on a local TV show. In preparation, I read as much as I could on Westheimer (and there was a lot). When she extended her hand to me in the grand ballroom at the Hilton Hotel, I was ready to fire questions at her.

The Joy of Dr. Ruth

America's in love with her—and she knows exactly why

SAN FRANCISCO—"Fantastic! Fantastic!" Dr. Ruth Westheimer says, barely able to contain her enthusiasm after finishing a sexually explicit speech to 500 prim-and-proper members of San Francisco's Commonwealth Club last week.

In the cavernous lobby of the Hilton Hotel, America's premier sex guru sinks into a beige sofa. Its oversized pillows dwarf the elfin Dr. Ruth, who bends down to change her size-4B Ferragamo black patent leather midheels to a pair of more sensible maroon, lace-up oxfords. Ash-blond, blue-eyed, twice-divorced Dr. Ruth is still charged with energy. A long, white limousine is about to whisk her off to a live television show that begins in 20 minutes.

In the meantime, she wants to walk through the lobby of the Hilton, something about buying a crystal knickknack. She gestures, strides, points like a pint-sized Gen. Norman Schwarzkopf.

A three-piece-suited man sees her and elbows his companion. "Dr. Ruth?" he asks timidly.

"Hello, hello," she sings like a parakeet to the couple. "And who are you? Vhat are your names?"

At least eight other people come up to Dr. Ruth. She stops for each, asking their names.

"Fantastic!" she says again for perhaps the twenty-fifth time during the last hour.

A bevy of women espies her. Ten paces past Dr. Ruth, one of the women, who is about five feet nine inches tall, turns around and asks, "How tall are you, anyway?"

"Four feet seven inches," Dr. Ruth answers without missing a beat, smiling as though she just downed a pint of matzo ball soup.

"Fantastic!" she says, and it becomes very clear that Dr. Ruth's response is really not directed at anyone. Rather, it's her own reaction to America's run-away love affair with her.

The author of five best sellers, she is host of a nationally syndicated television show, creator of a board and computer game ("It gives good orgasm!" she says), actor in two movies. She has appeared on thousands of TV and radio talk shows.

Dr. Ruth readily admits that she knows how to manipulate the media to her advantage. Her personal press agent for 10 years is, of course, "Fantastic!" but she also ascribes her blockbuster success to her German accent, her Munchkin size and her age (she is 62).

"Vhen a lady like me starts talking about erections, lubrication, premature ejaculation, masturbation, penises and vaginas, people listen!"

She smiles sweetly—and then, oh, no! She explodes with another "Fantastic!"

Dr. Ruth is indeed a multiple orgasm, a comparison no doubt she would wholeheartedly approve of. "People ask me, 'Dr. Ruth, vhat do you take for all your energy?' They think it's vitamins. Vhat do I need with vitamins? I love vhat I'm doing. Who vouldn't? I talk sex day and night."

Wearing a red linen blouse and black polka-dot skirt, Dr. Ruth started in right away at the Commonwealth Club, with its audience of affluent, well-heeled women. She climbed atop a pedestal in the ballroom of the Hilton and pulled the microphone down to her lips.

She related how two weeks ago she returned from Israel, during which there were dozens of Scud missile attacks. Dr. Ruth said she advised the Israelis not to have sex with gas masks on. She also drew the line when it came to lovemaking while hiding in a room sealed because of a possible poison gas attack.

A ripple of titters from the audience.

She recently talked to the Harvard Law School about masturbation, and said that for years people thought masturbation caused hair to grow on the palms of the hands. "And you know vhat? As soon as I said that, all the attorneys looked at their hands!"

Dr. Ruth's sexual magic was working again. She had turned this audience into willing slaves panting for more.

She told them that by thinking exotic thoughts and exercising certain pelvic muscles, some women in the audience may be able to experience orgasms. "But I don't vant to see a show of hands on how many that exercise vorked for."

A sea of laughter.

"Fantastic!" Dr. Ruth exclaimed, clapping her hands just as she does on TV.

"Anything that two consenting adults do in their bedroom, living room or kitchen is all right."

Dr. Ruth told another story about a man who wanted to make his wedding night special.

"I said after the vedding ceremony and after the party, you should go into the bathroom. Have your vife get into bed first. Vhen you valk out of the bathroom, do not vear pajamas. Vear only a tie and a top hat. Then he asked me, 'Vhere should I put the top hat?'"

Thirty seconds of applause. The audience belonged to Dr. Ruth.

Next, she offered up advice, recommending that husbands and wives take turns watching their spouses sleep. "People have orgasms during erotic dreams, so stay avake to see if your husband or vife is smiling."

Make one thing very clear: Dr. Ruth is no libertine. She says she is an old-fashioned square who believes in love and marriage. "Sex is not just intercourse. Sex is a smile, holding hands. Sex is a relationship."

She even confessed that she and her 69-year-old husband don't sleep together. "Ve don't even sleep in the same room. He snores too much and it's getting vorse. It goes to show that you can still have good sex and a good night's sleep."

Someone at the lecture asked about the fabled G Spot, the citadel of female pleasure.

"Fantastic question!" Dr. Ruth debunked the famed theory, blaming its promulgation on bogus research. "Unfortunately, no such thing as G Spot." She did assure the audience that when such a spot is found, Dr. Ruth will be there.

In some ways, Dr. Ruth is an explorer, charting familiar but seldom-discussed issues. She also is a female Horatio Alger. Rags-to-riches stories don't get much better than her own.

Born Karola Ruth Siegel in Frankfurt, Germany, her family died at Auschwitz while she was attending elementary school in Switzerland.

Orphaned, she moved to Palestine after the war and became a member of the Haganah, the Jewish underground movement fighting for Israel's statehood. She was trained to be a sniper.

At 22, she married an Israeli soldier and moved to Paris, where she earned a degree in psychology from the Sorbonne, even though she never graduated from high school. The marriage collapsed after five years.

In Paris she had an affair with a young Frenchman and the two married to legitimate a pregnancy. After moving to New York, that marriage, too, failed.

She supported her toddler daughter by working as a $1-per-hour housemaid in Manhattan, while earning a master's degree from the New School for Social Research and a doctorate from Columbia University.

Dr. Ruth met her third husband, Manfred (5 feet 5 inches tall) on a skiing trip in the Catskills in 1961. She tried to go up the mountain with her six-foot-tall boyfriend Hans. When the unbalanced couple found they couldn't negotiate the T-bar on the lift, she looked around and spotted the shorter Manfred, an engineer, and went up with him. The rest is history. These days, he calls Dr. Ruth his "little skiing accident."

She became project director of a Planned Parenthood clinic in Harlem, and has taught at Lehman College, Brooklyn College and West Point—which she loved, she says, "because of all the tall, handsome officers in their uniforms."

After her Commonwealth talk last week, Dr. Ruth didn't want to sit. "Come vith me to the hotel gift shop. I vant to buy a present."

In the gift shop, the clerk pulled out of the display case a small crystal castle. "How much?"

"That's $110."

"Vow!" Dr. Ruth exclaimed. She reconsidered and finally plunked down a credit card. She explained she has a grab bag at home, ready to give anyone a present.

"But this little castle, I think I'll keep it myself. Hee-hee-hee-hee!"

Back in the lobby, the limousine for the television show was waiting.

One last item before she went: Dr. Ruth wanted to talk about her grandson, Oli.

"Eight months ago my daughter had a baby boy. He is the most beautiful little baby I have ever seen. He is precious."

"Fantastic!" Dr. Ruth says, clapping her hands.

The Sacremento Bee, March 11, 1991

WRITING THE STORY

I seldom start stories with quotes, and I admonish beginning writers who attempt such sleazy, lazy openings to get serious about their writing. "You're telling a story, not publishing a Q and A!" is my stock exhortation. There is no context for the quote. The reader has to go to the end of the sentence to see who's speaking. There's got to be a better way to suck readers into a story than glibly quoting a person without first laying any foundation.

Out with such silly rules! There is only one way to start this story, and it's with Westheimer's mantra, "Fantastic!" It was a self-congratulatory dictum that Westheimer used not just to describe whatever situation was at hand, but her life and America's infatuation with it.

In the second graf of the story, I want to paint a detailed picture of Westheimer, and what first struck me upon seeing her was her size. Not someone to stand on ceremony, as she sat down after her lecture, she immediately pulled out a pair of shoes, slipped off the black pumps she was wearing, and in her stocking feet, exchanged one pair for the other. I broke the ice by asking Westheimer her shoe size and the brand she was wearing. She thrust one of the shoes into my face, extolling the virtues of Ferragamo mid-heels. "Expensive, and they pinch my toes, but they're beauties. Look at them!" she said, before intoning another "Fantastic!"

My own research had given me a working biography of Westheimer, but I want to sprinkle the top of the piece with reader nuggets: twice divorced, blue eyes, ash-blond hair. Almost as soon as we sit down, Westheimer has too much on her mind to chat. Now with the more sensible lace-ups on her feet, she bounces up from the sofa and says she wants to walk. I follow. I get the distinct impression that Westheimer wants to be seen. She wants to show me, maybe remind herself, of her amazing public persona. And within seconds, she gets the payoff. A dozen people strolling through the Hilton lobby spot her. Just as she notices their glances, she stops, sticks out her hand and introduces herself. To the one brazen onlooker who asks how tall Westheimer is, Dr. Ruth smiles and informs, then continues her strut, exclaiming one more time to no one in particular, "Fantastic!"

This is an interview on the fly. There is no subtle nuance with Westheimer. If I want to get anything, it's got to be following the one-woman Dr. Ruth parade. The first full Westheimer quote I use has got to be a zinger, and it is: "Vhen a lady like me starts talking about erections, lubrication, premature ejaculation, masturbation, penises and vaginas, people listen!"

Clearly, Dr. Ruth knows her shtik inside and out. She talks in quotable quotes. She is part sex meister, part comedian, part therapist, part grandmother. Her anecdotes about talking to Harvard Law School about masturbation, about the honeymooners and the top hat, about whether or not your spouse smiles when asleep, are calculated and well timed. And funny.

Outside the practiced nonstop show that Westheimer puts on, I dole out to the reader more nuggets: She and her husband don't sleep in the same bedroom; her parents were killed at Auschwitz; she used to work as a housemaid. Detail, as usual, is what sells the story. I ask Westheimer how tall her husband is, which leads to another anecdote on how the couple met ("the little skiing accident").

EPILOGUE

The one-person Dr. Ruth Show continues to flourish. Westheimer regularly hobnobs with the nation's power elite. In 2002, she was nominated for a Grammy for her CD reading "Little Red Riding Hood" and "Goldilocks." She recently co-wrote a book, *Power: The Ultimate Aphrodisiac,* in which she waxes rhapsodic with chapters such as "Sleeping Your Way to the Top" and "Trophy Wives." A previous book, *Sex for Dummies,* published in 1995, has been translated into 23 languages. Currently, she answers questions about sex on her own AOL site. The Dr. Ruth Page (http://www-2.cs.cmu.edu/~chuck/ruthpg), set up by an especially loyal fan, contains scores of downloadable video and sound clips. On her personal front, Westheimer's husband, Manfred, died in 1997. Last year, though, Westheimer starred in a jewelry company's national advertising campaign, modeling a bridal veil, with the slogan, "Suddenly, everybody wants to be a bride."

ASSIGNMENTS

1) The next time a celebrity comes to town, make arrangements to interview that person. Thoroughly research the person's career. Prepare a list of well-

thought-out questions. In your story, infuse the piece with the characteristics you discern from your interview.

2) Talk to students and others in your community about their own sexual practices. Are certain activities more popular than they may have been several years ago? Is abstinence a trend, and if so, is it politically, religiously, or culturally motivated? Assure those you interview that you will grant them anonymity, but make sure you record all quotes exactly as they are given to you.

3) Profile a local celebrity. Write a tick-tock on his or her daily life. If it's a writer, when does he get up, how long does he write every day, where does he hang out? Why does he choose to live in your community? If it's an artist, find out her inspirations, her mentors, where she buys her paints, what she wears while she paints. Demystify the person and any aura surrounding him or her.

12

GOTHIC REVIVAL

Ask anyone on either coast what Iowa brings to mind. After corn, pigs, perhaps "The Music Man" and "Field of Dreams," odds are you'll hear "American Gothic," the Grant Wood painting of the dour-faced farm woman and her pitchfork-toting husband. The painting has become one of the most recognizable pieces of art in the world; certainly, it's one of the most parodied.

So, naturally, when I moved to Iowa in the early 1990s, I wanted to go to the source, to the spot where Grant Wood conceived this American icon. The backdrop for the painting, I found out, was in a tiny, out-of-the-way southeast Iowa town called Eldon. The town has had two brushes with fame. In addition to Grant Wood's arrival in 1930, comedian Roseanne and her (now-former) husband, Iowa native Tom Arnold, bought a rundown pizzeria in Eldon in 1993 and converted it into an aluminum-sided restaurant called The Big Food Diner. The diner made *People* magazine, but after the couple divorced a year later, Eldon returned to its sleepy self. Residents, though, still report that every once in a while out-of-towners circle Eldon's four-block downtown grid in search of the old white-washed farmhouse that Wood used as the setting behind his two severe-looking models. The man and woman in "American Gothic," it turned out, were nothing like the stern and stoic characters Wood painted. The man was Wood's dentist, a live wire who used to zip around town in a red sports car. The woman was Wood's sister, a happy-go-lucky lady known for her hearty laugh.

I spent an afternoon in Eldon, interviewing locals as well as two visitors who happened into town and had me snap photographs of them in front of the farmhouse.

Gothic Revival

Grant Wood's painting may not be great art, but it certainly is popular

Grant Wood was driving through Eldon, a tiny Iowa town in the fall of 1930 when he pulled off Main Street and drove four blocks north. There he saw a small, white-washed house with Gothic windows. Wood took a fancy to the place, and hastily drew a 3-by-3-inch color sketch on the back of an envelope. That afternoon when the 39-year-old painter returned to his Cedar Rapids home, he asked his sister, Nan, and his dentist, Dr. Byron McKeeby, to pose.

Nan Wood Graham, 30 at the time, wore a brown apron over a plain black dress, adorned only by a cameo brooch. Her blond hair was pulled back tight against an oblong face. McKeeby, then 62, who was more accustomed to a dentist's white coat and drill, was painted in a black jacket and faded blue overalls while holding a pitchfork in his right hand. Although many viewers of the painting have assumed the couple to be husband and wife, Wood said he intended to show a stoic Iowa farmer and his daughter.

The small, 25-by-29-inch painting initially brought Wood a bronze medal and $300 from the Art Institute of Chicago in a contest that awarded $2,500 for the top prize. But as soon as the public saw "American Gothic," the painting caused a sensation.

"American Gothic" has become one of the world's most recognized paintings, as sure an American icon as the Statue of Liberty or the Golden Gate Bridge. Perhaps the only other painting more recognizable on the planet is the "Mona Lisa"—with Edvard Munch's "The Scream" a possible runner-up.

For a while, "American Gothic" also was one of this country's most misunderstood paintings—a characteristic of celebrated works of art. The depiction of Nan Wood Graham brought forth protests from hundreds of Iowa farm women who said her dour portrait would "sour milk."

Some viewers mistakenly figured the bald McKeeby to be a minister, an inference drawn because of the somber jacket he was wearing, and confusion that the tall vertical house and Gothic window in the background could be a church. Others looked at the symbolic importance of the pitchfork McKeeby was holding and thought the three tines represented the divine trinity.

Curiously, although Wood painted McKeeby as a stern Iowa farmer, the dentist was known as a live wire in that part of Iowa, a man who loved to speed around town in a red sports car.

The first time Nan Wood Graham ever saw the house in Eldon was in 1980, a half century after her brother painted her and McKeeby in separate sessions back in his studio in Cedar Rapids, 80 miles northeast of Eldon.

Graham said the painting "made a personality out of me." Without it, she said, she would have spent her days as "the world's worst stenographer." Her brother, who died of cancer in 1942, would never know the dizzying extent of the public's fascination worldwide with "America Gothic." The painting also has become a hearty symbol of American culture. On their White House bedroom wall, President and Mrs. Clinton have hung a parody of "America Gothic." Tens of thousands of such knockoffs of the painting have woven the simple portrait into the American tapestry. Although the painting made Wood an overnight celebrity, the parodies didn't start until the late 1950s.

Everyone from George Washington and Elizabeth Taylor to Miss Piggy, Kermit the Frog and the Wegman dogs have been pictured with the backdrop of the small Gothic house. In a 1961 *New Yorker* magazine cartoon, Charles Addams depicted the Gothic pair strolling down a museum corridor as though they had just stepped out of their portrait.

A memorable episode on TV's "Dick Van Dyke Show" had Van Dyke buying a clown painting at an auction, and—while dusting the canvas—he then thinks he has discovered "American Gothic" under the image. Dozens of commercials, including ones for corn flakes, corn oil and deodorant, further popularized the duo of Nan Wood Graham and Dr. Byron McKeeby.

Parodies of the painting continue to pop up everywhere. When *Time* magazine sought to illustrate a cover story last year on "Everyone's Hip [and that's not cool]," editors chose to use "American Gothic" adorned with various "hip" accouterments. And in the fall, the CBS network plans to debut a TV series entitled "American Gothic."

But some representations may have gone too far. In 1968, Graham sued *Playboy* and *Look* magazines, NBC and Johnny Carson for a topless parody of "American Gothic." Graham received an out-of-court settlement. Moral standards change, and several years later, when publisher Larry Flynt printed in *Hustler* magazine another more explicit version, Graham filed another lawsuit, this one for $10 million. The second case was thrown out of a Los Angeles Superior Court; the judge said the depiction was a parody and as such was not intended to be taken seriously.

Realizing that the parodies themselves were as much icons as the original, Edwin B. Green, the retired managing editor of the *Iowa City Press-Citizen,* started collecting "American Gothic" knockoffs in the mid-1950s. They first filled a shoe box, then a drawer, then a closet and finally an entire room. In 1979, Green donated the collection to the Davenport Museum of Art, which today houses the world's largest collection of parodies of the painting. In fact, the parodies have led to a renewed interest in Wood. In 1985 "Arbor Day" fetched $1.37 million, a record price for a Grant Wood. And an upcoming Grant Wood exhibit promises again to bring his name to more Americans.

In his day, Grant Wood's art scored a hit with actors, musicians and directors on both coasts. His paintings were snapped up by Edward G. Robinson,

Katharine Hepburn, Cole Porter and King Vidor. Such popularity irked critics, who even today still snicker at Wood's artistry, derisively labeling it "representational" and "regional." Throughout Wood's career, he was despised by the American art establishment. Such venom wasn't confined to elite New York art circles. While the soft-spoken, bespectacled Wood was a faculty member in the art department at the University of Iowa from 1934 to 1940, jealous colleagues repeatedly tried to get him fired. One of them, H.W. Janson, who later wrote a standard reference work, *The History of Art,* went so far as to call Wood's painting style similar to that of state art approved by the Nazis.

The hue and cry continued. When Wood's art became the subject of a massive one-man show at the Whitney Museum in New York in 1983, *Newsweek's* art critic John Ashbery took a verbal pitchfork to the exhibition.

"Few artists have managed to enter Parnassus on slimmer credentials," Ashbery wrote. "On the evidence of the Whitney show, it would seem that Wood's work must remain a dead letter, a cluster of prettily-made baubles that inspired no imitators and whose thinly veiled regional-chauvinist principles seem not only quaint but slightly distasteful today."

Grant Wood, who was born in 1891 in a farmhouse four miles from Anamosa, Iowa, is a native-son hero to Iowans. The two main repositories of his work are the Cedar Rapids School District, for whom Wood worked briefly as a high school teacher, and Turner Mortuary, the Cedar Rapids funeral parlor that once gave him free studio space.

Grant Wood elementary schools in Cedar Rapids, Iowa City and Bettendorf attest to his legacy. Byron McKeeby, one of the models, died at the age of 82 in 1950. Nan Wood Graham died at 91 in 1990.

Today fewer than a dozen tourists a week make the pilgrimage to see the 115-year-old "American Gothic" house in Eldon (population 1,255). The weekly trickle spurted in 1993 after Roseanne Barr and Tom Arnold bought a pizzeria and converted it to The Big Food Diner, complete with shiny aluminum siding and an entree called the Loose Meat Sandwich. The diner—patterned after the Lunch Box, the restaurant in Roseanne's television show—was situated four blocks from the "America Gothic" house. But now that Roseanne and Tom have called it quits, the diner is closed and boarded up. The last Loose Meat Sandwich was served the day before Valentine's Day this year, the same day Roseanne married her former bodyguard.

As for the nearby 28,000-square-foot mansion Tom was building for Roseanne and all their Hollywood buddies (it would have been the largest house in the state), that came to a halt after the foundation was laid and some walls were put up. Last spring, Tom gave the whole concrete mess to the local community college district, which doesn't know quite what to do with it.

Back in the '80s, a self-styled local entrepreneur erected tacky painted plywood cutouts of Graham and McKeeby and, for a price, tourists could stand behind them and have their photographs taken with the famous house as a back-drop. Hooligans vandalized the then-vacant house, and often held parties there. But in 1988, the Iowa State Historical Society acquired the house. These days, the only improvisation comes when tourists take out silverware from their picnic baskets and pose in front of the "American Gothic" house, holding table forks, rather than pitchforks, shoulder-high.

Although the house is owned by the state, it is closed to the public. The state rents the 1,000-square-foot, 1½-story house to Mari Beth Johnston, a nurse who pays $150 a month, excluding utilities. In a bizarre twist of fate, Johnston is the great-granddaughter of Gideon Jones, who owned the house when Wood painted it in 1930. Steven Ohrun, the historic site's coordinator for the State Historical Society, says the aesthetic value of the property is the house's exterior, not its interior.

Ohrun said tenant Johnston's lease does carry three special provisions: There can be no smoking in or around the premises; she must display the lace window curtains the Society provides (identical to those depicted in the painting); and she "shall treat the visiting public in an appreciative manner," although she "may deny access to the interior of the house."

The State Historical Society has poured $150,000 into the house in renovations, which include a new foundation, roof, heating and plumbing systems, as well as a fire sprinkler system. And that's not all. Ohrun's office made a request to the State Department of Cultural Affairs for almost a half-million dollars, as part of a development that would include bicycle paths, roads, a lake and a dam adjacent to the tiny historic house. Last April, the state legislature approved $225,000 to begin design and construction for a visitors center, but in June, Iowa Gov. Terry Branstad vetoed the appropriation.

Chicago Tribune Magazine, August 13, 1995

WRITING THE STORY

Stories start with the first word. I wanted to put readers into the artist's shoes, and whisk them off to Eldon, where everything started. What helps sell the lede is detail—"3-by-3-inch color sketch on the back of an envelope." The specificity is important. The graf ends with a teaser, a tantalizing allusion to the two unheralded models in the world-famous painting. Anyone who wants more on either will have to go to the second graf.

Ages are important in stories, and especially in this one. Readers want to know how old Nan Wood Graham and Byron McKeeby were when they posed. That Wood had intended the pair to be father and daughter, not husband and wife, also is significant. The actual size of the painting is relevant, too, since few people realize that the piece of art is relatively small. The greatest irony of "American Gothic" is that the Art Institute of Chicago bought it for a measly $300 in a contest in which the painting placed third.

As the story builds momentum, it details the public's wildly different interpretations of "American Gothic": that the Eldon house in the backdrop was a church, that McKeeby was a minister and the pitchfork he held represented the divine trinity. I continue with the same "misunderstood" thread when I write that the two models never even posed in front of the Eldon house, but that Wood juxtaposed the models (and he never even posed them together!) back in his studio in Cedar Rapids, 80 miles away. It took Nan Wood Graham a half century to visit the house in the painting that had made her so famous.

The centerpiece of the story, of course, is the dizzying popularity of "American Gothic," as well as the innumerable parodies and knockoffs of it. Finding many of the parodies was easy. In a local card store, I found a postcard of Bill and Hillary Clinton in an American Gothic pose. I surfed the Web. I went to the local library, where I found six source books on Wood, including a biography Nan Wood Graham wrote about her brother. For additional information, I interviewed the curator of an Iowa museum that planned to open a major retrospective of Wood's art.

As I wrap up the story, I take the reader back to where the story started—to write about the topsy-turvy history of the farmhouse. In a strange spin, I discover that the house, owned by the State of Iowa, is actually leased to a private citizen, a nurse. The tagline of the story nicely caps the controversial masterpiece. Citing budgetary considerations, Iowa's governor had recently vetoed funds to make a visitors center at the "American Gothic" site.

EPILOGUE

"American Gothic" was as misunderstood as Grant Wood himself and, in many ways, I grew to realize that Wood's famous portrait was an apt metaphor for his own life. As Norman Rockwell or Andrew Wyeth would later be categorized, Grant Wood was roundly condemned by the American art establishment as an "illustrator." At the University of Iowa where I teach, faculty members banded together to oust Wood from the art department. Wood's art was too popular for the highbrow professors whose names today largely are forgotten. I have a special fondness for Wood. The last house in which he lived is around the corner from where I live in Iowa City. When I walk by the stately red brick house and peer through it's Gothic windows, I often think about the heartache Wood must have felt. I wanted "Gothic Revival" to work as a long-overdue eulogy of Wood, a paean to a painter reviled by critics and artists, but adored by the public.

ASSIGNMENTS

1) Go to a local art museum and write a piece about one of the institution's famous paintings or sculptures. Include in your story where the artist started and completed the work, whether models were used (if so, who were they), the artist's career from anonymity to fame, and where the piece of art fits in with the artist's career and that of other artists. Peg your story to a museum opening or show featuring the artwork.

2) Write a story about the chain of owners of a particular piece of art in a local museum— from initial sale by the artist to how it found itself in the museum. Trace the ownership of the artwork, the roller-coaster ride from collector to collector, from institution to institution. Track the piece's appreciation in value.

3) Write a profile of gallery guards at the local museum. How do they stand for so long every day? In a job not punctuated with excitement, write about the rare occasions when they have been called into action. Who is cut out for such jobs? Are they art lovers, or is the museum venue coincidental to the job for most? What kind of shoes do they wear to protect against fallen arches?

13

KINGS OF THE MAT

Before Hulk Hogan, Ric "Nature Boy" Flair, Stone Cold Steve Austin—today's multimedia kings of the mat—professional wrestlers had long entertained legions of die-hard fans in search of athletic prowess and hokey theatrics. When I lived in Dallas, the biggest and most popular venue for professional wrestling was a dilapidated old arena with corrugated sheet-metal sides and roof, called the Sportatorium (located on Industrial Boulevard). The place was as low-rent as you could get. In the summer, there was no air-conditioning and if you sat up front ringside, you could see (and smell) the perspiration dripping from the wrestlers as they body-slammed and pile-drove each other onto the mat. Admission was cheap, as were the beer, hotdogs and peanuts. The fans were outrageously partisan. Wrestlers were cartoonish all-American heroes—or odious, foreign archvillains. There was no in between. Going to the Sportatorium was raw entertainment, a chance to witness a sliver of humanity at its best and worst.

I knew I had to do a story on wrestling as soon as I first breathed in the fetid air of the Sportatorium. But what was my angle? After several Friday-night forays, I settled on a profile of Dallas' first family of professional wrestlers, the Von Erichs. The three Von Erich boys, Kevin, David and Kerry, were hometown favorites, good guys who in the end always seemed to triumph over the forces of evil. But the Von Erich boys were only part of the story. The piece quite naturally focused on their father, Fritz, a master showman and wrestler who ran the family's international empire.

But how to reach Fritz? After flashing a press card to get me into the locker room, I introduced myself to Kevin, David and Kerry, and asked whether they'd consent to a story. Talk to our father, they shot back at me.

"But will he talk to me?" I asked.

"That'll be up to him," David said. "If he wants to follow up, he'll contact you."

When I heard nothing from Fritz, I asked the ringside announcer to see whether he'd contact Fritz on my behalf. Then I asked one of the ring referees. I got nowhere.

I tried to call Fritz, but, of course, the Von Erich family had an unlisted number. Then I put my reporter's hat on. Using Fritz's real name, Jack Adkisson, I went to the county administration building and, by looking up real estate records, located where the family lived. I wrote a letter directly to Fritz, pitching a story on the wrestling dynasty he had created. Within a week, Fritz wrote back. In the letter, he referred to himself in the third person. Attached to his letter was a map to his house and explicit instructions to destroy the map as soon as I got done with it.

Once I got to the house and started interviewing Fritz and his sons, I was nervous. Fritz had a way of staring you down. Certainly, his handshake demonstrated that he still possessed all the strength necessary to administer the Iron Claw to anyone who proved troublesome.

After some warm-up questions, I tossed out a question about whether matches were fixed or not. There were several seconds of silence, and then David asked in a testy tone, "Where'd that come from? Exactly what kind of story are you gonna write anyway?"

Before I could answer, Fritz angrily motioned to David to desist. "Let *me* answer that question for you," Fritz said with total authority.

Kings of the Mat

The map to his home is accompanied by explicit instructions: "Destroy the map once you're through with it. Don't make a copy of it. Fritz doesn't want it to get into the wrong hands."

Fritz is Fritz Von Erich, the hulking modern-day godfather of wrestling, best known for his once-deadly trademark: The Iron Claw. When Fritz used to spread his Paul Bunyan hands across an opponent's face and start squeezing, tighter and tighter, there never was a reprieve. Whether it was Bobo Brazil, Gorgeous George, Wild Bill Curry, Duke Keomuka or Wahoo McDaniel, they all used to scream in pain, shrieks so loud that the noise would pierce through all the stomping and cheering of fans gone berserk.

Nowadays, what keeps Fritz busy is managing his own dynasty—the wrestling careers of his three oldest sons, Kevin, David and Kerry, remarkable athletes in their own right who perform flying dropkicks, headlocks, sleepers—and the Claw—worldwide.

Wrestling, long associated with sleaze and sham as a sport, has brought wealth and respectability to the Von Erichs. Fritz is a self-made millionaire. Besides a 15-acre rambling estate, there are an additional 275 acres of Lake Dallas property, landholdings in Rowlett, on Lake Ray Hubbard in downtown Dallas, and acres scattered throughout the Midwest. Once he owned three airplanes, herds of cattle, 5,000 quail; but it all became too much to manage. Kevin, David and Kerry all drive Lincoln Continentals. The gold and diamond jewelry the family members wear is flashy and to the point: We are famous, we can't be ignored, no matter what anyone claims.

Their success—and accompanying popularity—is so intense it seems rivaled only by past pharaohs of rock 'n' roll music. Tens of thousands of groupies, mostly teenage girls, swarm with offerings of cakes, embroidered shirts, rings. They wait hour after hour outside the Von Erich dressing room at Dallas' grimy, corrugated-steel Sportatorium. Many have tears in their eyes. Many clutch photos. The more audacious ones lunge at the Von Erichs, grabbing them by their necks, planting wet kisses on their cheeks. There is no way the Von Erichs can answer the 800 fan letters they receive weekly.

Kerry has just returned from Japan, Kevin from Mexico, and all three plan to tour the Middle East this summer. And Fritz runs it all, the whole money-making, publicity-attracting dynasty, from his base of operations: a rifle-lined study with three phones at his home on Lake Dallas.

He didn't always go by the name Fritz Von Erich. When he played high school football for the old Crozier Tech Wolves in downtown Dallas, he went by his real name, Jack Adkisson.

As a hulking sophomore on an athletic scholarship at Southern Methodist University, he turned everyone's head. Jack played varsity football as a ferocious lineman, opening holes for Kyle Rote and Doak Walker. In the spring, he tossed a discus 162 feet, 2½ inches to set an SMU record that stood for more than a decade.

His SMU sports career ended when he married Doris, a 17-year-old girl from Woodrow Wilson High School. SMU forbade athletes on scholarships to be married. Jack was promptly told to pack his bags. With Doris in tow, he moved to the Texas Gulf, lured by the University of Corpus Christi—only to find that the school's football program was to be eliminated the next year. So instead, he signed as a free agent for the Dallas Texans, the team that eventually would move to Maryland and become the Baltimore Colts. But early in his first game, he tore a ligament. His career was shot.

"By then, I had enough of sports. I thought of going into life insurance," Jack says in a jagged voice that sounds as though it has been lubricated with dirty diesel oil. "But, you had to make money where you could," he says, pulling on a Pall Mall. With his awesome strength and imposing size, professional wrestling was a natural choice.

His parents were dead set against wrestling as a career for Jack, but Doris stuck by her husband's choice. "If he said a word, I believed him," she says now. "He had a presence about himself. I felt he was indestructible."

Jack worked out in an Oak Lawn gym for three months, then drove south to Austin for his debut in a ring, the green man on a six-wrestler tag team. "I stood there in the corner with a wild crowd shouting at me. I was so nervous that when they tagged me, I could hardly get through the ropes to get to the ring. I was already out of gas." A barrel-chested wrestler by the name of George Penchoff promptly pinned him. Jack got $25 for the bout.

Over the next 13 weeks, he lost every match. Desperate, he needed a new market, a new identity, someplace where no one knew him. He picked Boston, leaving Doris and their first child in Dallas. Jack was living on apples and peanut butter; he sent all his earnings back to Doris. It wasn't much help. Within three months, their television had been repossessed; the finance company had petitioned to take the car. "We almost starved to death," Doris says.

Then Jack came up with an idea: inflame the fans, make them hate him.

The name Adkisson was too bland. Memories of goose-stepping and swastikas were less than a decade old. Jack resurrected his mother's maiden name, Erich, and manufactured the Fritz and the Von to complete the German connection. "Fritz Von Erich beat the hell out of Jack Adkisson," he recalls.

Pitted against local favorites, he became a sinister villain hard to beat. Fans wanted someone to hate, someone on whom they could vent anger and frustration. They got it in Fritz Von Erich.

He moved farther north, to Canada, and joined the carnival circuit, traveling to lumber villages for one-week stands. Anyone who could survive more than five minutes in the ring with Fritz Von Erich would get $25. Fritz would take four or five comers a night. For the tough ones, he reserved the Claw, often drawing blood within 30 seconds. Between bouts, he packed tents on the midway, drawing rubber-necking onlookers by bending a silver dollar with his thumb and index finger. Sometimes he would squeeze an apple in his fist and drink the juice.

In June 1959, while Fritz was in Cleveland, he got an urgent call from Doris, who was then living in a Niagara Falls, N.Y., trailer camp. Their six-year-old son, Jack Jr., had been electrocuted in a freak accident.

Fritz redoubled his efforts to make himself a star to become more hated by the fans. Says ringside announcer Bill Mercer, who started broadcasting wrestling in 1953: "He was a holy terror. Once, I tried to interview him, and he told me to shut up. I thought he was going to kill me. After that, I stayed away from him." Mercer's dead-serious visage didn't betray whether the recollection was hype or fact.

That fans were reacting violently to Fritz was cause for celebration. "In our business, the crowd doesn't care about a blah," he says, hands outstretched, palms up. "You don't draw money that way. They either love you or hate you. There's no in-between. I didn't care just as long as I was making money."

Indeed, he was making more and more. He had a grueling schedule, five or six matches a week, up to 300 bouts a year, on the road almost every day. "When Fritz was wrestling in the '50s and '60s, he was one of maybe 10 or 20 main eventers who made over $100,000 a year. It wasn't unusual for him to get 10 percent of the gate," recalls Norman Kietzer, editor of *Wrestling* magazine.

Occasionally, he wore a black mask and fought incognito so he could wrestle twice a night. Promoters held Fritz for the last event to build suspense and to allow fans enough time to stew themselves with concession-stand beer.

Fritz became known in the trade as "a rule breaker," says Bill Apter, managing editor of *Sports Review Wrestling* magazine. He often pulled opponents down by their hair, by their pants, by their neck—all technically "illegal" moves tolerated in professional wrestling. "He was one of the most feared men. Promoters had to dig up opponents to fight him," says Apter.

They did not have to look for fans, though, most of whom hated Fritz with a passion. Doris remembers when a horrified neighbor discovered she was the wife of evil Fritz Von Erich. "Well, he wins, doesn't he?" Doris said. Then she walked away quickly.

During an upper New York State match with Bobo Brazil, a seething spectator grabbed a ball-peen hammer at ringside, climbed between the ropes and walloped Fritz six inches above his nose.

Another time, in Detroit, Fritz had just beaten a favorite, and the crowd was hot. A fan flicked what felt like burning cigar ashes on him. But when Fritz got to the dressing room, he felt a little knob protruding from his derrière and saw his thigh covered with blood. He had been stuck with a six-inch hat pin, pushed in all the way.

In the Cleveland Arena, where Fritz was the main eventer in the biggest card ever held, he started to cover his opponent's face with his giant hands to apply the dreaded Claw. "Suddenly, I sensed a change in the crowd's mood," he recalls. "I looked around and saw this guy with a knife coming straight into the ring." He left his opponent, kicked the fan in the chin, then pitched the knife out of the ring.

But Fritz did more. "When he was down, I stomped him. It was just a reflex action. Then I picked him up, and this is where I was wrong. I turned him upside down, and slammed him over the ropes onto the cement floor head first. He went out like a light." The interloper was not killed if only, perhaps, because he was drunk at the time. Fritz was fined $100.

On the road, he was a bad guy, but back home in Dallas, Fritz could do no wrong. One night in the Sportatorium, Fritz had finished squeezing blood from an opponent and was heading to the dressing room. Suddenly, he felt a big, flabby hand seize him by the neck, choking him. Fritz reacted, knocking over a security guard and the attacker, a huge, overweight woman. From the floor, she looked up and cried, "But Mr. Fritz, I love you. I love you."

The events that always touched fans the most, that were guaranteed to pump adrenaline into anyone's bloodstream, were the Texas Death Matches—two wrestlers locked in an iron cage, where, as the promoters say, there would be "no disqualifications, no time limits, nothing illegal, finished only when one man can't defend himself any longer."

By his own count, Fritz was the main event in more of these gruesome bouts than anyone in the history of the sport. "You knock the hell out of each other in these things. What's especially bad about them is it takes such a long time to recover. But the fans will pay for them, and that's what's important."

Fritz Von Erich climbed out of the ring for the last time in June 1982 at Texas Stadium. Fifteen thousand fans were on hand for the match, a savage bout with King Kong Bundy, an awesome 420-pound wrestler with a shaved head. After Fritz lifted his opponent and tossed him bodily out of the ring, Bundy picked up a steel chair and braced to bring it down on Von Erich's head. Fritz vaulted the ropes, kicked Bundy in the stomach, grabbed the chair, and, to the cheers of wild fans, slammed it over Bundy's head. Then, exhausted, he fell on top of his opponent's heaving stomach and claimed victory.

The brutality of his career shows. At 51, his hearing is impaired. Each wrist and every finger has been broken at least twice, both shoulders separated. He still complains of the torn ligaments in his knees.

Now, nearly all of Fritz's time is occupied with molding the careers of his sons, who have catapulted their father's wild success into further fame.

All of them have bodies like Greek gods—for good reason, Fritz says. "These boys were raised to be jocks. When they were youngsters, there were no kids scrawnier than mine. They were made into champions."

Fritz set up a ring at the Lake Dallas estate, and each son began wrestling at six. They lifted barbells before most youngsters ride a bicycle. By the time they graduated from Lake Dallas High School, they were recognized as the finest athletes in the history of the school, excelling in football, track and basketball. Fritz kept pushing them harder and harder, a round-the-clock coach who never let up.

"I'd catch a touchdown pass in high school," says David, now 24. "The coach would go crazy, the fans would go crazy. But it didn't mean anything unless I saw my dad in the stands clapping. We'd always know where he was sitting, and we'd always be looking up toward him. If we weren't hustling, we'd hear him. It would be like a bolt of lightning."

Make no mistake about who was—and is—in charge of the Von Erich boys. Pointing a gnarled index finger, Fritz says: "These boys were never raised as bullies. If they ever pushed their weight around, their dad kicked their butts. They also got kicked if they ever stepped down when they had to fight."

When Kevin, now 26, went to his high school prom, two drunks tried to dance with a friend's date. Kevin went to her aid, they yanked a hank of hair from his scalp, and he sent them both to a hospital emergency room.

Kerry, 23, went to the University of Houston, where, like his father at SMU, he set a collegiate discus record; he also was an All-American. Kevin and David enrolled at North Texas State University. Bill Brazier, at the time assistant football coach there, remembers one characteristic about the pair. "They were a pleasure to coach because I never had to worry whether they'd hit hard enough. They had the ability to punish their opponents and take the punishment back."

Another coach, Bill Blakeley, says the same. "They're super-tough, hard-nosed kids who stick together no matter what. If you try to whip one, you have to whip them all."

But it is Fritz who has controlled the shots. "They still worship their father. Everything always is 'Yes, sir,' or 'No, sir,'" says Blakeley.

Fritz's idea of creating a wrestling dynasty became a reality when the boys quit college to join the wrestling circuit. "It wasn't a question of their not being smart," recalls Blakeley. "They just weren't interested in academics. They had grown up in the shadow of their father, and they wanted to show off for him in the ring."

Each has his own distinctive style. Kevin's trademark is a numbing flying body press. He goes outside the ring, climbs atop the turnbuckle and then, in a perfect swan dive, leaps onto his opponent for a sure pin. David is a close-in body fighter, able to apply arm and leg locks so tight they stop the flow of blood. Kerry's forte is a flying drop kick. He has the most developed body of the three, a compact version of Arnold Schwarzenegger's. And, of course, all of them know the Claw.

The three try to keep their marital status quiet, so as not to cause anguish among some of their fans—the adoring high school coeds who paste photos of the Von Erichs inside loose-leaf notebooks and wear lockets in which Kevin's, David's or Kerry's name is engraved. Kevin and David are married; Kerry is engaged. Kevin and his wife have a two-year-old daughter.

To ensure privacy, the Von Erich estate is surrounded by a wire fence and gates. The family tries to keep its location from the public, but on weekends, dozens of cars snake by, with fans hoping to get a glimpse of Fritz or the sons.

It is not just teenage girls who enjoy looking at the Von Erichs. *Playgirl* magazine made an offer to Kevin to pose nude for its centerfold, but he refused. Dallas' male stripper club, La Bare, wooed all three brothers with a package proposal they also turned down. Then there were two movie offers—a martial arts, blood-and-guts film and a motorcycle-beachboy script. But none involved enough money to make up for what the brothers would lose by not wrestling.

They still hone their public image, assuaging even the most protective mother's objection to a daughter's adoration of the trio. They often appear at sports clinics and are featured speakers at high school assemblies. They attend church every Sunday and, along with their parents, are born-again Christians. Each prays before and after every bout in the ring, and actively tries to convert fellow wrestlers.

Says their mother, Doris: "There are so few heroes these days. These boys give young people an image to emulate, someone they can look up to. Each of them takes that responsibility very seriously."

Not everyone adores them, particularly the wrestlers who climb into the ring and trade hammerlocks with the Von Erichs. Gorgeous Jimmy Garvin, 30, a boisterous showman with a lion's curly mane, thinks the brothers got a free ride on their father's trunks. "I started out with nothing. They had their daddy to pave the way for them," he says. "The only difference between them and me is that when I try to break the rules, I get fined. When they break them, they get away with it. Texas and the Von Erichs are one and the same." Bravado or not, Garvin's complaint sounds real.

Garvin's latest run-in with the family centered around his "personal valet," a flashy blonde who goes by the name Sunshine and accompanies Garvin everywhere. In April while wrestling David Von Erich at the Sportatorium, Garvin yanked Sunshine into the ring and used her as a shield against body punches. David let up, but after the match, he dragged a kicking and screaming Sunshine into the ring, bent her over his knee and spanked her. The crowd loved it.

Garvin, who comes from Tampa, did not. "I hate his guts," he says with theatrical rage. "David knew that spanking my chick would press my button. Man, was I ever angry! As I explained to her, it just shows what an uncouth individual he is."

Despite the blue sequined bow tie, white gloves and cutaway formal jacket Garvin wears into the ring, he makes no claims to being a gentleman. Last month in Corpus Christi, Garvin was fined $500 for punching a referee. In Australia last year, he was stabbed in the back twice by angry fans, an event that caused a riot.

Someone else who doesn't mince words about the Von Erichs is King Kong Bundy, the 420-pounder who lost to Fritz last June. Although Bundy is currently a villain, he and Fritz once were good friends. In fact, it was Fritz who introduced Bundy to the ring. The friendship, though, is now over. Kevin smashed a chair over his head while the two were wrestling in the Sportatorium last year. Bundy says he has nine stitches to show for the real-life altercation.

Bundy, 21, knows about the swooning Von Erich cult. Usually on the losing side of any Von Erich match, he often is portrayed as a slow-moving, sure-footed plodder, waging battle against the popular Von Erichs and their quick aerial moves. While wrestling David before a standing-room-only crowd at Williams School in Plano recently, he returned twice to the locker room before the match started. The crowd, mostly teenagers, kept taunting him, chanting over and over, "Bundy is a pig. Bundy is a pig."

"It's just like going against a home court advantage," he says. "It bugs me. The Von Erichs are just a bunch of pretty boys."

After the match, in which Bundy got pinned, he stomped out of the gymnasium, retreating to the locker room. With sweat dripping from his face and doubled-over belly, he looked up, his stubby hands wiping his face. "Hell, I'm making money at this. Fans are morons, but they recognize and remember me. That's what's important. If they don't know who you are, how can you attract a crowd?"

Suspicion that the sport is choreographed by zealous promoters and fixed to stretch suspense is why wrestling is largely boycotted by almost every newspaper sports page. Print coverage of wrestling is limited to a half-dozen tawdry wrestling magazines, which often lure readers with grisly stories, features about blood-worshipping women wrestlers and violence-prone bullies who stick their thumbs in opponents' eyes.

Showmanship, the ability to inflame a crowd, to pit the forces of good versus evil, indeed underscores the sport. Although tremendous athletic prowess is demonstrated in the ring, so is a well-timed sense of drama—something that even Fritz does not dismiss.

"It's not all phony at all, no way, shape or form," he says. "You're seeing real wrestling out there the majority of the time, as far as I'm concerned. The real thing is taking place out there a helluva lot more than anyone seems to realize."

To Fritz, the success of the sport has as much to do with the spectator's perception of what he *believes* goes on in the ring as with what actually *does* go on there. "It comes down to this: If you just let yourself go and enjoy it, you'll never be more entertained anywhere. That's God's honest truth. We sell out everywhere we go; the arenas aren't big enough to hold all the fans."

When asked if winners are ever picked in advance, even an old pro like broadcaster Bill Mercer backs away. "I'd just as soon not answer that question. It's something I really don't get into. But it's crossed my mind."

In no way, though, is all wrestling theatrical. Broken bones, stitches, an occasional blood-splattered wrestler or spectator indicate otherwise. "Why don't you put on a pair of tights and climb into the ring to find out whether it's fake or not?" Fritz suggests pointedly, flashing that big half-menacing smile of his.

While Mercer might hedge on whether matches are fixed, he is emphatic about the authenticity of what goes on in the ring. "I've never witnessed fake blood. All you have to do is look at the faces of some of these wrestlers. They look like road maps." The reason blood flows easier, according to Mercer, is that when athletes hyperventilate, their blood becomes thinner and tends to run faster.

"The sportswriters say wrestling is a 'gray area,' not a real sport," says Fritz. "But you know what? We don't need the papers, we've gone to the medium of the people, and TV does it all for us. God bless television."

Ted Turner's Atlanta-based station, WTBS, regularly broadcasts wrestling. Dallas' KXTX, channel 39, syndicates telecasts of Sportatorium matches to 21 stations across the United States, the Virgin Islands and in Puerto Rico. KXTX's Sunday morning broadcast, admittedly not the hottest prime-time slot, often pulls in a 30-percent share of the TV audience, says Terry Noble, KXTX's local sales manager. "Wrestling has an extremely loyal audience; they are the people TV never has really gone after. They've always been neglected," Noble says. Station manager Roger Baerwolf is pushing to sell the matches to more affiliates. He calls the sport "cartoons for adults."

KXTX is owned by the Christian Broadcasting Network, a nationwide syndicate of television stations that features fundamentalist religious programming. It's a good fit. Since 1964, when Fritz attended a Christian revival at Dallas' First Baptist Church, where he was "born again," he has devoted a substantial part of his life to spreading the gospel. "Anyone who tells me he's not a Christian makes my heart bleed," he says.

Since January 1982, Fritz says he has given 10 percent of his annual gross income to the church and says that someday he hopes to raise the tithe to 50 percent.

The family's sizable income should get even larger as the Von Erich dynasty expands. Two sons are still at home, Chris, 13, and Michael, 19, who both aspire to become—what else?—wrestlers. Fritz says he may allow Michael to make his wrestling debut this summer.

Someone who won't be there to watch is Michael's mother, who seldom attends matches, and never when her sons are on the card. "It's too painful. I learned a long time ago that I didn't want to go through that experience. It was too nerve-racking. I just wait at home to hear about it."

Fritz, though, does attend. "But I can't get near the ring, I'm too tempted to jump in," he says.

Clearly, Fritz still loves the sport, but beyond all its violence and hucksterism, the fans who worship him, the wrestlers who despise him, is his religion.

"I have a joy and an inner peace," Fritz Von Erich says, leaning back and smiling.

The Dallas Morning News, May 29, 1983

WRITING THE STORY

The way to open this extended story has to be the cloak-and-dagger manner in which I was invited to Fritz's house. Then it's laying out the facts—about violence, groupies, hype. Details help sell the story. From the rifles that line Fritz's study to his three phones, to the description of Fritz's jagged voice. It's all there to suck the reader into the world of sham and show that Fritz Von Erich cornered as his own. The summing up of Fritz's career then segues to his personal history, which to no one's surprise is full of requisite melodrama. Fritz's career details (whether they're true or not) help sell the story: rabid fans with hammers, knives and hat pins.

Once I finish with Fritz, then it's on to his sons. The subtext of the story is a disturbing tale of how Fritz raised his boys to follow in the one profession that meant anything to their father. Physical violence was central to their lives. I buttress this thesis with interviews with football coaches who give their takes on Fritz's sons.

Then it's on to the Von Erich boys' rivals, and that's where I have the most fun with the story. Gorgeous Jimmy Garvin's talking about his personal valet, "Sunshine," is one of my favorites: "David knew that spanking my chick would press my button. Man, was I ever angry! As I explained to her, it just shows what an uncouth individual he is." I also interview King Kong Bundy at a local high school benefit, and it's Bundy who perhaps best defines the essence of any kind of publicity: "Fans ... recognize and remember me. That's what's important. If they don't know who you are, how can you attract a crowd?"

Perhaps the most interesting part of the story is an issue I choose to gloss over: the marketing of wrestling through Christian television. I neglect that potential lode, and instead close with Fritz's summation of his career and his life. I erroneously go for the easy way out.

Nine months after the piece appeared, I was called upon to cover another wrestling main event: the funeral of David Von Erich, who died in 1984 while on tour in Japan. The official cause of death was acute inflammation of his intestines, but most fellow wrestlers knew what killed David: a drug overdose.

Three years later, Mike Von Erich committed suicide with an overdose of tranquilizers. Months later his younger brother, Chris, fatally shot himself. And, in 1993, Kerry Von Erich, facing a prison term for illegal possession of narcotics, killed himself with a gun.

Fritz and Doris divorced soon thereafter amid persistent rumors that Doris had been the victim of domestic abuse for years. In 1997, Fritz died two months after he was diagnosed with lung cancer.

The one remaining Von Erich is Kevin, who retired from wrestling in 1995. Today, Kevin walks with a shuffle, the result of seven knee operations and five concussions.

And the dank Sportatorium? It lies vacant. The last Sportatorium wrestling match took place in 1998. In December 2000, firefighters responded to a minor fire at the abandoned arena and found three homeless people sleeping inside.

ASSIGNMENTS

1) Write a story about a nontraditional spectator sports event, e.g., Battle-Bots, motorcycles on ice, skateboarding, demolition derby, when an event comes to a nearby arena. Focus on the spectators as well as the aura surrounding the megastars performing.

2) Profile a popular professional wrestler who has a connection to your community. Spend several days with the wrestler, following him from match to match, from town to town, to get an understanding of what life is like as a professional wrestler. Interview fans, supporters and enemies in the ring, any groupies who follow his career. Alternatively, find a former wrestler with ties to your community. Find out what kind of life awaits wrestlers after they leave the ring.

3) Report on the state regulatory board or commission that oversees professional wrestlers in your area. Report what responsibilities the body has, who is on the oversight commission, whether there are any possible conflicts of interest in the exercise of its authority. For years, the sport of professional wrestling has been associated with the illegal use of steroids. Find out what measures, if any, are taken to ensure that professional wrestlers stay clean.

14

SAN FRANCISCO'S
WORST KEPT SECRET

I usually don't know where my next story is going to come from, but if I keep my eyes and ears open, I always find a story lurking somewhere not far away. Still, I was caught off guard when Linda, a reflexologist who for years had pinched and pressed the soles of my feet whenever I could afford her, told me that one of her clients had an unbelievable story to tell.

Linda said she didn't know much, only that it involved her client's dead grandmother, who had been a notorious abortionist in San Francisco from 1920-1955, and who had performed more than 50,000 abortions, some of them on famous Hollywood stars. The self-described abortion queen had operated with the tacit approval of the police (through bribes), physicians (through kickbacks and gifts of premium liquor), and the Catholic Church (by providing favors to pregnant nuns, as well as to priests whose illicit liaisons resulted in unwanted pregnancies).

"Would you be interested?" Linda asked, as she lowered my right foot into a bowl of warm, rose-scented water, in preparation for another reflexology session.

Despite my relaxed state, my adrenaline started flowing. After I dried my feet and put my socks back on, I wrote down the name of Linda's client, and that evening I called Caroline Carlisle. Within five minutes, I knew I had to meet Carlisle and scheduled a face-to-face interview with the next day.

San Francisco's Worst-Kept Secret:

The Untold Story of Millionaire Abortion Queen Inez Brown Burns

The tools might have been found in a secret sliding panel in the upstairs linen closet. Or they could have been stashed in the hollowed-out banister used to hide hundreds of thousands of dollars. Bruce McGee is not sure.

When McGee sold the San Francisco house in 1990, he took the tools with him. He kept them in a cupboard, under a stack of dishrags and potholders. They were a bizarre curio no more.

"So you came to see the instruments," says McGee, a man not quite certain why a stranger would spend months tracking him down, just to glimpse 17 half-century-old medical tools buried in the bottom of a kitchen cabinet.

McGee unties the canvas carrying case, gingerly lifting out from each pocket a different instrument, still shiny, without traces of rust. Each measures eight to 18 inches long.

And there they are: forceps, dilators, tenaculum, curette. Tools of the trade for an abortionist.

They are no ordinary instruments. These tools of pain and relief, of destruction and guilt, were used illegally inside the bodies of as many as 50,000 women over a 35-year period.

They were not wielded by some back-alley abortionist with nicotine stains on his fingers and blood streaks on a dirty smock. As McGee rolls up the carrying case of the German-made instruments, a name scratched in faded India ink is still visible: "Inez Brown."

From 1920 to 1955, Inez Brown Burns (she married in 1932) performed eight, a dozen, up to 30 illegal abortions a day. Most were performed in her clinic at 327 Fillmore Street, in what eventually was known as the Lower Haight neighborhood. Her business was one of the worst-kept secrets in California.

Tens of thousands of women paid visits to her makeshift hospital. They included the rich and famous. Rita Hayworth, Lana Turner and Sonja Henie were just three of the movie stars Burns said received abortions at her hands.

Burns also performed abortions on poor women, those barely able to afford her not-inexpensive fees, let alone another child. Scared single and married women came to her clinic, and some to her house on Guerrero Street, located in San Francisco's oldest neighborhood, known as the Mission District. Madam Sally Stanford sent her prostitutes to Burns. Cigar-chomping industrialists sent their mistresses. Politicians sent their "secretaries." Occasionally, even a shamedfaced nun would walk through the front door.

Through it all, Burns amassed millions of dollars. Aside from a handful of Hollywood stars, Burns became one of California's wealthiest self-made women.

To ensure that her operations ran smoothly, Burns paid off scores of police officers, politicians and physicians. It took an obscure San Francisco district attorney by the name of Edmund G. (Pat) Brown, on a relentless campaign touting family values, to prosecute Burns three times before a jury eventually convicted her.

Inez Burns' high-profile conviction ultimately catapulted politician Brown to statewide office, first as attorney general and later as governor.

"I had the zeal of a new D.A.," said Brown, 90, in a telephone interview. "I was looked at as a fighting D.A., and the rest of the state thought that was good."

Brown recalls Burns as "a very good abortionist with a good reputation. Everyone thought she was a necessary evil. But when I became D.A. her business had become flagrant."

Burns served four years in two state prisons and one year in federal prison for tax evasion. She didn't start serving time until she was 60, after having performed tens of thousands of abortions for decades.

But for all her wealth and fame, Inez Burns died in 1976 at age 87, a poor, broken woman alone in a Moss Beach nursing home. Although once a millionaire, at the time of her death she was destitute, a ward of the state, dependent on welfare for her rent.

Few then knew, and even fewer today know of her awesome influence and power. Probably no one in California history performed more abortions. Whether Inez Burns was a monster living among the ghosts of aborted fetuses or a pioneering, self-reliant woman decades ahead of her time depends on the beholder's point of view.

Today, more than two decades after the U.S. Supreme Court declared abortion legal, fewer and fewer physicians are performing the relatively simple procedure. Hospitals and clinics are eliminating abortions, and the pool of physicians able to perform them is shrinking. In 1991, only 13 percent of the nations' OB-GYN residency programs required training in first-trimester abortion, and only 7 percent required second-trimester instruction.

The fact is that during the era of Inez Burns, even though abortions were illegal, they were easier to obtain than they are today in many communities. In describing Burns' operation, the San Francisco *News* in 1946 called the clinic, "one of San Francisco's oldest and best-known institutions." For three decades, Burns was dubbed "the abortion queen."

Inez Brown was less a rebel or a reformer than an opportunist, someone out to help women, but also out to help herself. She earned so much money that in 1922, when she was 33, she had the Guerrero Street house built to her own specifications. She decorated the stately home with life-size statues, including a replica of Venus de Milo, which lined the sunny living room facing Valencia Gardens across the street. Dozens of hidden compartments concealed bundles of cash.

But the money she lavished on building the Guerrero Street house barely dented the amplitude of abortion fees flowing in. She couldn't put the cash in the bank, so she spent it, buying a 1,000-acre ranch near Half Moon Bay where she bred race horses. She owned homes in Atherton and in the posh San Francisco enclave of St. Francis Woods.

Burns' hospital on Fillmore Street was staffed with registered nurses who dressed in spotless white uniforms, matching hats perched atop netted heads of hair. Burns required them to wear polished white shoes and seamed white stockings.

Once or twice a year, Burns went on "business" trips to Los Angeles and Seattle and on at least one occasion she went to New York State, where she set up a temporary clinic in Syracuse.

Her clients were referred to her, not just through word-of-mouth recommendations, but by physicians and attorneys. Anxious husbands and boyfriends— even mothers and fathers—often paced the waiting room.

By most accounts, Burns' operation was clean and effective. Like a rabbi who performs circumcisions even though he is not a physician, the self-taught Burns boasted that she had "the touch," an instinctive skill to perform abortions. If there were complications, she had a long list of cooperating physicians who could patch up any problems.

But she was aware of the risks involved—not so much to her patients, but from police. Performing an abortion was a felony punishable by a prison term of two to five years. That's why at both her home and the clinic, Burns had installed trap doors for fast escapes. Burns also installed large concrete incinerators in the backyards. It was in these large, fiery vats that Burns destroyed fetal remains.

Burns in her hey-day was a gracious, elegant, refined woman. When not working, she wore designer gowns and matching hats. Her clothes were made to order by her personal seamstress at San Francisco's fashionable Ransohoff's department store on Union Square. She had a chauffeur who drove her to the opera in her 1936 Pierce-Arrow.

Burns flourished in part because of the nature of pre-World War II San Francisco. Ask any old-time San Franciscan what life in the city was like before the War exposed thousands upon thousands of servicemen, ship-building workers and their families to the Bay Area for the duration, many of whom later decided to settle in the city by the bay. San Francisco was politically dominated by Irish and Italians and was predominately Catholic. It was a small, friendly family town that distrusted outsiders.

"Steeped in a tradition of gold rush and Barbary Coast license, nineteenth- and early twentieth-century San Franciscans took a perverse pride in their reputation for naughtiness," says historian Kevin Mullen, who retired in 1986 as deputy chief of police in San Francisco.

Mullen says that unlike in other cities, puritanical blue laws never got much of a hearing in San Francisco. "Discreet vice was permitted to operate in the European tradition, just as long as no one was hurt too badly." In fact, San Francisco was known throughout the United States as "the place to go for 'women in trouble.'"

Burns was able to stay in business so long because she was good at what she did. She quietly performed a public need. Righteous society vilified her, but her clients needed her and went to great lengths to protect her—and themselves.

To prosecute her, authorities needed credible witnesses who would testify that Burns performed abortions on them— but these women, let alone the men and madams who paid the fees, would be the last to talk. Burns' real ace-in-the-hole was the implicit threat of her going public with everything she knew. In short, hanging over San Francisco's rich and mighty was the possibility of a "little black book" filled with scores of names. If the sensational San Francisco newspapers had a field day covering Burns once she was on trial, imagine the stories they'd have if Burns sang.

Of course Burns was the soul of discretion—she kept no records, no lists of names (at least none was ever uncovered). As Tallulah Bankhead once observed dryly, "It's the good girls who keep the diaries; the bad girls never had the time."

Even the existence of a diary probably wouldn't have made Burns worthy of a chapter in California history. But today, she isn't even a footnote. Little information remains about her. Practically all of Burns' contemporaries have died. The impression Burns so indelibly left on her own generation is almost obliterated today. Unlike births, no one kept records of abortions.

Old newspaper clippings link dozens and dozens of people to Burns, but few are living today. Pat Brown's chief prosecutor, Thomas Lynch, died in 1986. Police Inspector Frank Ahern, who was offered a $225,000 bribe by Burns, and who went on to become San Francisco's chief of police, died in 1958. Burns' own defense attorney, Walter McGovern, died in 1975. Judges William Traverso and Herbert Kaufman, who presided over Burns' sensational trials that ended in hung juries, are also dead. So are the physicians who testified at her trials, Frank Pagett, Theodore Diller and Adolphus Berger.

In October 1992, when I asked to interview 96-year-old Vincent Hallinan, a lawyer who had befriended Burns, his son, Terence, now San Francisco District Attorney, said that his father was in ill health, but he would ask about any reminiscences. Three days later, Vincent Hallinan died.

Visits to both the grand house Burns built on Guerrero Street and the Fillmore abortion clinic brought bemused smiles from their current tenants, but little information.

"Really? So that rumor's true?" asked Hollyce Fagerhaugh, a costume designer in her early 20s who lives on the top floor of the Fillmore duplex. "I've never felt anything but comfortable in the house. It's always had a good feeling."

"We love the house," said the owner of the Guerrero Street mansion. "And no, we never get anyone knocking at the door asking us for an abortion."

At the Fillmore Street venue, the trap door inside the back closet has been boarded over. In the Guerrero Street house, the sliding panel in the upstairs linen closet still works; the banister has been painted shut to prevent stashing of anything inside. At both places, the outdoor incinerators have been covered and filled with cement.

Pondering whether someone still lived in San Francisco who knew Inez Burns, someone with personal recollections or memorable encounters with her, the name of a genteel, elderly woman came to mind. A San Francisco native, Edith Patchen has a memory like a Shakespearean actor; she can recall verbatim lines from 50 years ago.

Asked if the name Inez Burns meant anything to Patchen, her pause seemed to last forever, at least 20 seconds. Then Edith Pachen (a pseudonym, used at her request) said quietly, "I went to Inez Burns in the '40s to get an abortion." Patchen said she hadn't thought about Inez Bruns for 30 years.

At 22, Patchen had married a soldier in a euphoric post-World War II binge. But the match was a fiasco, and when Patchen filed for divorce in 1947, she found herself pregnant. Panicked, she went to a North Beach attorney, who referred her to Inez Burns.

"I remember going to her Guerrero Street house, and sitting in the front room, a beautiful, elegant room. And I remember seeing Mrs. Burns, a pleasant, kind woman, who sat down in the parlor with me."

The first thing she asked me was, "Do you want this baby?"

"Yes!" Patchen blurted out without a moment's hesitation.

"Well, dear, you don't belong here," Edith remembers Burns saying. "Then she took me by the hand and showed me the door."

Patchen's son was born in 1948, and today is 48.

"In San Francisco then, everyone knew everyone else, and we looked out for everyone," she said. "We protected each other. There was nothing sinister about Inez Burns. She was like your grandmother."

●　　●　　●

"Do I remember my grandma? You're asking if I remember grandma?" Caroline Carlisle asked. "How could anyone ever forget her?"

Carlisle lives alone in a Pacifica apartment. She is a walking encyclopedia on her grandmother. From age 16 on she was raised by Inez Burns.

Carlisle pulls out a rotogravure photo of her grandmother. Taken when Burns was 19, it shows a woman with full, sensual lips and large almond-shaped eyes. Her auburn hair is swept back in a Gibson-girl coiffure. Her skin appears creamy soft.

Burns was born in Philadelphia in 1889, one of four children. Forced to quit school, she worked in a pickle factory at age seven and stank of garlic when she came home every night.

Her father abandoned the family, leaving the mother, a seamstress, as the sole supporter. In 1901, Burns' mother remarried and the family packed their belongings and took the Southern Pacific's Zephyr to San Francisco. Her stepfather died shortly after their arrival. Burns' mother found a job running a boarding house on Perry Street in the Mission District.

The 16-year-old Burns worked as a manicurist at the opulent Palace Hotel on Market Street. She had long, golden-reddish tresses, which she proudly called titian-colored. Burns was a striking, shapely woman with a captivating smile, and quickly built up a clientele of adoring male customers who gladly forked over $1.50 for the pleasure of her holding their hands. Burns used her charms to her advantage. She accumulated furs, dinner invitations, pearl necklaces. She also, according to stories she told Carlisle, had several abortions.

One of her customers at the Palace was an elderly San Francisco physician by the name of Dr. West, Carlisle recalls her grandmother telling her.

Burns used Dr. West's services for her abortions, as did other girls at the Palace. Whether his motivations were romantic or professional, West took a liking to Burns, and offered her a job at his clinic.

West, it turned out, was a full-time abortionist, and Burns started as his assistant. After attending a year's worth of abortions, she figured she could perform the same procedure herself.

So sometime in the 1920s, Burns started her own clinic on Fillmore Street in a two-flat house. There were eight full-time employees, including nurses, and a man who drew blood. Burns was the sole abortionist. No one else ever did the abortions, says Carlisle.

In and outside of her clinic, Burns was one of a kind. "She told me that you tell how much a man loves you by what he gives you," Carlisle recalls her grandmother telling her. Burns was a flirt and, learning from her days at the Palace, wouldn't continue going out with a man unless he showered her with gifts. And the presents required weren't little trinkets.

Carlisle recalls that one of her grandmother's callers bought her a diamond ring, and she threw it back at him because it was too small.

And although married, "Grandma liked a lot of men at the same time," Carlisle says somewhat cheerfully.

Burns was moody, bawdy, authoritarian and opinionated. Her granddaughter says that psychiatrists today would classify her as having a multiple personality. Almost daily Burns would take Dexedrine (amphetamines) in the morning, and at night three Nembutal (barbiturates).

"She once came after me with a frying pan in her right hand. I remember grandma telling me, 'Never slap with an open hand. Always fight with a fist, and go first for the stomach, then hit 'em in the chin.'"

Her knockdown and drag-out arguments with her third husband, Joe Burns, a red-faced Irishman who was a former San Francisco assemblyman, were legendary among friends and neighbors. Burns was clearly in the driver' s seat.

"You f...... b....!" he would shout at her in a drunken slur.

"If there's any f...... going on here, I wanna be in on it!" she would reply.

In the early 1930s, she laundered some of her abortion money by buying Burns a Mission District tavern called Kavanaugh's. To evade arguments with his powerful wife, Burns would simply leave, driving his long sedan to the bar to play poker and supervise book making.

"Who bought that big diamond ring on your finger?" Burns would rail at Joe unmercifully. "Who bought that big ranch in Half Moon Bay?"

Burns was a shocker. Outside of her clinic, those who spent time with her knew it was going to be a bumpy ride. Even Carlisle was not exempt from grandma's verve. Once, Carlisle recalls, she asked one of her boyfriends over to Burns' Guerrero Street house, and Burns said to the young man, "Forget Caroline. I want you for myself!" No one was quite sure whether she was serious.

Burns professed to believe in reincarnation, claiming that in her previous lives she had been both a Rumanian gypsy and a slave master. As a young woman, Burns had her two small toes removed from both her feet, so she could fit into the stylish, pointy shoes of that day. Carlisle recalls, "She always asked me anxiously, 'How do I look?' How do I look?' "

Starting when she was 50 years old, Burns had three face lifts. She got on the scale every morning, and if she weighed over 125 pounds, she wouldn't eat. On some days, she would crack six eggs and down the yolks raw.

When Carlisle was 12, she began to realize what her grandmother did for a living. Carlisle often served coffee, tea and home-made bread to resting women recuperating after their abortions.

At age 16, after both her parents died, Carlisle began living with Burns and her husband, attending Mission High School two blocks away from the Guerrero Street house. She also started serving as her grandmother's assistant.

To avoid detection by strangers, Carlisle recalls that Burns made up her own words to describe things. "Glantham" meant money, and "nidash" meant, "Don't open your mouth!"—both of which Burns often whispered to Carlisle whenever strangers were around.

Burns charged standard rates to all her patients, Carlisle recalls. There was no sliding scale. When she started in the 1920s, her fee was $50 per abortion. At the clinic, prior to World War II, the standard fee was $300. She rarely came down from her price—only when a truly destitute woman would appear at her door. Poor women could do no wrong, in Burns' eyes, and occasionally—but only very occasionally—she would charge them nothing.

Burns was proud of what she had accomplished. What other profession was open to women that paid nearly as well? Certainly not teaching or nursing. As she saw it, being an abortionist allowed her not only to help women, but also to protect them from men, who, she thought, pulled all the strings in American society. And she became a millionaire in the process.

Burns demanded an eccentric oath from Carlisle. For years, she made Carlisle promise over and over that when she, Burns, died, Carlisle would bury her medical instruments in her grandmother's coffin.

"Don't just say yes and forget about it," Burns sharply warned Carlisle repeatedly. "I don't care what anyone says. These tools have made me millions of dollars in my lifetime, and I want them to go with me!"

● ● ●

For at least 15 years, Inez Burns operated her Fillmore abortion clinic with complete immunity from the law. Long-time District Attorney Matthew Brady, who had been the county's chief prosecutor for two decades, presided over a San Francisco that in many ways was as corrupt as the town's old Barbary Coast. Former newspaper reporter Charles Raudebaugh, now 82, remembers San Francisco rife with bribes, run by beat cops who decided whether to file charges against anyone they picked up. "There were 150 whorehouses in the city and bookie joints were everywhere," says Raudebaugh, who started working for the *Examiner* in 1926.

"Sure I remember Inez Burns. Ran an abortion mill at 327 Fillmore, right?"

In the spring of 1938, when authorities finally succeeded in raiding the clinic, Inez Burns made banner headlines in all the San Francisco papers. The San Francisco *News* called the hospital "a flourishing abortion mill, reputedly the city's most prosperous." At the time of the raid, 10 patients had either undergone abortions or were waiting to have abortions performed. The women were described by the *News* as "attractive and all over the age of 30."

Two weeks later, all charges were dropped when prosecutors were unable to convince any of the patients to swear to complaints.

The federal government retaliated a year later and indicted Burns for tax evasion, charging that she had earned more than $77,000 in 1934 and 1935, but paid only $157.25 in income tax. She settled by paying a fine of $10,000.

It was all the cost of doing business in San Francisco—until Pat Brown decided he wanted to get started in politics.

Brown took his political cues from across the Bay from "a young broad-shouldered district attorney named Earl Warren [who] was building a marketable reputation by relentlessly prosecuting con men and women, bunco artists, prostitutes, bookies and racketeers," according to Roger Rapoport in his biography *California Dreaming: The Political Odyssey of Pat & Jerry Brown*. "Warren had been hailed for running the best D.A.'s office in America." Not a bad role model, Brown figured.

In 1939, Brown lost his first race to unseat D.A. Brady. Four years later, he challenged Brady again, this time with the slogan: "Crack Down on Crime. Pick Brown This Time."

While campaigning, Brown told packed war-time rallies that, "There is no organized crime in San Francisco; the crime is all organized by the police department." He charged that cops winked at favored abortionists, bookmakers, gambling parlors and two-dollar whorehouses.

Brown beat Brady handily this time and continued to import from across the Bay his Oakland mentor's successes. In 1943, Warren was elected governor. "If a train called 'reform' could carry Earl Warren to Sacramento, Pat reasoned, he might as well buy a ticket on the same line," writes Rapoport.

From then on, Brown went after Inez Burns with a vengeance. In 1945, police discovered a cache of $300,000 in secret panels at Burns' Guerrero Street house after they first raided the Fillmore clinic.

Brown said Inez Burns performed 20 to 30 abortions a day, grossing $50,000 a month. She and four others, including receptionist Mabel Spaulding, blood technician Joe Hoff, gofer Musette Briggs and anesthesiologist Myrtle Ramsey were charged with felonies.

A sensational trial followed. To the disappointment of the hungry newspapers, Inez Burns never took the witness stand. Her attorney, Walter McGovern, knew the trial was political and pleaded with the jury to consider Brown's motive.

"Don't be pawns in a dirty political fight! Don't make these defendants the goats on the sacrificial altar of the political ambitions of Mr. Brown. He is using these women as a springboard to attain higher office through publicity!"

McGovern, a former president of the San Francisco Police Commission, wasn't finished. He played on a sense of complicity that San Franciscans shared. "If Inez Burns is punished," he told the jury, "I say the overwhelming majority of the people of San Francisco are guilty. How can the ladies and gentlemen of San Francisco excuse themselves? How can the people look at her as she sits there and say that for 15 years she has gone and done these things and not say, 'We permitted you to do it.'"

Then, before closing, McGovern exploited post-War racial prejudice, heightened by the thousands of blacks who were migrating to San Francisco. "Women are the particular victims of war," the booming attorney told the jury. "They wanted to do something that was patriotic and some of them went overboard. Other women went into bars and were seduced. There are still other women of middle age, on respectable missions, who became victims of the rapist!"

He went on: "Picture some girl close to you, the victim of an assault by a man whose race, color or physical background she did not know. If you were responsible for that girl, would you allow her to bring this child into the world? To ask this question is to answer it."

It was a shameless performance, but the jury bought it. After 30 hours, the jurors announced they were "hopelessly deadlocked." Burns and the four other defendants were released.

Vowing to retry the case, District Attorney Brown petitioned the Board of Supervisors for a supplemental appropriation of $12,500 to launch another investigation.

At the second trial, the jury deadlocked again.

Pat Brown wanted a conviction. In the fall of 1946, Burns was tried a third time. And this time it was an event few in San Francisco would ever forget. Operating tables, anesthetic machines, tanks of oxygen, nitrous oxide and carbon dioxide, along with Burns' instruments, were on display in the courtroom.

Two prospective witnesses, both of whom reportedly had undergone abortions at Burns' clinic, "disappeared under mysterious circumstances, and were unable to testify," according to the account in the *News*.

After six and a half hours of deliberation, the jury found Burns and her co-defendants guilty. The *Chronicle*'s lead paragraph the following day read, "One of San Francisco's oldest and best known institutions came to the end of the road yesterday."

Burns was sentenced to two to five years in Tehachapi State Prison. After more than a year of legal maneuvering, Burns, at age 60, went to prison. She served two years.

With Inez Burns behind bars, Pat Brown's career took off. "Closing down card games, brothels and abortionists was only the beginning," says Rapoport. "Pat needed more causes to keep his eager young staff busy and, of course, to keep his name in the headlines."

Brown, a Catholic, appealed to his San Francisco constituency by proclaiming family values. He began waging a war against pornography, trying to shut down the Howard Hughes film "The Outlaw", starring Jane Russell.

In 1946, Brown lost his bid against State Attorney General Frederick Howser. Four years later, he came back to get elected attorney general, the only Democratic candidate to survive the 1950 Republican landslide.

San Francisco's days as the Barbary Coast were coming to an end by the time Inez Burns was released from prison in 1949. In 1951 she pleaded guilty to tax evasion and began serving a one-year sentence at Alderson Federal Prison in West Virginia.

In 1952, she was arrested again for performing another abortion, this time with former city autopsy surgeon Dr. Adolphus Berger. She was arrested in a Richmond district home with tools in hand. The new district attorney, Thomas Lynch, had used a decoy as a patient.

Burns was convicted and again sent to prison for a two-to-five-year term, this time to the California Institution for Women at Corona.

Wracked with arthritis by this time, Burns weighed 105 pounds. She complained of repeated health problems stemming from a virus. She was released after 14 months, in February 1955, at age 66. Still the authorities were not finished with her: After being hounded by the Internal Revenue Service for decades, in 1956 she signed a promissory note to pay $745,325 in back taxes and penalties.

For the next 20 years, Inez Burns was an embittered woman. Someone who saw her weekly was Andy Roach, now 68. A lifelong bachelor who came to America from Dublin in 1958, he used to eat at the Burns' house often in the mid-1960s. Burns would call Roach on the phone three, four times a week, and talk for hours.

"She'd call at 10, and I couldn't get off until noon or sometimes 1 p.m. She said her children were ingrates, no one appreciated her any more." She used to harangue Roach about how she was stabbed in the back.

"I just listened to her. Really I never could get a word in edgewise," he said, sipping black coffee in a Mission dive called Kenny's.

"Everyone was afraid of her. The look that woman could give—no Hollywood actress could scare you any more.

"Whenever I'd go over there, you'd smell the smell of bread baking. She'd give me two or three loaves to take home."

The end was near for Burns. She refused to leave her house on Guerrero Street, and would spend hours listlessly staring out the large bay windows that overlooked a rundown housing project built in the early 1950s.

"Every time I saw her she was in a nightgown and slippers," said Bob Collen, a retired San Francisco county employee who got to know Burns in the early 1970s. "She would sit in the front room, looking at the street. She was always angry at the world."

One thing that hadn't changed was Burns' relationship to her husband Joe. She berated him constantly, Collen remembers. "You felt sorry for them, two old people lost in a world of their own. Once in a while, she'd bake a little bread. But basically, she would look out that front window, in some sort of reverie of the past."

In 1974, Burns and her husband Joe moved to the Moss Beach Hospital and Rehabilitation Center, both infirmed, their health failing fast. Joe died first in late 1975, and six months later, Burns died at age 87. Bob Collen was one of the pall-bearers at Burns' funeral at Skylawn Memorial Park in Moss Beach. Fewer than a dozen people showed up.

The grand Guerrero house Burns built 52 years ago was ignominiously auctioned off by the IRS one year after Burns died, for past taxes due. An attorney who specialized in sex cases placed a sealed bid of $80,000 at the IRS auction, and came away with the house, which soon turned into a venue for nocturnal gay gatherings. The house's peculiar legacy continued when its next owner, Dr. Robert Shank, opened the door to more parties. When Shank died in 1989, he bequeathed the building to his friend, Bruce McGee. McGee sold the house within a year, taking Burns' abortion instruments with him.

After Burns died in 1976, Carlisle sought to heed her grandmother's wishes and bury the instruments in her coffin, but other members of the family refused to go along.

"Why would you want to do that?" one asked. It just wouldn't be dignified, they told Carlisle, who eventually lost track of the tools.

No one else in the family even liked to acknowledge that Burns had been an abortionist; embarrassed, they used to refer to her as a "foot doctor."

The Californians, March/April, 1996

WRITING THE STORY

The first day of reporting the story, I awakened early. Through friends at the San Francisco newspapers, I was able to get two boxes full of clippings on Carlisle's grandmother. The brittle, brown-edged clips were a gold mine. There were scores of stories about police raids of Burns' clinic, about hung juries, a zealous prosecutor by the name of Edmund G. Brown and the high-rolling life Burns led.

The clips supplied me with addresses of where Burns had lived and where her clinic used to be located. I took out a legal pad and wrote down notes, with names and addresses highlighted by a yellow marker. My interview with Carlisle supplied me with more names and addresses. Burns had adopted and raised Carlisle as a child, and Carlisle's colorful stories of growing up with an abortionist grandmother were explicit and rich in detail.

While the story would keep, I knew I had to work it fast. Many of these who had known Burns were dead or in their nineties. I wanted to get as many live quotes as possible. One of the first calls I made was to Edmund Brown, who at the time was 90. When I got the former California governor (as well as father of another former governor) on the phone, he distinctly remembered Burns. Brown told me that his dogged prosecution of Burns had helped create a statewide platform for him, which he freely admitted he used to catapult himself to statewide office.

I called several retired newspapermen who had covered Burns. I interviewed a former deputy police chief, now retired, who had arrested Burns several times in her heyday. I went to the location of the abortion clinic Burns once operated, and interviewed surprised residents there. One interview I hoped to pursue was with a 96-year-old attorney who had represented Burns in her third trial nearly half a century earlier. The day before our interview, the attorney died.

The shocker of the piece came when I interviewed the woman I identify in the piece as Edith Pachen. Pachen was a newspaper reporter's dream source. She was an armchair historian, and there was little she didn't know about San Francisco. Pachen had files and files of newspaper clippings, hundreds of out-of-print books, posters and correspondence—anything that had anything remotely to do with San Francisco history. I had interviewed Pachen many times before for other stories and knew she'd be a good source for this piece since Inez Burns had played such a central role in San Francisco mid-century history.

As I wrote in the story, when I asked Pachen over the telephone about Burns, Pachen paused. It was a pause that seemed to last forever. No one had mentioned the name Inez Burns to her for decades, and Pachen had kept her connection secret for good reason. Pachen had once visited Burns' clinic for an abortion, and after Burns talked her out of the abortion, Pachen subsequently gave birth to a son. To this day, Pachen's grown son, now in his fifties, has no idea that his birth nearly never took place.

After several weeks of interviewing more than three dozen people, as well as poring over newspaper clips and reading accounts of similar well-heeled abortionists operating during the same era in other cities, a less fuzzy picture emerged of Burns.

But how to write it?

This story, like all of them, presented its own set of problems. The most immediate: How was I going to suck readers into such a long profile about an abortionist who had been dead for almost 30 years? Who'd be interested?

During our interviews, Caroline Carlisle had mentioned to me her grandmother's instruments, the tools she used to perform so many abortions. Carlisle said Burns had made one final request before dying: that the instruments be buried with her. But when Carlisle had tried to find them, she came up empty-handed.

That was all I needed. It was a self-imposed challenge I gratefully accepted. *I* wanted to find those instruments. If they hadn't been thrown away or sold at some garage sale, I wanted to get a glimpse of these tools of pain and relief. To me, the instruments were at the core of the story. I would use them as my own tools to tell the tale.

I made a cold call during the middle of the day to Burns' old house. I didn't expect the owners to be there, and was relieved when no one answered the door. I slipped a note under the door, explaining my purpose in an oblique way, and asking the current residents to call me. They did in several days, and when I returned, I interviewed the two men who had lived in the San Francisco Mission-District home for more than a decade. When I told them about Inez Burns, they weren't shocked. Instead, they seemed pleased that they lived in a house that, as one of them put it, "just became a landmark." The owners took me on a tour of the house, and showed me several secret panels and hollowed-out banisters. "So, that explains why she had so many places to hide things," one of the men said.

Then, I went after the long shot: Had either of them ever come across any instruments, any medical tools? They looked at me strangely, and shook their heads. I asked them whom they had bought the house from, and they gave me the name, Bruce McGee.

I knew it was an implausibly long, long shot, but after searching real estate records, I was able to contact McGee, who still lived in San Francisco. I initially interviewed McGee over the phone, and when I asked him about any instruments he might have taken from the Mission-District house, he, not unlike Edith Pachen, paused.

"Why do you want to know?"

"Just so I can have a look at them."

"You want to buy them?" he asked.

"I just want to look a look at them, that's all."

McGee paused again. "Well, I've got a canvas carrying case that wraps up, and inside it, there are tools that sorta look like dentist's instruments. I took them from the old house I used to own."

I had goose bumps when I walked into the McGee house the next day. I presented myself, I must say, in a rather strange manner. All I wanted of this stranger was to take a look at this curio—old medical instruments. I explained to McGee about Burns and what the instruments had been used for, and he, like the owners of the Mission-District home, didn't seemed shocked or offended in the least.

I told him I just wanted to look at the instruments, perhaps take a picture of them. Would that be okay?

McGee said yes, but make it snappy. He was in a hurry. I thought for a minute that McGee might ask me to pay for the right to take the photos, but he didn't.

As I walked out of the house that night, I was euphoric over the thrill of finding something only I could understand. I dropped the roll of film off at a corner Walgreen's, and after I picked up the photographs the next morning, I drove over to my wife's gynecologist. I wanted him to identify the instruments. Morey Filler shook his head, his eyes bulging a little.

"Where in the world did you ever find these?"

Dr. Filler, a man in his fifties, had never seen anything quite like them, but he was able to identify each instrument.

That's how I got the story's lede.

EPILOGUE

My portrait of Burns may be contrary to the today's popular image of a big-city abortionist who practiced her craft from 1920-1955, but I'm convinced I got the

Burns story right. For 35 years, she was California's worst-kept secret. It wasn't until the above piece was published that any appraisal of Burns' life had ever been aired. Burns' story was history, but the kind of history that few wanted anything written about.

From a personal point of view, I was deeply moved by the Burns story. Here was a woman who had succeeded—and succeeded wildly—in a man's world. Inez Burns was smart, powerful, wealthy, witty, influential. And if you extrapolate from Edith Pachen's memory of her, Burns also had heart. I consciously wrote the piece as a teaser for a screenplay or book proposal. The story had everything. Or so I thought.

Perhaps it had too much. No commercial publisher or studio bit on turning Inez Burns' story into anything more than what I had written: a journalistic piece for California history buffs. Inez Burns and her life were too controversial, too purulent, too local for mass appeal.

ASSIGNMENTS

1) Interview several retired local reporters and find out the favorite stories of their careers. Such journalists are often fonts of information. Ask if they can provide information on local issues and personalities in the news today. Were there any stories that got away from these reporters, relevant stories that could be updated today?

2) Profile a local abortion clinic, as well as a local agency that works with pregnant women to help place infants up for adoption. Select a woman at each facility and follow her pregnancy through termination or to adoption.

3) Who was the most famous—or notorious—woman in your city's history? Talk to local historians, relatives, those who may have known her. Resurrect the woman's life through a thoughtful appraisal.

15

THE BIG CHILL

While on vacation in Southern California, just as I checked into a hotel, I noticed in the lobby a poster advertising a lecture to be given by John Robbins, someone I had never heard of. The poster had a photograph of Robbins (rail-thin in his early forties), a description of his lecture topic ("how organic, vegetarian food choices can improve health and happiness"), and a biographical sketch ("author and lecturer," then in small type, "heir to the Baskin-Robbins ice cream fortune). I was floored. The guy who stood to inherit millions from the world's largest ice cream empire was on the lecture circuit, apparently denouncing high-cholesterol food.

Robbins spoke at the hotel after I had checked out, so I never got to hear his lecture. But as soon as I got home, I searched databases and clips for anything on him. Robbins had just written a book, *Diet for a New America,* a scathing critique of the U.S. food-processing industry and the diet Americans follow, fueled by greedy corporate interests. But I found nothing about Robbins' intriguing background: how a child whose millionaire father had a kid's dream job—taste-testing new flavors and selling that ice cream—grew up and turned against much of what his father stood for. That was enough of a peg for the story. But I soon got another. Robbins lived in the hills overlooking Santa Cruz, California, and I lived less than 75 miles away. I called Robbins and pitched my story to him. He was more interested in talking about his new book and his crusade against processed food than his own personal history. But Robbins consented to an interview, and within a week I was driving the winding roads in the Santa Cruz Mountains to his house.

The Big Chill

Think ice cream. Think chocolate, vanilla, strawberry. Think Rocky Road, Jamoca Almond Fudge, Pralines 'n' Cream. Think 31 flavors. Think Baskin-Robbins.

Think money.

Baskin-Robbins is the largest chain of ice-cream stores in the world. Its creamy aroma wafts around the globe and has become as much an elixir to those with a sweet tooth in Abu Dhabi as it is in America. In the United States, there are 2,429 Baskin-Robbins parlors spread in a swath as thick as Chewy Gooey Chocolate. Outside the States, there are 937 Baskin-Robbins outlets, dotted in 41 countries with more stores than there are chocolate morsels in a gallon of Fudge Chunks 'n' Chips.

And the whole sweet multimillion-dollar empire could have gone to 41-year-old John Robbins just for the asking.

Of all the heirs to great American fortunes, John Robbins is the only one practiaclly born with a silver spoon in his mouth. As the car was to the Fords, and oil was to the Gettys, ice cream was to the Robbins family.

John Robbins, heir apparent to the world's largest ice-cream empire, was groomed to take over his family's business from birth. From his days as a toddler, ice cream was larger than life to Robbins. The family freezer was perpetually stocked with ice cream. Robbins and his two sisters taste-tested the company's new concoctions.

While growing up, Robbins worked summers at the burgeoning business his father founded in 1945 in the Los Angeles suburb of Glendale. His apprenticeship included sampling butter-brickle bits, diced black walnuts or slivers of English toffee before they were swirled into yet another vat of frosty cream. Robbins tinkered with old standards and helped invent new taste sensations that wound up on the tips of billions of tongues. When Robbins apprenticed with the company's advertising division, he helped create a jingle that only an ice-cream company could get away with: "We Make People Happy."

Robbins lived and breathed ice cream. He even swam in it. In the backyard of the family estate in the wealthy San Fernando Valley enclave of Encino, founder-and-president Irvin Robbins basked in his fortune by building an ice-cream-cone–shaped swimming pool.

It was an undeniable monument to ice cream's glory, as well as to the opulence the treat that "everyone screams for" had created for one family. On approach to Burbank Airport, commercial airline pilots routinely pointed out the pool to planeloads of transplanted families arriving in Southern California in the 1950s.

The pool—and attendant wealth—was no mirage. The fantasy pool and inviting turquoise water glittering inside were testimony to what could happen to anyone who believed in this most Californian of all American dreams.

That dream turned out to be a nightmare for John Robbins.

When he was 20, Robbins told his father he wanted nothing to do with the family fortune. He moved to a remote island in British Columbia for a decade and practiced Zen meditation and yoga. The family, which included his wife Deo and son, whose name is Ocean, lived on a yearly income of $600. They made pilgrimages to India to discover true wisdom.

For the last two decades, Robbins has been a strict vegetarian, swearing off all forms of meat, poultry and fish. He has dropped dairy products from his diet and hasn't eaten a grain of sugar for years. He eats no cheese or milk.

He hates ice cream.

In fact, John Robbins has come to believe that ice cream is a curse to mankind. America's treat, he says, causes a host of deadly illnesses, including stroke, diabetes and cardiovascular diseases (the nation's No. 1 killer).

Burt Baskin and Irv Robbins, the brothers-in-law who started the company and amply indulged in the product they sold, are examples of the accumulated ravages of a lifetime of ice cream.

In 1967, Baskin died at age 54 of heart disease.

Irv Robbins, now 72, living in retirement near Palm Springs, has diabetes, coronary artery disease and high blood pressure. For much of his adult life, he has been chronically overweight. On instructions from his cardiologist, Irv Robbins today follows a no-fat diet and avoids all dairy products. Ice cream has no place in his life.

Lean, angular John Robbins, a marathon runner and accomplished modern dancer, has become an evangelist for healthy eating. Now a psychotherapist living in the rural Santa Cruz County community of Felton, Robbins has written a stinging exposé of the food-processing business, *Diet for a New America* (Stillpoint Publishing: $12.95), in which he explores how food choices affect our health and happiness.

The 423-page tome is a deeply reasoned treatise that blasts corporate greed as the motive behind the public's addiction to processed food. Printed two years ago by a small New Hampshire publishing house dedicated to "books that explore the expanding frontiers of human consciousness," Robbins' work has become an underground classic of sorts, garnering praise from such diverse quarters as Frances Moore Lappe, author of *Diet for a Small Planet;* Ram Dass, the former Harvard professor turned guru; and Dr. Michael Fox, the scientific director of the Humane Society of America.

In the same muckraking manner that Upton Sinclair exposed slaughterhouses in *The Jungle* and Rachel Carson took to task the pesticide industry in *Silent Spring,* Robbins excoriates America's modern food machine—from the overcrowded conditions in poultry and cattle factories to corporate lies used in marketing products that are bad for our health.

Ice cream does not escape Robbins' rapier-edged scoop. With an undercurrent of guilt and scorn, Robbins cites National Dairy Council campaigns aimed at exhorting impressionable children to devour ice cream. A Dairy Council brochure states flatly, "Ice cream is a healthful food made from milk and cream along with other good food." In a section on weight loss, Robbins includes a suggestion from the Dairy Council that urges overweight teenagers to eat "stay-slim sundaes" (with fruit toppings instead of chocolate sauce) or angel food cake and ice cream.

"It's hard to avoid the conclusion that the Dairy Council is more concerned with getting youngsters hooked on a lifetime of high-fat dairy-product consumption than with providing sound nutritional education," Robbins writes.

Robbins should know. For years, ice cream was touted by his family's business as harmless, good, wholesome fun. Not to like ice cream, not to be hooked on the stuff, was somehow very wrong. But John Robbins is up to the task of shocking anyone out of another double-dip cone.

In his sparsely furnished home, visitors are politely instructed to take off their shoes before entering. Robbins wears only "natural fibers": white cotton socks, New Age Chi-brand pants and a blue work shirt that matches his eyes. Two satisfied cats roam the living room.

F. Scott Fitzgerald's oft-quoted observation, "The very rich are different from you and me," is still true for Robbins, even though he now rents a small, paint-peeled house and drives a 10-year-old, beat-up Datsun. Robbins, who carries 155 pounds on his 6-foot-1-inch frame, comes across as monastic, an ascetic with little sense of humor. He seems to be an intense, private man consumed with a mission. He lives a fringe life, visibly rejecting all that is opulent, comfortable, in the least bit materialistic. He proudly points out that he rents and doesn't own the home he shares with his wife and son. Robbins lifts his nose and eyebrows in disdain when asked about movies or television, activities in which he has absolutely no interest.

Robbins' speech is peppered with New Age shibboleths. Shirley MacLaine would feel at home here discussing chakras. A handmade pyramid adorns a corner of the kitchen. A '60s-style, tie-dyed sheet is pinned to the living-room door. Robbins brews mint tea and talks about his journey to rejecting ice cream for an inner warmth that gave meaning to his life.

"If I had done the obvious, my success would have been built on selling ice cream," he says. "Ice cream is basically frozen butterfat and sugar. I knew it wasn't good for anybody. I would have looked in the mirror and seen a man whose prosperity was contributing to disease, and ethically I didn't want to be in that situation."

Except for being able to offer friends a dip in an ice-cream-cone–shaped pool,

Robbins' life wasn't terribly different from that of any other wealthy kid growing up in the San Fernando Valley during the boom years. He attended Grant High School in Van Nuys, and then enrolled at the University of California, Berkeley, during the dawning of the Free Speech Movement.

In 1967, when Robbins was 20, Uncle Burt had just been felled by a massive coronary, and Irv Robbins had received a buyout offer from United Fruit Company. Irv Robbins summoned his only son to Los Angeles to spring the question millions of children could only dream their father might someday ask: Are you ready to become an ice-cream mogul?

If John said no, Irv Robbins would sell the private company for a staggering amount. If he said yes, the vast multimillion-dollar empire would be his.

"That was a milestone in my life, and freed me from the expectation my father and I had for years," Robbins recalls. "On that day, a bell had rung. The time had come for me to leave everything I had ever known that was secure."

The younger Robbins' decision broke his father's heart—a rupture that only in recent years has been mended. Not only was he rejecting immense wealth, he was rejecting his father and everything his father had so ingeniously built.

Irv Robbins' own story was one of hard work and savvy deals. Home from World War II, Robbins opened a hole-in-the-wall ice-cream store in Glendale in 1945, and called it Snowbird. Brother-in-law Baskin opened another store in Pasadena, and by 1948, the two men owned eight Los Angeles stores that offered not just ice-cream cones and sundaes in Dixie cups, but takeout containers.

Such rapid expansion was phenomenal for a very fundamental reason: Prior to the war, ice cream was not the dessert of choice among Americans. Pie was queen as the after-dinner treat in the 1940s and '50s, and nothing came close to knocking her off the throne. When served at home, ice cream was a treat reserved for special occasions. It was hand-cranked by someone with strong arms during a tiring process that took hours. Since there was no way to keep ice cream frozen at home for any length of time, it had to be eaten in one serving.

But technology helped ice cream melt its way into the American diet, and turned Burt Baskin and Irv Robbins into millionaires. Starting in the late '40s, refrigerator manufacturers such as General Electric and Westinghouse started selling their home models with tiny compartments, called freezers, designed to keep items especially cold.

Baskin and Robbins could not have asked for better timing. The postwar economic boom, particularly in California, allowed millions of Americans to buy refrigerators.

With demand up, Baskin and Robbins set out to increase supply. They hit upon an idea that would fundamentally change not just the takeout ice-cream business, but the very nature of U.S. commerce: franchises.

Years before Ray Kroc did the same thing with hamburger stands, Baskin and Robbins opted for control instead of ownership—the cornerstone of franchising.

In exchange for owning a Baskin-Robbins store, each manager would buy all the ice cream, supplies, even advertising, from the company headquartered in Burbank.

And with dollars pumped into national advertising campaigns, ice cream became fun. It turned into the nation's first impulse food. Standard vanilla, chocolate and strawberry gave way to such concoctions as Mississippi Mud, Pink Bubblegum and Can't Stop the Nuts. By 1967, when Baskin died, the pair had franchised 500 stores across the nation.

After John Robbins thumbed his nose at the offer to take over the business, he admits his father kept him at arm's length. "He was offering me what 99 percent of the men in the country would give their right arm for, and I said, no thanks."

Robbins describes his parents as members of "the country-club set." Their lifestyle, he says, "was one that very few people ever obtain. I had the privilege of growing up with people who could buy anything they ever wanted. Roughing it meant calling the maid's quarters for room service. I was born on top of the ladder."

Up there, it was tough to balance. At home there was that ice-cream-cone–shaped pool, yet during the summer of 1965, 18-year-old Robbins marched in freedom crusades in Selma, Ala., and Jackson, Miss.

His parents' opulence repelled him. "It was the lifestyle of the rich and nervous. The people I saw growing up were not the people I wanted to be. Their lives were not exemplary. I released myself from the hypnosis of our society: If you want to be happy, make a lot of money."

While at UC–Berkeley, Robbins concealed his family's wealth from his friends for fear they'd be more interested in his wallet than in him. "I never ever, ever told people about my background. No one ever knew," he says. "It was a total secret."

Armed with a Berkeley degree in the history of political consciousness, Robbins and his wife, a fellow Berkeley student, moved to a tiny island off the coast of British Columbia in 1969. Ardent vegetarians, they built a four-room log cabin five miles from the nearest neighbor and grew all their own food. They had no electricity or running water. Their son, Ocean, was born in 1973.

"We lived the way human beings had lived for centuries," says Robbins, sounding like a cross between Thoreau and a *nouveau* swami. "We wanted isolation. I wanted to do things with great depth and concentration. I was on a human journey, working out my emotional blocks." He obtained a master's in psychology on the British Columbian mainland and became a psychotherapist. On the island, Robbins started a yoga and meditation retreat called Rising Spirits.

He became infatuated with trees and animals and fell in love with, as he puts it, the fertility of the earth and its creatures. "I became deeply attached to animals. They have faces and eyes, and mothers and fathers, and certainly the ability to feel pain."

The decade of isolation ended in 1979 with a commitment to return to California and become a full-time proselytizer of a spiritual radicalism based on vegetarianism and animal rights, which culminated in *Diet for a New America.*

"I started having a series of dreams in which a giant cow appeared to me," he told *Yoga Times* magazine recently. "Then I saw a giant pig. And they would say things to me, powerful things about life and our relationship to them and to the natural world. Finally, I received a very clear message that said: 'You are to write this book. You will be guided the entire way.'"

After finishing the book, Robbins started an environmental, pro-vegetarian group called EarthSave, funded primarily with profits from the book.

While his father lives in Rancho Mirage where conspicuous consumption is king, John Robbins' life today is devoted to what he calls "voluntary simplicity." He says he doesn't want more than he needs. "If I don't need it, I don't want it. We don't pursue objects. We would never have an object that is costly. The richness of the inner life is really what's paramount."

Meanwhile, the ice-cream company his father founded has undergone a host of permutations since it left the family. United Fruit Company unloaded Baskin-Robbins to United Brands, which, in turn, sold it in 1971 to J. Lyons Ltd., a British multinational. Lyons was subsequently taken over by another British firm, Allied Corp., maker of Tetley Tea and Teacher's Scotch.

Baskin-Robbins is a profitable subsidiary, but its parent company releases no figures on its revenues. Irv Robbins estimates profits from the subsidiary to be "so high, they must be in the jillions."

Irv Robbins stayed on as president of Baskin-Robbins for 11 years, and retired in 1978, when there were 2,300 ice-cream franchises worldwide.

Although he no longer has any connection with the ice-cream company, Irv Robbins is careful when asked about endorsing his son's campaign against high-fat dairy products.

"Eating excess ice cream is bad," he says in a telephone interview, tiptoeing and pausing. "But eating anything in excess is bad. Moderation is the key. We have to move closer to the vegetarian concept.

"The only reason I don't eat any (ice cream) today is because of what's happened through the years to me."

Cardiologists aren't so charitable in their view of ice cream. Today, most wholeheartedly agree with the younger Robbins that high-fat dairy items can be primary contributors to heart disease.

"After all these years of thinking that milk with butterfat is an essential food, maybe it isn't so," says Dr. William P. Castelli, the medical director of the Framingham Heart Study, and lecturer at Harvard Medical School, the University of Massachusetts and Boston University. "Is it a coincidence that the traditional Japanese who have so few heart attacks don't drink milk or eat much cheese or cream?"

In fact, in April, Baskin-Robbins introduced a new low-calorie, low-cholesterol frozen dairy dessert. But John Robbins is having none of it. His typical daily diet is not for everyone: orange juice and protein powder for breakfast; whole-grain bread with pickles, tofu and vegetable spread for lunch; potatoes, pasta, homegrown vegetables and salad for dinner.

Robbins' 15-year-old son is as staunch a vegetarian as his father. But Robbins wanted Ocean at least once to taste a piece of meat. Ocean refused.

"I felt very strongly that he should make his own decision; that's why I insisted he try meat. But he told me, 'You can't lay your trip on me, Dad.'"

At one time, Robbins considered becoming a closet revolutionary. Like Patrick Reynolds, grandson of the Reynolds Tobacco founder, Robbins thought of giving Baskin-Robbins profits to good causes.

"But I didn't want to answer to my parents. I realized there would be too many strings attached. They wouldn't even be strings, they'd be ropes and chains."

Robbins says he feels vindicated for leaving the wealth behind. He has inner peace, and over the last two years, he and his father have come to respect each other at a distance.

"After all these years, it shows that blood is thicker than ice cream," John Robbins says with only the slightest trace of a smile.

The Sacramento Bee, May 7, 1989

WRITING THE STORY

The first three words of the story explicitly exhort the reader to do something: Think. That short first sentence is an imperative—a command I'm giving the reader. It's also an unconventional way to start a story, and I'm banking that the novelty of such an opening will work to suck the reader into the story. I want readers with me from the very first word, and that's why I choose to start the piece with ice-cream flavors. Who won't read a story about ice cream? That the story was published in early May didn't hurt either. People start thinking ice cream as the summer approaches, and I want the article to shadow their inclination for the frosty stuff.

After I implore the reader to think "ice cream," I narrow my focus—"chocolate, vanilla, strawberry." I further narrow that focus to ice cream exotica—"Jamoca Almond Fudge, Pralines 'n' Cream," original Baskin-Robbins' concoctions. With that progression, it's time to spring the number "31," and follow with the name of the largest ice cream chain in the world.

The second graf is a mere two-word single sentence, which jumps out typographically. It's followed by a long graf that sets up the tension in the story: a worldwide empire of ice cream parlors—and John Robbins' complete rejection of not only his father and the business, but the very product itself.

The next graf torques up the news value of the story and places Robbins' life in context with other American-made family fortunes: automobiles and Ford; oil and Getty; ice cream and Robbins.

I continue with the family angle, segueing to Robbins' ice cream-centric childhood. Detail, as always, is essential, and I can think of nothing more visual in conveying that detail than the delightful image of an ice-cream-cone–shaped swimming pool, as well as the planeloads of transplanted families arriving in California peering down and seeing that indelible picture frozen in their minds.

The turn of the story—what makes it a story—is Robbins' revulsion of that ice-cream-driven wealth. The next portion of the piece describes the ascetic life Robbins has chosen, all the way to another short, one-sentence graf—that Robbins hates ice cream. No surprise, but talk about irony.

I follow with Robbins' staunch stand and then introduce something startling: that co-founder Burt Baskin died of heart disease at 54, and Robbins' own father, Irv, has coronary artery disease, is overweight and on doctor's orders, avoids all dairy products, *including ice cream.*

Then it's time to fold in Robbins' crusade against the corporate food machine. His book is well thought out and does, in fact, squarely fall in the same category as some of the great muckraking efforts of our time. Once I've established Robbins' credentials and his ability to deliver on them, it's time to return to Robbins' life and the difficult choices he had to make to become the person I found myself interviewing. Theatrically, I set the denouement as a key element in the story—when Robbins' father offers his son the corporation, and the younger Robbins walks away. Such drama rings like a Greek tragedy, with the son rejecting not only his father but all his father believed in.

Woven into that narrative is some interesting social history: How the brothers unwittingly were beneficiaries of 1940s technology, as well as a sea-change in American eating habits and business practices. In a sense, both Robbins and his father were classic reflections of their times. I recall the utter disdain Robbins had in his eyes when he categorized his parents and their ilk as living the "lifestyle of the rich and nervous."

Robbins and I had something in common, having gone to the same university, and when I asked him how he dealt with revealing his wealthy origins to friends at Berkeley, I was rewarded with a telling anecdote. Robbins' wealth was a total secret.

I let Robbins talk, and his thoughts come across especially well when he waxes about mothers and fathers in domesticated animal families, as well as when he talks about seeing the animals' faces and knowing intuitively that they feel pain.

Near the close of the story, I write about a reconciliation between Robbins and his father. I interview Irv Robbins, and when I ask him point-blank whether ice cream can lead to a host of heart ailments, the senior Robbins toes the line as adroitly as any corporate spokesman. The piece ends in an unsettling way—just as Robbins is in real life—deeply serious, still troubled over the wealth that his legacy has brought him. He has found inner peace, Robbins tells me, yet even when he cracks a joke about blood being thicker than ice cream, there is no laughter, just a slight smile.

EPILOGUE

After my story appeared, I never heard from Robbins. Today, he continues to write and lecture about transforming American diets from high-cholesterol processed meats and their by-products to healthy, low-impact vegetarian meals. He has appeared on the Oprah Winfrey show and has spoken at the United Nations. Robbins, though, remains a controversial figure. The National Cattlemen's Beef Association continues its attempt to discredit Robbins and his message. Recently, Robbins found himself under attack by a University of Minnesota scientist of environment and occupational health who challenged the veracity of Robbins' findings. Robbins and his wife, Deo, continue to live in Santa Cruz, but now with their son Ocean and his wife, and grandsons Bodhi and River.

ASSIGNMENTS

1) Interview the grown son or daughter of a very wealthy family in your area. Focus on how different his/her childhood was and any hardships that such wealth may have posed while growing up. Discuss in your story the choices the heir made to become a part of such wealth or to reject it.

2) Work in a local fast-food restaurant. Report on the working conditions, as well as sanitation and food preparation at the restaurant.

3) Go to the county or city board of health and review health-code violations at local restaurants and markets. Find out who inspects those venues, as well as the regularity of his or her rounds. Consider doing a ride-along with an inspector.

16

YUGOSLAV PRINCE COVETS A CROWN

Everyone in the news business is accustomed to getting bombarded by public-relations executives. Such personnel—"flaks" as they're called by journalists—are endemic to the news business. Skilled flaks know how to play the media, as well as how to spin any and all related events to their clients' advantage. Getting a client's name and message inserted in the media's daily menu of news and filler generally costs plenty of money, but such publicity is invaluable. "Press kits," those colored binders filled with press releases that litter reporters' desks, have become a staple of the nexus between the news business and the public-relations trade. The entertainment industry, politicians and drug companies seem to be the most common purveyors of public-relations campaigns these days, but almost any sizable business employs flaks to ensure that its products get exposed in just the right way.

Still, I was surprised one summer morning to get a call from a public-relations firm hawking a story about a former Yugoslav prince. Brad Pit, Bob Dole, Prozac, yes, but selling a story about the man who wanted to be king? This was something I *had* to cover. But I was going to cover it my way.

Yugoslav Prince Covets a Crown

Though he's never seen a divided country, he longs to rule

SAN FRANCISCO—Explaining the woes of royalty, Yugoslav Crown Prince Alexander, whose cousins include Prince Charles and King Juan Carlos, moaned Monday, "It's hard to go into Macy's and buy a pair of underpants, and say you're a king."

But these days Prince Alexander has weightier issues on his mind than Jockeys or BVD's. The prince believes that the civil unrest in his country may set the stage for a dramatic return to his family's homeland so that he could become king.

There are several impediments—aside from the wild political instability in Yugoslavia—before the prince dons crown and cape.

For one, the man who would be king has never been in Yugoslavia.

And he speaks only halting Serbo-Croatian, the main language of the nation's 24 million people.

Not to worry, though. The prince said he is brushing up on the language by listening to tapes several hours a day.

Prince Alexander, 46, was in San Francisco to drum up support for his plan to assume the throne. He had just come from a three-day stay at the Bohemian Grove along the Russian River, the famous conclave for the rich and powerful.

The prince plans to carry his campaign to Los Angeles, New York, Washington, D.C., and Canada, before returning home to London.

Speaking in a clipped British accent at a news conference on Monday, the prince said he is the logical choice to head the country.

"I'm the only one not tarnished by politics. I served in the British Army. I've had the best education offered. I have first-hand knowledge of market economies. … I was brought up in democracy. I don't think you could find many people with that knowledge in Yugoslavia."

Moreover, said the beefy prince with a three-dial gold watch, "I'm very well-known. My movements are being followed. We are very historically connected."

The prince's father, King Peter II, was banished from Yugoslavia in 1945 when the monarchy was abolished and Communist leader Josip Tito took control.

While his parents were living in exile in London, the prince was born in Suite 212 at the Claridge Hotel. Since Yugoslav law required that royalty be born on national soil to retain title, the British government temporarily declared the hotel room to be Yugoslav territory.

In 1948, the royal family moved to New York, but Alexander stayed in Europe, enrolling at the exclusive Swiss boarding school, Le Rosey. He later was a student at Culver Military Academy in Indiana, as well as at boarding schools in Scotland and England.

When King Peter II died in 1970, the prince was formally eligible to take on the title of king, but the prince preferred to retain the title he was born with. He then became, as described in his resume, "a successful businessman."

The prince says he "was involved" with advertising in Great Britain and Brazil, as well as insurance brokering in the United States, he said. Back in London, he expanded his horizons in shipping and construction.

Between ventures, in 1972 he married Princess Maria da Gloria of Orleans and Braganca of the deposed Imperial House of Brazil. The couple had three children and divorced in 1983. In 1985, the prince married Athens-born Katherine Batis.

Prince Alexander said Monday that he is devoting his full-time attention to the turmoil in his family's homeland. "I meet with people regularly. I meet with representatives all the time. I want my education to do some good."

Yugoslavia's six republics are threatening to break apart and become sovereign nations. As the country moves toward civil strife, experts say the chance of ethnic and political violence becomes increasingly likely.

Although they caution that political unrest in Yugoslavia makes prognosticating difficult, many academics in the United States don't give much credence to the idea of the prince ever returning to his family's homeland.

"He has a very slim chance," said Wayne Vucinich, a professor emeritus of Eastern European history at Stanford University. "I think he is well-intentioned, but what he is suggesting is not politically practical. He's been so out of it for so long, people don't know him."

Ken Jowiett, professor of history at the University of California, Berkeley, said, "The chances are he's going to be spending a lot more time at the Bohemian Grove than in Yugoslavia."

Jowiett said the prince has no leverage or independent weight in Yugoslavia. "I don't see it," Jowiett said. "It's a fanciful notion."

Meanwhile, the prince said Monday, "It's in my blood to be of service to my country."

The Sacramento Bee, July 23, 1991

WRITING THE STORY

At first, I thought the flak was lucky. The morning he pitched his client's story was shaping up to be a slow news day. But more likely, the flak wasn't lucky at all. That's *why* he was hitting me up with the story.

Five or six other journalists bit on the story, and we were all ceremoniously ushered into a suite of rooms at a swanky hotel. Seated behind a polished mahogany table sat the would-be king. Good reporters are supposed to be able to cover a fire one day—and the prince of Yugoslavia the next day. Before making my way to the hotel, I had spent an hour getting as much information as I could on Prince Alexander. From my research, there were two aspects of the story that immediately grabbed me: The prince had never lived in the country he hoped to someday govern, and he hardly spoke a word of Serbo-Croatian, the language most of his would-be subjects speak.

How pragmatic could the prince's conquest really be?

I created my own angle to the story. Here was a prince without a country, a royal polo player who would never likely rule any country. What was it like to be blue-blood royalty whose cousins included Prince Charles and King Juan Carlos?

I asked the prince whether he carried such privilege and burden with him everywhere he went. Indeed the prince did, he said. I wanted to go deeper, to get the prince on the record, reflecting his own personal issue of identity.

"Could you give us an example of the anonymity to which you've been relegated because of the political unrest in Yugoslavia?" I asked, pressing the prince.

At that point, Prince Alexander put his hands together, then showed an uncomfortable smile, and came out with what became the lede to the story.

The story took a surreal turn after I queried the prince on his nonexistent native language abilities. The prince vaguely told the assembled reporters that he was "practicing" Serbo-Croatian.

"But how and with whom" I persisted.

With no one, Prince Alexander said.

"Then how are you practicing?"

Again came the uncomfortable smile. The prince said he was trying to learn the language of his motherland by listening to language tapes several hours a day.

The rest of the story is filled with detail (three-dial gold watch; Suite 212 of London's Claridge Hotel), as well as reaction from scholars who gave the prince a zero-to-none chance of ever assuming power.

EPILOGUE

What did the scholars know? As it turns out, Prince Alexander and his family moved back to the prince's ancestral palace in Belgrade in the summer of 2001, and he is now positioning himself to assume, as he sees it, his rightful place in Yugoslav history. During 1999, the prince brought together opposition leaders at well-publicized conferences outside Yugoslavia, setting the stage for the ouster of President Slobadan Milosevic. With Milosevic later deposed, the prince, his wife and three American-born children returned to Yugoslavia. These days, the prince and his family are busy touring Yugoslavia, appearing at hospitals, airports, shopping malls, their photos popping up in newspapers and television news shows daily. The prince and his family have even set up a Web site (http://www.royalfamily.org).

Political analysts today agree that Prince Alexander is indeed a player in shaping Yugoslavia's future and could someday assume the throne.

Who would have thought it? No one—except perhaps some savvy flaks.

ASSIGNMENTS

1) Try something different. The next time you're on the receiving end of a public-relations campaign urging you to write favorably about a product, write about the publicity campaign itself and the hoped-for hyped results. Go into detail on costs, messages, branding, the stakes involved. The product can be anything—from soap to sandwich bags.

2) Spend a day at a local public-relations firm. Find out what account executives do to brand product names into the collective public consciousness. Write a compelling narrative about the strategies and politics that exist in mounting a successful campaign.

3) Interview local nationals from a foreign country whose nation is undergoing political turmoil. Are they worried they will no longer be allowed to return home? Profile three such residents in your area, focusing on the human toll global political maneuvering takes on families.

17

EVICTION BRINGS
MOUNTAIN MAN DOWN

One spring afternoon, I was hiking 10 miles south of my San Francisco home in a county park near San Bruno Mountain, just northwest of San Francisco International Airport. I had brought with me a loaf of sourdough bread and Monterey jack cheese, and just as I was about to sit down to enjoy my meal, I heard rustling in the woods nearby. Out from some gnarled, thorny bushes, a grizzled man with a scraggly beard emerged. The intruder to my picnic began walking toward me. At first, I was alarmed, but as the man got closer, there was something about him that allayed my fears. He stuck out his hand and smiled. He had a gentle, almost sweet way. We talked, and after a while, I asked him to join me. As it turned out, *I* was the intruder. This was Dwight Taylor's backyard, and this is his story.

Eviction Brings Mountain Man Down

Dwight Taylor was a junior high school music teacher until one restless summer night eight years ago.

He got out his sleeping bag, laid it in his backyard and climbed in. Taylor's life was never to be the same.

"The trees blew gently in the breeze. I could see the fog pass the moon and the seagulls float by. I found it delightful," recalls Taylor, 43.

He soon found that he was unable to sleep back inside his house. Despite protests from students and parents because he was so popular, Taylor quit his job at Westborough Junior High School in South San Francisco. He sold his car, rented out his San Francisco home and hired a secretary to take care of his finances.

Then he moved to a remote part of San Bruno Mountain, the rugged 2,226-acre San Mateo County parkland just southwest of Candlestick Park, to the west of the Bayshore Freeway. Taylor became an urban mountain man, a modern-day Davy Crockett, a real-life Grizzly Adams without the bear.

Between two freshwater springs, he constructed an A-frame shack thatched with willow wands and eucalyptus branches. During the day, he foraged for greens and berries. At night, he lulled himself to sleep playing the flute or recorder.

That's the way Taylor lived for more than seven years—until last week, when park officials evicted him.

"He was as close to nature as any camper I'd ever seen," says David Christie, director of the San Mateo County Department of Parks and Recreation, which oversees the mountain. "But we allow campers only in designated areas. We had no choice. He broke the law."

Park rangers had known about Taylor for years but looked the other way, until a Brisbane city councilman hiking in the area noticed signs of makeshift civilization. He complained, and Christie says he was forced to post Taylor's eviction notice.

Taylor is undecided about where to go. He has hauled down the mountain all his belongings—his musical instruments, his sleeping bag, his books—and intends to relocate farther from civilization.

"They say I'm marring the area, but for the seven years I've been here, no one said I hurt the mountain," Taylor says, "I've blended in. This is my home."

Before Taylor climbed the mountain, he found himself the victim of teacher burnout. "The kids test your mettle," he says with a smile. Westborough teacher

Joe Neynaben remembers Taylor as "gentle and friendly, always interested in his kids."

Neynaben says the pressures of everyday life were more than Taylor wanted. "He decided he had enough money to live on, so he quit his job and started living the way he wanted to live."

Taylor found a spot both remote and practical—a steep, wooded area three-fourths of a mile up the mountain. The first few months, he retained the appetites of city life. He hauled up eggs and bacon, apples and oranges. The eggs broke and the bacon attracted bugs. The apples and oranges were too bulky to carry.

So, he simplified his diet: brown rice and rolled oats, supplemented with wild mustard greens, mushrooms, miner's lettuce and watercress.

Gradually, Taylor got mountain living down to a science. He laid a rock floor that served as a sleeping platform. His kitchen was a hut of scrap tin and canvas. He made a stove by wedging molded pieces of metal against a boulder. He hid his encampment within a grove of native scrub oak trees.

Occasionally, Taylor would make repairs to the house he owns in San Francisco, collect his rent and check his savings, including a money-market fund. Frequently he'd walk to church services in San Francisco.

Mountain life, though it may sound idyllic, had its responsibilities. "During the winter months, there was nothing certain. Everything was crucial; everything had to be done," he says. Firewood had to be collected and meticulously stored. Rainwater drains had to be in order. Repairs had to be made.

When his work was done, Taylor read and meditated. He made friends with butterflies, blue jays and gray foxes. His favorite activity, though, was sitting still.

"It was the most important part of my life up there," he says, pointing to the mountain that rises off Guadalupe Canyon Parkway in Brisbane.

"It's easier to sit still than to get your mind still. But if you can get no thoughts for five minutes, then you'll feel so sweet. You'll never let go. It's a sweeter feeling than any drug."

Last year park rangers posted an eviction notice on Taylor's campsite, based on the county regulation prohibiting camping in undesignated areas.

But David Christie relented when his department received hundreds of letters from Taylor's supporters.

"I told our rangers not to cause a controversy. We thought he would move on," he says.

Last month, Brisbane City Councilman Fred Smith filed a complaint against Taylor. While hiking on the mountain, Smith said in his complaint, "I felt as if I was trespassing on someone's homestead."

Smith called Taylor a "squatter" and demanded that "swift and vigorous action" be taken to remove the "trespasser."

Christie had no choice. Rangers dismantled Taylor's home last week, while

Taylor sat on a boulder watching silently.

"I sympathize with Dwight, but a county or state park just isn't appropriate for him," Christie says.

Smith said Friday he remains convinced that Taylor should go. "The park is to preserve the natural environment, not the human environment. I don't see why Taylor is so special."

Since Taylor's eviction, Christie has received at least 28 letters of protest. But Christie says his rangers will continue to patrol the area for overnight campers.

Throughout his years on the mountain, Taylor welcomed visitors, some of whom called him the "people's ranger." He took hikers through his wilds, showing off the land like a proud father.

Joe Neynaber, who teaches science, occasionally led his students on field trips to see Taylor and his natural home. "He was a living textbook of the mountain," Neynaber said.

David Schooley, who heads a group called Bay Area Mountain Watch, remembers meeting Taylor on a hike. "It was a foggy day, and there he was jumping from rock to rock like he was king of the forest."

"I had grown to love that place," Taylor says, "Especially the colors. There is a time every day when the rosiness of dusk matches the rosy tint of the rocks, when the white water cascades down the ravine."

Taylor says that in the city his mind would fill with the buzzing sound of a tape player, with events and conversations played garbled and fast-forward.

After the first month on the mountain, Taylor says, he experienced a soothing sense of solitude. "I felt lonely from time to time, but it never was a bad feeling. You get an emotional charge from living next to trees," he says.

Taylor says he will miss the lizards, "who really got to know me," and a jay "who had chosen me as his very own. It isn't that I don't like people. I just came to the discovery one day that I crave solitude more. After two or three days, time becomes liquid."

San Jose Mercury News, July 23, 1991

WRITING THE STORY

I didn't have a reporter's notebook with me that day at the park, but I did have a pen. After Taylor and I started talking, I started scribbling notes on napkins I had stuffed in my knapsack. I was uncertain whether Taylor sought me out because he figured I had food, because he was lonely and wanted to talk, or because he wanted to drum up support for his cause. Whichever it was, Taylor struck the jackpot with me. I was moved by his transformation from junior high teacher to urban mountain man. At first, I didn't believe his story, so I asked him for names of fellow teachers at his old junior high school, as well as the county officials who were trying to evict him from his mountain home.

Taylor had done what millions of urban dwellers only dream about. He had given up his day job to live out a fantasy. Granted, few would want to live the way Taylor lived, but that wasn't the point. He epitomized what was in the hearts of millions of urban dwellers. Here was a story about why a seemingly reasonable man had chosen to alter his life in a most radical way.

I began the piece with Taylor's lovely epiphany of what took place that summer night eight years earlier when he rolled out his sleeping bag in his backyard. In the following grafs, I broadened the piece to put Taylor's new life in perspective, and that's why I cited Davy Crockett and Grizzly Adams. Granted, those comparisons are cheesy, but by the fifth graf, it's make or break time. The story has got to hook readers by then—or all my work would be for naught. Taylor, damnit, had an amazing story to tell, and my job was to tell it in the most tantalizing way I could. I owed that much to Taylor, as to readers.

After I got the basic outline of his story, I worked the piece from home. I bid Taylor good-bye and wished him luck. I told him that I hoped a newspaper story I could write would help him. On Monday, I called and interviewed the county bureaucrat who said he had been forced to bust Taylor. David Christie came across as humane as any public official could possibly sound. I called Taylor's old school and interviewed a fellow teacher who remembered him.

Then I wove my napkin notes into the narrative about how Taylor had set up his home. I wanted to make sure that I didn't make his life sound too idyllic, too much like a single-man's version of the Swiss Family Robinson. I knew I was romanticizing Taylor and what he had done, but I wanted to make sure the story reflected the realities of his squatter status. Taylor talked in a lyrical way about his companions—the butterflies, blue jays and gray foxes. His quotes might or might not have deflected reader inference that he was off his rocker, and that's just how I want them to read. The reader would have to infer whether Taylor was a modern-day Henry Thoreau or a budding Theodore Kaczynski.

Then it was off to more officialdom and the city councilman who upset Taylor's hideaway and instructed Christie to oust the mountain man. I chose to ease out of the piece with one of Taylor's best quotes for the clincher. There was a shade of doubt of Taylor's rationality as I let him talk, particularly when said he was going to miss all his friends, especially the lizards. Taylor's final quote— about life turning into liquid (and remember, he says, he did not take drugs)—fits in with the story I was weaving. That's the impression I wanted to leave with the readers, so it's up to them to render the final verdict.

EPILOGUE

Shortly after my story appeared, Dwight Taylor was evicted from his makeshift home near San Bruno Mountain. He moved to a nearby canyon, where he set up another rustic wilderness home. Word of Taylor's ecological habitats spread, and the elementary school teachers often would take their students on environmental tours that included visits to Taylor's home. On one such tour, a second-grade teacher hiking with her Brisbane, California, elementary school students met Taylor, and immediately sparks flew back and forth. Taylor and the teacher started dating. The teacher started spending afternoons, then evenings, at Taylor's rustic home. Eventually, Taylor and the teacher were married. Today they live (in a house) in the beach community of Pacifica with 10 cats. Taylor spends most of his days organic gardening.

ASSIGNMENTS

1) Find out whether there are squatters in your regional parks. Talk to hikers, park personnel and campers. Write about rules against long-term camping, and whether officials ignore such regulations to accommodate rustic residents.

2) Talk to former urban dwellers who gave up wealth and material success to lead simpler lives elsewhere. Write about how they planned their exoduses and what their new lives brought.

3) Interview rural residents who leave the countryside for the big city. Find out what brought them to urban life. Focus your story on the non-economic issues that contributed to their decision to leave rural America. In addition to jobs, lifestyle and family, what factors led them to move to the congested city?

18

SNEAKING SCRIPTURE INTO THE SPOTLIGHT

Anyone vaguely familiar with sports, television and celebrity during the 1980s probably remembers the name Rollen Stewart. If, by chance, the name has slipped from memory, then Stewart's indelible image could not. Stewart, also known as Rainbow Man, Rainbow Head, Rock-N-Rollen, and the "John 3:16 guy," used to show up every weekend at nationally televised sporting events, wearing a rainbow-colored Afro wig and holding up a hand-painted placard or bed sheet that read "John 3:16."

Stewart was a self-styled, New Age missionary who said his God-mandated purpose in life was bringing the New Testament's message to the masses. With religious zeal, Stewart angled and elbowed his way into prime locations in stadiums, and just as television cameras were panning the crowd, he would pop up smiling, banner in hand. For baseball games, Stewart would position himself behind home plate; for football games, he'd make his way behind the goalpost uprights.

Stewart was a kind of bottom-up media maven. His image appeared nonstop everywhere America looked. Although sporting events were his main calling, Stewart also dropped in on Ronald Reagan's inauguration, the Academy Awards, and the wedding of Prince Charles and Diana Spencer. Stewart bedeviled network executives and camera operators who did everything to avoid beaming his image to tens of millions of viewers each week.

Who was Stewart and what made him tick? How'd he plan his strategic attacks every week? Who financed him?

Short of shadowing Stewart around the country and then waylaying him at a stadium one weekend, I needed a conduit, someone who knew Stewart and could put me in touch with him. While at *The Dallas Morning News*, I had written a story on the resurgent fundamentalist movement known as creationism. I kept the business card of a pastor I had interviewed. On a lark, I called the pastor and asked whether he knew Stewart.

The pastor didn't, but said he could put me in contact with people who did. Thus began two weeks of elaborate third-party negotiations that ultimately led to a pay phone in Houston. I was to call Stewart at the pay phone at a predetermined hour. But when I called, no one answered. I called back the intermediaries the Dallas pastor had put me in touch with, and soon got another phone number, this one at a rest stop on Highway 101 in Santa Maria, California. This time when I called, Stewart answered and we talked for more than an hour. I could hear cars whizzing by in the background. Over the next three weeks, Stewart and I connected for a total of six hours from pay phones in New York, Miami and Seattle.

Sneaking Scripture Into the Spotlight

The vision came in a Technicolor dream a decade ago.

Rollen Stewart's hair turned the color of a tutti-frutti rainbow. The 31-year-old man imagined himself an international celebrity, showing up at sporting events, beauty pageants, parades around the world.

His image would be beamed to millions. He would have instant recognition. He would have an agent.

Stewart would appear on Budweiser television commercials. He would drop in at the Royal Wedding, Ronald Reagan's inauguration, the Kentucky Derby, the Indianapolis 500, the Academy Awards.

His character would be featured on "Saturday Night Live," on "St. Elsewhere," on "The Tonight Show." Cartoonist Charles Schulz would draw Stewart alongside Charlie Brown.

It was a heady dream. It came true.

Stewart, now 41, is the man who shows up at sports stadiums wearing a rainbow-colored fright wig, who holds a banner spray-painted with cryptic messages—"Eph. 2:8,9" or "John 3:16."

"Eph. 2:8,9" is not a coded football play to be run in the second quarter with eight minutes, nine seconds left. Nor is "John 3:16" a reference to John Madden's weight.

Stewart's favorite and most frequently flashed message, John 3:16, is from Chapter 3, Verse 16 of the Gospel of John: "For God so loved the world that he gave his only Son, that whoever believeth in him should not perish, but have everlasting life." Similarly, Eph. 2:8,9 refers to Ephesians, Chapter 2, Verses 8,9.

Stewart received a "call from the Lord" in a motel room in Pasadena six years ago, just hours after Super Bowl XIV had ended. While on his knees, he says he accepted a mission that would give new purpose to his life. Already known as a sports gadfly, Stewart became a cheerleader for Christ.

Since then, he has appeared at so many televised events that he's lost count. Highlights of his career include:

- Being arrested during both the 1980 Olympic Games in Moscow and the 1984 Olympic Games in Sarajevo, Yugoslavia, for displaying religious banners made of bed sheets.

- Showing up during every World Series, Super Bowl, NBA Championship Series, NCAA title basketball game, and most major PGA golf tournaments since 1977.

- Getting camera time at both the Ariel Sharon and William Westmoreland libel trials in New York City in 1984.

- Maneuvering appearances at four nationally televised college football bowl games in 1983—in Atlanta, Houston, Dallas and New Orleans—all within a 24-hour period.

- Attending 31 of the 52 games at the 1986 World Cup Soccer Championship in Mexico City.

Stewart, known as "Rainbow Man," "Rainbow Head" and "Rock-N-Rollen," has become an international performance artist. "I'm probably the most famous person in the world who no one knows anything about," Stewart said recently from a pay phone along Highway 101 in Santa Maria.

He and his bride of two months, Elsie, were en route from last Sunday's Los Angeles Rams game in Anaheim as part of a Western swing that included appearances at football, basketball and hockey games every three or four days.

Not bad for someone who hates sports.

"I don't care who wins or even who plays," Stewart says.

As with most events they attend, he and Elsie left Anaheim Stadium Sunday evening without knowing which team won. "I really despise the games I go to. They're all greed-oriented," he says.

Stewart feels the same way about TV. "I realize now that television is a tool of Satan. I never watch TV unless it's to figure out my own strategy so that I can appear on it."

Before his conversion, he wore his trademark wig for one reason: to attract attention so that he could break into commercials and become independently wealthy.

"It was a calculated career move to make money," Stewart says. "I was trying to make a buck. I thought that by wearing the wig and acting crazy I could make a lot of money promoting products."

Stewart's agent, Reg Hamman, says his client used the wig and the media to create a national character. "He saw the money potential, the fame, the power."

At that point, the life of Rollen Stewart—a former linen salesman, drag-car racer and rancher—revolved around sex, drugs, disco dancing and partying. He used to call himself "a smoker and joker," someone who "loved to drool at the cheerleaders."

But after his conversion, he returned to his home in Cle Elum, Wash., and sold his 76-acre ranch. For the past six years, he has used the money to finance his evangelist campaign.

Now, with his life savings almost depleted, Stewart and Elsie crisscross the nation, driving 60,000 miles a year. They live on a $600-a-month budget, which covers food and tickets, as well as the loan payment, insurance and gas for their 1986 Toyota. They avoid motels, opting to sleep in the back of the van.

Their diet consists of vegetables, orange juice and nuts. They allot themselves $6 a day for food—which usually includes two salads at fast-food restaurants.

Stewart says that almost every religious sign carried at a major sporting event is the work of either himself or Elsie; Bill King, an associate Stewart met in Dallas while working the 1984 Republican National Convention; or a Los Angeles evangelist who calls himself Bob Bible.

"I'd say that 99 percent of the time, they're holding the bed sheets," says Hamman, who owns an Arkansas public relations firm, and who edits a nationally distributed newsletter about Rock-N-Rollen. "In the other 1 percent, it's someone else who has told us in advance."

The group does have its imitators. At a recent 49ers game in Candlestick Park, there were signs that said "Fred 3:16," "Raoul 3:16" and "Al 3:16."

Each week, Stewart and his wife decide which events to attend, based on which contests will generate the largest television audience.

They read *TV Guide* on Monday and *USA Today* on Friday. *TV Guide* gives them the coming week's events; *USA Today* tells them the size of the events' televised markets.

But how does Stewart manage to get such good seats?

He generally buys the cheapest tickets he can find from scalpers outside the stadium on the day of the event.

He and Elsie fold the banner and squish the wig, hiding them under their clothes. They take along duct tape and a collapsible curtain rod from which the banner is hung.

Once the pair gets in, they locate empty front-row seats and sneak down after the game begins.

Stewart carries a Sony Watchman TV to figure out where the network cameras are located and how tight the camera angles are.

Stewart manages to foil network camera operators by securing a strategic seat, donning the rainbow wig, and then flashing his evangelical message.

For football games, he usually tries for front-row seats in the end zone. That way, after a touchdown, there's the replay of the pass or run, as well as a camera shot of the extra-point attempt—which means he and his message may be shown three times.

Lopsided scores upset him. "I pray for tight games, extra innings, double overtimes, extra holes on golf matches," he says. "Anything that makes people not turn the channel."

Network executives admit their crews try to shoot around Rock-N-Rollen. "We don't zoom in on him, but if we catch him in the camera range, there's nothing we can do," says Pam Haslam, director of communications for CBS.

"We do what we can to avoid him, but it's not always easy," says Irv Brodsky, public relations director at ABC Sports. "We aren't going to miss a winning touchdown just because he's there."

Once past the ushers and in front of the cameras, the next obstacle is the stadium security guards. Stewart is usually thrown out of stadiums after flashing the banner several times. But as long as the message gets on television, he says he doesn't care.

Candlestick Park, he says, is among the least sympathetic to his mission. As soon as the security guards there see him pulling out a banner, Stewart says he is escorted out of the park. The reasons include obstructing spectators' views and interfering with play of the game.

The most cooperative venues are Pittsburgh's Three Rivers Stadium and St. Louis' Busch Memorial Stadium.

In fact, it was in St. Louis last Oct. 2, three days after the Dallas Cowboys beat the Cardinals in a nationally televised game, that Stewart married Elsie Hockridge, 36, another itinerant evangelist.

Elsie's first assignment for Stewart had been in 1985 in Lakeland, Fla., where she carried a John 3:16 banner during the 1985 Miss USA Pageant.

The two occasionally traveled together in a car supplied by the New Testament Church of Williamsburg, Va., but when reports got back of that arrangement, church elders "thought that Elsie and I were living in sin, and they called back the car," says Stewart, who denies the accusation.

The marriage is Stewart's second, Elsie's first. His first ended in divorce in 1968, when he worked selling housewares and linen for a Seattle department store.

A drag and stock-car racer, Stewart next went into business for himself starting up two automotive-supply stores near Seattle.

In less than a year, he says, his mother perished in a house fire and his sister was murdered. "I became disenchanted with the business world. I am a quiet, shy, introverted person. I wanted to move away, drop out and be a hermit."

Stewart bought the ranch in Cle Elum, population 1,800, east of the Cascade Mountains, and tried for a while to be a gentleman farmer.

Then on Jan. 30, 1976, came the Technicolor dream.

He bought the zany multicolored wig, grew a 36-inch moustache and started showing up regularly at the SuperSonics basketball games in the Seattle Coliseum. Management was so taken with Stewart's ability as a mascot that they allowed him into the games free.

He attended other events, including the 1977 World Series in New York and Los Angeles, where he sat directly behind home plate.

Stewart had his strategy carefully mapped out. "I wanted to join the Screen Actors Guild and do television commercials," he says. "I figured with millions of people watching, someone would call me with a contract."

Someone did: an advertising executive from D'Arcy, McManus, the agency representing Anheuser-Busch. In the spring of 1978, Stewart was hired to stand and smile in the Los Angeles Coliseum for a Budweiser commercial.

The commercial ran for two years. Stewart says he earned about $12,000 per year from the spot.

His life was cushy for the next few years, but he felt—so the cliché goes—empty. "The Hollywood high started to get to me," he says.

Then came his conversion while watching Dr. Charles Taylor, a television minister who hosts "Today in Bible Prophecy."

Stewart promptly sold his ranch, turning the $50,000 he got for it into silver coins, which he hid and buried in different places because he doesn't trust banks.

He expanded his traveling schedule and now is gone about 50 weeks of the year. Almost all of his money is gone, and apart from fans who slip him dollar bills, he says there's not much money left to continue his campaign.

While his scripture-bearing image has saturated the media, he receives no remuneration when actors impersonate him on television shows.

He is frequently mentioned and mimicked on late-night TV programs. On Oct. 1, 1986, the Rock-N-Rollen character was featured in an episode of "St. Elsewhere."

John Tinker, the writer who devised the "St. Elsewhere" subplot, says the frizzy-haired character with the John 3:16 sign was included in the script because, "He shows up everywhere else, why not in the waiting area of the emergency room at the St. Elsewhere hospital?"

Stewart has created controversy in his mission—and not just from fans who sit behind him, whose views are occasionally blocked by his sign.

John White, first vice president of the National Association of Evangelicals, says he doesn't approve of Stewart's methods.

"The significance of Christianity is more than a flash on a television screen. It tends to cheapen and truncate the message of Christianity," says White, professor of biblical studies at Geneva College in Beaver Falls, Pa.

Stewart is not to be deterred. He says his subliminal advertising works. "People look up the scripture cited on the banners weeks after they first see it on television."

He is tired, though, of all the travel. He hopes to take a lesser role in his mission by the end of 1987.

"I'm getting older and burned out. We need younger zealots," he says.

In the meantime, Stewart plans to be on the road through the World Series next fall, outfoxing television camera operators and stadium security officers.

"It's a joy to get on television and be used by the media."

San Jose Mercury News, December 13, 1987

WRITING THE STORY

The lede to the piece—the first six grafs—works as a stanza, neatly introducing Stewart to the reader, and laying out his resume of credits. During each of my interviews with Stewart, I was stuck with disconnections in his life. I weave these disconnects throughout the story. Stewart's first quote is an example: He hates sports. Then we learn that Stewart thinks TV is a "tool of Satan," yet it is a tool that Stewart embraces with glee.

The piece is Stewart's roller-coaster rags-to-wigs story. Stewart certainly sounds like a con man, but most comers in Hollywood would sound the same. Stewart talks the talk. His quotes come out practiced, just as anyone who works the media: "a smoker and a joker," someone who "loved to drool at the cheerleaders."

After writing about Stewart's conversion to Jesus, I delve into the details of his crusade: How exactly he and his wife, Elsie, are able to pull off their missionary capers every week. Much of the story is a behind-the-scene look at Stewart's guerrilla strategy. Throughout, he remains devoted to his cause, explaining, for example, why he hates lopsided scores and prefers football stadiums in Pittsburgh and St. Louis. Peppered throughout are comments from his nemeses, heathen executives from television networks.

Stewart's meager financial status adds to the story, as do comments from a variety of sources, including the Hollywood writer who folded Stewart's character into a plot on the television show, "St. Elsewhere," and John White, an evangelical leader who doesn't approve of Stewart's methods.

EPILOGUE

I never met Stewart, but grew to appreciate the intensity of his mission over the course of our interviews. The piece would have fared better if I could have accompanied Stewart as he delayed security guards or as he traveled cross-country, living out of his car. Deadlines on other stories, though, as well as Stewart's unpredictable, hectic schedule, conspired against up-close reporting. But for what it is, a series of seat-of-your-pants phoners, buttressed with detailed background reporting, the story is a snapshot of an icon of our times. Even without a face-to-face interview and no personal observation of Stewart in action, there was something immensely likable about him. Perhaps if I had met him, my perceptions would have been different. Perhaps *because* I never met him, I found myself impressed with his verve and intensity.

As often is the case, the power of Stewart's message ultimately became less important than the power of his ego. His wife, Elsie, left him shortly after the couple married, saying Stewart had choked her because she held up a sign in the wrong place during a World Series game. By the late 1980s, Stewart's car had been totaled and his money had run out. He found himself abandoned by the zealots who had once so embraced him. Stewart also had been virtually shut out of the media spotlight by television technicians and stadium personnel now savvy to his tactics.

By the early 1990s, Stewart had reached his lowest point: homeless in Los Angeles. His pranks, though, soon began escalating from harmless to potentially dangerous. In 1991, he was charged with detonating four stink bombs in Orange County: at the Crystal Cathedral, a Christian bookstore, a Christian broadcasting studio, and the offices of the Orange County *Register*. Later that year, he was detained for setting off an air horn and smoke bombs at the Master's Golf Tournament just as Jack Nicklaus was about to putt on the sixteenth green. He threw skunk entrails into the audience at The American Music Awards, saying to police that he wanted to show everyone that "God thinks this stinks."

A darker, psychotic side of Stewart also began to take hold. Police said Stewart took steps to assassinate then-presidential candidate Bill Clinton while in Los Angeles, but was thwarted by heavy security. Stewart's denouement came in 1992, when he held a hotel maid hostage at gunpoint, leading to a nine-hour standoff with Los Angeles police. Stewart said he would release the woman only if he were granted a televised press conference to call attention to his prophecy that the world would end in six days.

On July 13, 1993, Stewart was found guilty in Los Angeles Superior Court and sentenced to three concurrent life prison terms. At his sentencing, sheriff's deputies wrestled Stewart to the floor when he refused to refrain from screaming that the world would soon end in a nuclear holocaust. He currently is an inmate at the California Men's Colony in San Luis Obispo.

ASSIGNMENTS

1) Interview a clergyperson whose sermons are aired on television. In choosing whom to write about, select someone who has ties to your community— currently or historically. Research all you can on the preacher, talking to allies and adversaries, reading clippings, searching the Internet. Write a compelling story on the man or woman's rise from bricks-and-mortar congregation to sanctuary of the airwaves.

2) Familiarize yourself with a powerful local church or synagogue. Find out what role this house of worship plays in your community in terms of political and economic power. Determine the extent and value of its land holdings,

as well as any plans for expansion. Talk to the leaders as well as current and former members to determine the organization's strategies to further its clout and influence.

3) With their consent, accompany followers of either The Church of Latter Day Saints or Jehovah Witnesses as they attempt to proselytize non-believers. Spend a day with disciples on their rounds. Write about their beliefs and missionary activities, as well as the reactions they receive.

EXTRAORDINARY CIRCUMSTANCES

19

18 YEARS ON A
LONG, BOOZY ROAD

Rounding the corner to my cubicle in the windowless press office of the Van Nuys Courthouse, I saw a deputy district attorney wheeling a chrome cart, stacked precariously high with court folders.

"Looks like you're gonna be busy today," I said.

"No kidding."

"What cases are they?"

"You mean, what *case* is this?

"One case?"

"Yeah. Crazy, repeat drunk driver—but it's just a misdemeanor. You probably got better things to write about."

I stopped in my tracks. "All that's *one* drunk driver?"

"Yep."

I paused. "Mind if I take a look?"

Thus was my introduction to the Gary Christopher story. I had the amazing story all to myself. No other media bit at the story—at first.

18 Years on a Long, Boozy Road

At 2 a.m. on March 28, police officers stopped a black Camaro that had been speeding and weaving along Hollywood Boulevard without headlights. The driver's face was flushed, his eyes bloodshot. Asked to touch his nose, he missed.

"He was close to being comatose," officer Wayne DeBord recalled. "Without a doubt he was the drunkest driver I've ever seen."

Within six months the driver would earn another distinction.

Gary Lin Christopher, a 38-year-old hot tub salesman from Encino with a penchant for fast cars and strong screwdrivers, would receive what apparently is the longest U.S. jail sentence for drunk driving.

For convictions stemming from the incident on Hollywood Boulevard and three other drunk-driving arrests the previous six weeks, Christopher was sentenced to nine years, 220 days in jail.

None of the incidents involved injury or damage to property. But the legal proceedings last month resembled those for a murderer. Municipal Court Judge Suzanne Person set Christopher's bail at $500,000. The prosecutor asked to be notified immediately if he was released.

At a time of increasing public attention to the problem of drunk driving, Gary Christopher's case had pushed participants in the criminal justice system past their point of tolerance. A stack of court records shows why: Over an 18-year period, this San Fernando Valley man had foiled every type of official effort to stop his drunk driving. Fines, jail, license suspension, alcoholism treatment—none had worked.

To City Attorney Ira Reiner and others, the case was an embodiment of the frustrations posed by drunk drivers, who account for about 300 arrests each day in Los Angeles County. "There are a lot of Gary Christophers on the road," Reiner said. "What is unusual about him is that he has been caught so often."

Christopher's record began to emerge that night in Hollywood as soon as the police punched his name into their squad-car computer. Since 1966, Christopher had been convicted 27 times of driving while intoxicated.

Although Christopher occasionally had been fined small amounts or allowed to enter alcoholic rehabilitation programs, he was no stranger to jail, having served more than three years in California and Texas institutions.

"I should be punished," Christopher says. "I know that."

But Christopher, a quiet man with a cropped gray mustache, was unprepared for the sentence he was handed Sept. 10. Along with his wife, his lawyer and a psychiatrist hired by the defense, he had hoped for commitment to a therapy program. They recounted the life story Christopher had repeatedly told policemen, probation officers and others: how he became an alcoholic after an accident cost him three fingers and his life's dream of becoming a professional bowler.

"What are they going to do when my sentence is up and I'm back on the road again?" Christopher asked a few days ago, dressed in blue prison overalls at the Los Angeles County Jail, where he is being held while he appeals his latest conviction. "Are they just going to put me back in here each time? Are they going to do that for all drunk drivers? I'm sick. I need treatment."

Christopher's attorney portrays his client as a political prisoner of sorts, a victim of a national frenetic crusade against drunk driving.

"Christopher is behind bars based not on what he has done, but what he may do in the future," defense lawyer Leonard Chaitin said. "He hasn't hurt anyone. He hasn't committed a crime commensurate with the punishment. His sentence is more than some people serve for murder."

Although Christopher has never been convicted of injuring another person, twice this year he has come close, according to police reports.

On Feb. 1 he was arrested after he barely missed colliding with an ambulance on the Harbor Freeway. His last arrest, on July 27 in Marina del Rey, stemmed from a hit-and-run accident that sent a 23-year-old woman to a hospital for treatment of bruises, cuts and a loss of hearing. He has not come to trial in that case.

Christopher says he is aware of the harm that drunk drivers can inflict. A decade ago, an accident caused by a drunk driver damaged the spine of the woman who eventually became his wife. When the woman went looking for a hot tub to ease the pain, Christopher was the salesman sent to her home. Four weeks later they were married.

With a $250,000 settlement from the accident, Brenda Christopher bought a house in Encino. In the ensuing years her husband used it as a security bond for bail release after his drunk-driving arrests.

Brenda Christopher says she still hurts when she walks; the spinal injury caused by a drunk driver "has ruined my life." But she has stood by her husband.

"Just this one time, let there be another chance," she wrote to a judge two years ago. "I'll put my life on the line as a security that my husband will never appear in your court or any other court again. All I can give you is my word."

That pledge was no more successful than the fines, jail and treatments. Christopher's release was followed quickly by the latest flurry of arrests.

The son of a retired army officer, Gary Christopher was born in Junction City, Kan., and was reared in Texas, Montana, Japan and Germany. His family moved to Southern California in 1960. Four years later, Christopher graduated from Granada Hills High School. He attended Pierce College in Woodland Hills irregularly for five semesters before dropping out.

Christopher has always traced his problems to the summer of 1965, when he worked as a punch press operator for Federal Stamping Co. in North Hollywood.

A machine accident ripped three fingers from his right hand.

Christopher later told probation officers that he was devastated by the realization that he would never be able to join the professional bowlers circuit. The night after the bandages were removed from his hand, he said, he became intoxicated for the first time.

"What got me on the road of drinking was the loss of my fingers," Christopher said last week. "I can cope with it for a period of time, then I can't any longer."

Area bowlers don't remember him as a potential star. "I know all the top bowlers, and Christopher wasn't one of them," said Walter Bloch, president of Los Angeles-based Professional Coast Bowlers. Officials for the Professional Bowlers Association and Professional Coast Bowlers say Christopher never applied for membership.

But, according to his mother, "What he wanted most was to make it as a pro bowler. That's all he ever talked about." The trophies he won as a younger man are on a bookshelf in the Encino house she shares with Brenda. To this day, as Christopher talks, he shields his damaged right hand.

His first drunk-driving arrest came in Los Angeles, 17 months after the loss of his fingers. In 1969, Christopher moved to Canyon, Texas, where he enrolled at West Texas State University. By May he was arrested for drunk driving and by fall he had been placed on academic suspension, according to the university's registrar. He left the school in 1971.

In the next decade, convictions led to widely varying fines and sentences. He got off once with a $92 fine, another time with probation. Jail terms ranged from one day to 358 days.

By 1979 his driver's license had been suspended five times. When he did not get his license back legally, he used aliases to get new ones in Texas and California, according to charges filed in both states.

City Attorney Reiner called Christopher's the worst drunk-driving record he has encountered. But, he added, "People like Christopher ... aren't rare."

"Hard-core alcoholics get up, they get drunk and they go to sleep," Reiner said. "These kinds of people pick up a lot of DUIs (driving under the influence), maybe six or seven. But for someone to pick up 27, that is exceedingly rare. ... Drunk drivers rarely get caught. Someone who has been convicted 27 times has probably been driving under the influence almost every day he's ever been on the road."

Christopher insisted that he does not recall the details of his drinking. "It's a complete blank to me," he said.

Brenda Christopher said that her husband never drinks at home, pursuing his habit alone in bars in the late evening, ordering screwdrivers. He would stagger back to his car, she said, sometimes sleeping in the vehicle before driving home.

Brenda Christopher said that when her husband would not return home when expected, she would "start calling all the jails and morgues in the area to see if he was there."

When Christopher telephoned her from a police station after being arrested, she said, "I'd just be glad it was Gary calling, not some police officer telling me he was dead from a car accident."

Christopher at times earned a living as a loan consultant and a supervisor at a vending machine company. According to documents filed with the court, he would sometimes earn more than $3,000 a month as a salesman of hot tubs. He drove a succession of expensive, sporty coupes—a Porsche, a Corvette, the Camaro.

Since 1970, Christopher has undergone a series of court-ordered counseling programs. The court record lists him as having attended Alcoholic Anonymous meetings, receiving treatment from at least two psychiatrists and spending more than 75 hours at a Van Nuys alcohol program called The High Road.

In 1979, a physician prescribed the drug Antabuse, which makes the user ill if alcohol is ingested. The medication was administered by Christopher's wife without official monitoring, however, and its effect was short-lived.

In Christopher's latest case, defense psychiatrist Elizabeth Anne Swann, who is on the UCLA medical faculty, recommended that he be sent to a locked psychiatric facility. Her recommendation was not taken seriously by prosecutors.

"You finally reach the point when you think this man cannot be rehabilitated, and he has to be punished for his conduct," said Deputy City Attorney Kevin Young, who prosecuted Christopher. "We've given him chances to reform, and he continues to drive drunk."

Judge Person evidently agreed. The sentence she gave Christopher was the maximum for the charges he faced for his four arrests early this year: four counts of driving under the influence and four counts of driving with a suspended license. He also was ordered to serve additional time for a past conviction.

Reiner called the sentence the toughest ever for drunk driving, a statement echoed by Robert Reeder, a consultant to the American Bar Association on driving issues. "It's certainly the longest term we've ever heard about," Reeder said. Four-time drunk-driving offenders typically serve 180 days in jail, an official of the Los Angeles Municipal Court said.

Even with time off for good behavior, Christopher cannot be freed before January 1991, according to Neil Rincover, a spokesman for the city attorney's office.

Besides the stiff sentence, Person set Christopher's bond, pending appeal, at $500,000, the second highest bail ever imposed in Los Angeles County for a misdemeanor. (The highest was in a case of a flagrant slumlord.)

Late last month, Christopher was back in court, appealing unsuccessfully for a reduction of the bail before Los Angeles Superior Court Judge James N. Reese.

"Mr. Christopher is being held on preventive detention, which is inconsistent with American democracy," said defense attorney Chaitin, who asked that bail be reduced to $40,000 or less. "This excessive appeal bond goes against years of American justice. It is higher than for most serious felonies."

Looking downcast throughout the 50-minute hearing, Christopher covered the right side of his face to a television camera. He wore sneakers, jeans and a Hawaiian shirt and awkwardly shifted position in a straight-backed chair. When the judge refused to reduce his bail, he winced.

Tricia Higgins, a Mothers Against Drunk Driving representative who attended the hearing, applauded the sentence and bond. "It's just luck that Christopher hasn't hurt anyone yet," she said. "He's a time bomb ready to go off."

At first, Christopher was embarrassed and reluctant to discuss his case. In recent days, however, he has become angry. From behind bulletproof glass in the county jail, Christopher complained that he had been singled out for special punishment.

Christopher speculated that his sentence "would have been the same if I had told Person that I had a .357 Magnum and then she convicted me of robbing a bank."

"I don't know why I drink," he said. "If I knew, I wouldn't be here now. Go ask 50 alcoholics why they drink. They don't know. ... Being locked behind bars isn't going to help me. I'm an alcoholic, and I need counseling."

Both sides agreed that his drinking and driving are likely to resume when he is released.

"We know that as soon as he's out, he'll probably be out and drunk the same afternoon, and he might kill someone," Reiner said. "At least we're protecting ourselves while he's in jail."

"Putting him in jail isn't going to stop his problem," Brenda Christopher said. "It's failed in the past. As soon as he gets out, he'll start all over again. He's not a skid-row Ripple wino. This is a serious man with a medical problem that needs correcting," she said.

When Christopher went to jail this time, his wife said that she worried he might not make it out and that he talked about suicide.

After visiting her husband in jail Wednesday, however, Brenda Christopher said his spirits had improved. "He's not happy, but if he has to do the time, he'll do it."

Los Angeles Times, October 4, 1984

WRITING THE STORY

Detail works in the lede (black Camaro, speeding and weaving along Hollywood Boulevard, without headlights, flushed face, bloodshot eyes). The last sentence in the lede, though, is what sells the story. In seven words, the reader understands exactly how plastered Gary Christopher was that night.

The arresting officer corroborates with a solid, convincing quote, followed by a set-up transition that leads to the story's nut graf.

The details of Christopher's life fall into my lap. Is there any way I could possibly bury Christopher's profession—hot tub salesman? That, coupled with "a penchant for fast cars and strong screwdrivers," leads to the reason for the story—that Christopher is about to set his dubious record. Notice the wiggle word, "apparently." I need that, even though, with a deadline looming, I talk to as many authorities as possible (cited later in the piece).

What amazed me in covering this story is reflected in how the legal establishment regarded Christopher. That the judge set bail at $500,000 was outrageous to me; her action demanded that in the story I make the comparison between a murderer and an alcoholic.

I broaden the piece in subsequent paragraphs, and extract from an hour-long interview with City Attorney Ira Reiner the one quote that grabbed me: "There are a lot of Gary Christophers on the road. What is unusual about him is that he has been caught so often."

Then, it's Christopher's turn. His words have a poignant, fatalistic ring: "Are they just going to put me back in here each time? ... I'm sick. I need treatment."

Christopher's bizarre story takes on a bizarre twist when he blames his alcoholism on the industrial accident that ripped off three fingers from his right hand, thereby ending his dreams of becoming a professional bowler.

But, folks, there's more.

In reading voluminous police reports and court records, as well as interviewing Christopher's wife, the story gets stranger. Brenda Christopher tells me she was almost paralyzed when an automobile—driven by a drunk driver—broadsided her car. As therapeutic treatment for her spinal condition caused by the collision, she wants to buy a hot tub. Guess who comes knocking at her door?

A month later the couple gets married. With the settlement from the drunk-driving accident, Brenda Christopher buys a house—the same house that her husband would later use as collateral to get out of jail each time he is arrested for drunk driving.

I am not making this up.

Although Brenda Christopher tells me during our interview that her spinal injury "has ruined my life," she stands by her man and gives her word to the judge that her husband "will never appear in your court or any other court again."

Because Christopher blamed his alcoholic descent on the industrial accident that ended his bowling career, I talk to bowlers on the local circuit, and Walter Bloch shakes his head no. I talk to Christopher's mother (I make a mistake when I don't quote her by her full name) and she toes Christopher's line: that all her son ever wanted to do was be the next Don Weber. From my interview at the jail, I notice that Christopher shields his right hand from view, and I insert that observation into the piece.

But it is Brenda Christopher who ultimately raises the most important issue in the entire piece (which I mistakenly buried): "Putting him in jail isn't going to stop his problem. It's failed in the past. This is a serious man with a medical problem that needs correcting."

Prosecutors, the judge or anyone else climbing aboard this railroad did not share any such concerns.

EPILOGUE

Almost two decades after Gary Christopher was sentenced to serve the longest penalty for drunk driving in the United States, I tried to find him. But I struck out. Christopher was nowhere to be found. I did, though, find the attorney who had represented him.

Leonard Chaitin said that if he had had more experience as a criminal-defense attorney at the time, he would have pushed for a different outcome. The city attorney's office had offered Christopher a plea bargain of three years in jail, instead of the more than nine years Christopher eventually received from Judge Person. "I had been doing criminal work for less than a year at the time," Chaitin told me. "I was severely inexperienced." Chaitin said both he and his client should have jumped at the deal.

Chaitin appealed Judge Person's sentence, and an appellate court reduced Christopher's jail term by one year. Chaitin, who hasn't talked to Christopher in more than 15 years, said he was uncertain how much time his client eventually served. Chaitin said he believes that after Christopher served his jail sentence, he left the United States for either Germany or Japan, where he had spent his childhood.

The Christopher conviction and my coverage of it helped create a national furor over penalties for drunk driving. Prior to Christopher, there had been plenty of media coverage of victims killed by drunk drivers and the prison terms those drunk drivers received. But Christopher's protracted jail sentence was ground-breaking. Judge Person had punished him for driving drunk, not for killing or injuring anyone while driving drunk. His sentence was longer than what most defendants convicted of vehicular manslaughter would have received.

"18 Years on a Long, Boozy Road" and the attendant publicity it generated made then-Los Angeles City Attorney Ira Reiner look like a protector of the people. Reiner maximized the story to further his political agenda. One month after the piece appeared, he took over as Los Angeles district attorney, heading the nation's largest district attorney's office. Political longevity is ephemeral. Six years after the Christopher case, Reiner was trounced when he ran in the Democratic primary for California attorney general. These days, Reiner is an attorney in private practice in Los Angeles. He recently represented a Hollywood scriptwriter who sued Steven Spielberg, charging that Spielberg had stolen his idea for a movie and turned it into the 1998 film, "Small Soldiers."

As for defense attorney Chaitin, the Christopher case propelled his career, as well. Chaitin went on to stitch together a host of other high-publicity clients, including a man convicted of assault during the 1992 Los Angeles race riots, two men charged in two gang-related murders, a court commissioner who sued a radio talk-show host for slander, and a family evicted from its federally subsidized home because of allegations of gang membership.

ASSIGNMENTS

1) Locate your region's version of Gary Christopher. Talk to local prosecutors, judges and police officers. Contact the driver whose criminal record most closely resembles Christopher's. Contact the driver's attorney. Write a story that gets at the driver's incessant need to drink and drive despite the penalties he or she has faced.

2) Interview local prosecutors to understand the cost of prosecuting drunk drivers. What are penalties for first-, second-, third-, and fourth-time offenders? Write about diversion programs for first-time offenders, designed, in part, to lessen the load on jails, prosecutors and judges. What is the impact of such programs? Interview defense attorneys who specialize in drunk-driving cases. Find out what they charge, and which defenses they most often employ.

3) Look into medical solutions for repeat drunk drivers. Some jurisdictions require repeat offenders to be administered a drug such as Antabuse that makes the drinker ill. Find out what, if any, innovative methods officials, psychologists or physicians are recommending to deter alcoholics from getting behind the wheel of a car.

20

STREETS OF SAN FRANCISCO
TEEM WITH TEEN RUNAWAYS

When I worked as a reporter in *The Sacramento Bee*'s San Francisco's bureau, the newspaper's office was located six blocks away from a seedy downtown neighborhood with a burgeoning Vietnamese community. A by-product of such population shift was the proliferation of hole-in-the-wall Vietnamese restaurants—great places that I began frequenting three or four times a week for lunch. On my walks to and from the *Bee*'s bureau, I began noticing young men, most of them teenagers, hanging out on street corners, leaning against buildings. They were not waiting for buses. I was intrigued and soon realized that each corner had a young man who had staked out the area as his own turf. Drivers would cruise by slowly, occasionally pulling into an adjacent alley, where the teenage boys would often hop into the cars.

Prostitution isn't a new story. But when the prostitutes are runaway teenage boys often under 16 years old, elements of a story begin materializing. When I discovered that in San Francisco, there were only 37 emergency beds to accommodate an estimated 2,000 runaways, I realized the story was waiting to be written.

Streets of San Francisco Teem with Teen Runaways

SAN FRANCISCO—Nikki Goldfoot's immediate problem is whether to step inside a white Peugeot parked around the corner. It he does, he'll make $50.

Since arriving in San Francisco five weeks ago, Nikki, 18, has traded sex for money or drugs 27 times.

Apart from its famous tourist attractions, San Francisco has another distinction: teenagers on their own and on the run. Nikki is one of the city's estimated 2,000 teenage runaways who, on any given night, prostitute themselves or sell drugs on the streets of San Francisco to survive.

Officials say San Francisco has now joined Los Angeles and New York as the nation's premier havens for at-large teenagers.

Runaway teenagers on San Francisco streets are a swelling burden few know how to handle. There are only 37 emergency beds for out-of-town runaways here. They are always filled, and city officials expect the problem to grow soon—as it does every year—with the onset of summer and no school.

Because they are not adults, runaways are not eligible for government assistance; because they are considered children, they are still the legal responsibility of parents who are sometimes thousands of miles away.

"The object is to survive," said Kiko, a 17-year-old friend of Nikki's, who has a diamond stud in his left ear and crude gang tattoos on his wrist and knuckles. "Without money, you can't get anything."

In San Francisco, runaways gravitate to six downtown blocks of Polk Street—a raunchy area where male prostitutes over 16 are considered old. San Francisco's bright lights have always attracted wanderers—from gold-prospecting 49ers to beatniks of the '60s and hippies who followed. But today's runaways are not modern-day Huck Finns, happily lighting out to explore America, nor are they contemporary Jack Kerouacs on the road.

They have come to San Francisco by way of running away from somewhere else—members of a tribe with neither home nor destination. Many meander along the Interstate 5 corridor, moving from Seattle to San Diego, stopping off at large cities.

In Sacramento, many hang out at Plaza Park across from City Hall, where they hustle and then turn tricks in vehicles or in the motels on 16th Street or on West Capitol Avenue in West Sacramento.

With just minimal programs to get them trained for employment, mentally treated or sent back home, the majority have no choice but to stay on the run.

At San Francisco's Larkin Street Youth Center, two-thirds of the calls made on behalf of children who want to return home yield the same answer from parents: Keep the kids.

Nikki, tall and lanky with green eyes and a crew cut, said he stays in contact with his parents, who gladly accept collect calls whenever he phones.

They freely admit that their son is a prostitute, a thief, a liar, a reckless juvenile with a penchant for Satan worship, Mohawk haircuts and drug dealing.

"We're always preparing ourselves for that call we'll get some day," said his father, Nathan, a 53-year-old automobile restorer who worked for Ford Motor Co. for 30 years. "We know, sooner or later, someone will call and report him dead."

Lorraine Goldfoot, 42, said that each time she and her husband talk to Nikki, they tell him, "Behave yourself, don't steal, eat well, stay well. Take care of yourself, and call whenever you want."

Their calls always end with Nikki's saying "I love you." Their response is always "We love you," she said.

Like many runaways, Nikki is a fugitive. He uses an alias among street friends; his real name is Charles. A warrant has been issued for his arrest. Committed twice to an Oregon state juvenile detention center, MacLaren School for Boys, he escaped last April while on cleanup detail.

Nikki said he then hitchhiked to Portland, and with three friends, stole a car and drove to San Francisco, where they abandoned the vehicle.

By all accounts, the Goldfoots were loving, supportive, attentive parents. The family is still close-knit.

Nikki's problems, both he and his parents said, date back more than a decade.

Adopted when he was 3 days old, Nikki was the first son of Nathan and Lorraine. Her father was a cantor in a prominent Portland synagogue. The family lived in a farmhouse on 4½ acres with blueberry bushes and dozens of sheep.

By age 11, Nikki remembers, he was cutting school regularly, smoking pot, drinking heavily and occasionally running away to 82nd Avenue, a gritty transient area in Portland filled with prostitutes and panhandlers.

Nikki's first trick, he recalled, took place at age 12. A businessman in a black Corvette asked Nikki if he wanted a lift. "He said to me, 'I'll give you 50 bucks for oral sex,' and I said to myself, 'What the hell?' I didn't want to do it, but I also did want to do it. I really didn't have to do anything for the money, just lie there."

With the sexual transaction completed, the man pulled a wad of bills out of his pocket and, Nikki recalled, "I bashed him with my portable radio. I grabbed $600 and ran off down the street to a dance club. I got a real adrenaline rush. Wow, it was so cool. I was counting out all the money and handing it out like it was fake."

After stealing his father's coin collection in 1984, his parents pressed charges and Nikki was sentenced to MacLaren School, followed by a private psychiatric facility. Whenever he was discharged to live at home, Nikki ran away. At age 15, he lived on Portland streets for two months. He eventually made so much money as a prostitute that he rented an apartment.

His parents said they knew where he was. "We'd go down and talk to him, we'd bring him food, we'd bring him home, but the next day, he'd be gone. So we just let him do his own thing," Lorraine Goldfoot said.

With fake identification, Nikki said, he bought a car and for several months transported drugs between Portland and Seattle.

Arrested for stealing a moped, he was sentenced to three years in various state youth detention centers, including a 12-bed home in Junction City, Ore. Its director, Harold Haig, remembers Nikki as smart, congenial—"someone who could make it."

Haig said that Nikki came in with his hair dyed white and styled in punk-rock spikes. When Haig explained that the unorthodox style would draw attention to him in the small farming community, Nikki then cut his hair into a Mohawk, and finally he shaved his head entirely.

He was arrested for drug possession, transferred back to the higher-security MacLaren School, and then escaped last April.

Nikki said that he is not homosexual, "just gay for pay." He said he knows he should stop his prostitution but that he's not ready to yet.

"The money is just too good. You walk around here and you see something you want, a jacket and pair of shoes, and you only have to work two or three nights to make enough money to get it," he said.

On a recent Friday night, Nikki was working Polk Street when a tan Buick pulled into an alley. Nikki sauntered over, opened the door and got inside. After 15 seconds of negotiating price, he and the driver, a thirtyish man dressed in a suit, took off for the evening.

"You don't put any passion into anything. All you are really is just a zombie," he said the next morning.

Since 1984, 11,216 runaways—two-thirds of them male—have either been reported or booked by police in San Francisco. Last year alone, there were almost 3,000, said San Francisco patrolman Floyd Moon, the officer assigned to tracking missing juveniles.

But that increase is deceptive. Few runaways have any contact with police; most blend in fast to the street scene. Some sleep at the beach, in parks, abandoned cars and buildings; others with money band together to rent cheap hotel rooms. About one-third, Moon said, find themselves in the "worst-case scenario." Within one week, Moon said, almost all runaways are introduced to prostitution and drug addiction.

At the bus station near Seventh and Market streets, or the TransBay Transit Terminal near First and Mission streets, "They are hit up by an adult, a guy who says he will take care of them. He may wine and dine them, and then in a couple of days, he says, 'I've been good to you. I've got this guy coming to town, and I want you to entertain him.'"

Leon, 17, left his home in Sacramento two years ago, and never thought he'd end up trading sexual favors for money. But after 10 days in San Francisco, he ran out of his $140 life savings and said he had no choice.

He now rents a room in a Tenderloin hotel with a 25-year-old nude dancer, a 17-year-old female prostitute who works for a pimp, and another 17-year-old male prostitute.

At any given time, there are between 20,000 and 25,000 runaways throughout California, said Wimsey Wrede, who directs a Sacramento-based state hot line for runaways and their families. Over the course of one year, there are close to 400,000, Wrede said.

"The average age used to be 14, 15, 16, but now that's shifting downward to 12 and 13," said Wrede, whose organization fields about 800 calls a month.

Life on the streets is its own world, complete with its own lingo. "Up Six," and "Miss Tilley" are codes for police. "Old Trolls" are men who desire young boys.

On most evenings, there are about 60 runaways hustling on Polk Street. Most work two or three tricks a night. Transactions take place in parked cars, in nearby hotel rooms, at the customers' homes.

No one income level or racial background predominates among runaways. At San Francisco's largest temporary home for them, Diamond Youth Shelter near Golden Gate Park, 51 percent are white, 29 percent are Hispanic and 16 percent are black.

Nikki, who stayed at the shelter when he first arrived here, said he hopes to leave street hustling by the next month. For now, he said he is staying with a 33-year-old, self-described drag queen. Nikki said he'll work until he's earned enough to rent an apartment for him self and his girlfriend, Tammy, who is due to arrive from Portland during the summer.

"As soon as she arrives, I'll quit," Nikki said dreamily. "We'll get married, have children, and my parents will be proud of me."

For now, Nikki has a steady customer he sees weekly, a 50-year-old man who rents pornographic movies. "I get paid $100 and there is no sex," he said.

Nikki admitted that unless he gets off Polk Street soon, he may never ever leave. "Money, money, money, that's all you have in your mind," he said. Then he ran off to get into the Peugeot.

The Sacramento Bee, June 13, 1988

WRITING THE STORY

Instead of returning to my office after lunch, I started hanging out around lower Polk Street, where the largest concentration of young male prostitutes congregated. One of the oldest was a guy who looked no more than 18. Since he and I often passed each other on the street, I began nodding, then talking, to him. At first, Nikki Goldfoot said he thought I wanted to hire him for an hour or so. When I said I wanted to talk to him for a newspaper story, he was suspicious. We ducked into a coffee shop, and Nikki was still wary. But after two or three more encounters, he was convinced that all I wanted was an interview.

It turned out that Nikki's story was as compelling as it was heartbreaking. Nikki said he didn't mind if I hung out with him on his street corner one night, just as long as I stayed in the shadows; he didn't want me to put the kibosh on business. That's where the lede of the piece comes from, as well as the detail that provides the spine of the story. Lingo, something that has always fascinated me, helps sell the story with shorthand like "Up Six," "Miss Tilley" and "Old Trolls." The story is buttressed with grim statistics and interviews with police officers, social-service personnel, as well as other male teenage prostitutes.

But the centerpiece of the story is Nikki and his dicey prospects for survival. Nikki provided me with his parents' names, and when I contacted them, they refused to talk. I followed our abrupt conversation with a letter in which I explained what I wanted and why. I wrote that I would read back to them their comments before I included them in my story; this way they could alter their quotes should they want to rethink what they had told me. In a week, the Goldfoots called me and we had a lengthy conversation. Through them, I talked with Harold Haig, the director of the juvenile detention center where Nikki once lived. The structure of the story is a circular tease. The lede introduces the main character and a decision that Nikki must make—does he get into the white Peugeot? Forty-nine paragraphs later, the reader finds out.

Originally, the piece was twice as long as what eventually was published. One of the important elements of the story was AIDS—Nikki's increased risk for contracting the disease, and what precautions he takes to guard against the disease. My editor wanted to place all the references to AIDS in one section of the story, a suggestion I thought was good. But when the piece appeared, the editor somehow had forgotten to reinsert the AIDS section in the story. That's why there is no mention of AIDS—a glaring omission in a story about street prostitution in San Francisco.

It is the comment that Nikki's father made to me that makes the story, and I wonder if I should have used it to more advantage than burying it in the interior of the piece: "We know, sooner or later, someone will call and report him dead."

EPILOGUE

For this book, I wanted to locate Nikki. But given Nikki's fast life on the streets, I was doubtful whether he'd still be alive. I sent a letter to his parents and, within a week, I got an unexpected response. Nikki was alive and well, still living in the San Francisco Bay Area. I sent him an e-mail and, several hours later, Nikki called me.

It had been 14 years since my story had appeared, and Nikki was now 31. Within a year of my writing the piece, Nikki had been able to save enough money from tricks on the street to find an apartment and become a bartender. But in 1991, he was convicted of burglary and forgery and sentenced to prison. After his release, he was twice sent back to prison for drug possession and spent a total of four years in three California correctional facilities. He and his girlfriend had a son, but the woman and Chazz (as Nikki prefers to be called these days) split up, and he has not seen the boy for more than eight years.

Nikki said for more than a decade he had been addicted to amphetamines and the designer drug known as ecstasy, but today has kicked the habit and is enrolled in City College of San Francisco, studying photography. "I've been through a lot, but living drug-free is the hardest thing to do. Having to pay the rent every month, saving each month for food, that's really hard. Responsibilities like that are the hardest things to keep up with."

Nikki said he recently had a blood test and is HIV/AIDS-free. "By all accounts, I should probably be dead. I know I'm lucky. I like being sober. After being high on drugs for so long, being totally out of control for so long, life is the real high."

As Nikki was about to hang up the phone, he paused. I sensed he wanted to say something else. "You know that story you did on me? That's what really changed my life."

"How?" I asked.

The story had won an award and had been reprinted in an annual review of prize-winning newspaper pieces. "I was in Portland hanging out at the university, and a student photographer came up to me and said he had seen my photograph before. When I said I didn't believe him, he got the book with the photograph of me, and I stared at it for a long, long time. I reread the story, and I thought, 'Hey, this is about me and everything I went through.' Then and there, I decided to learn photography so I could catch people at different stages of their lives, as you had done."

These days, Nikki and his fiancé own a photography business, and specialize in shooting musical groups. "I'm so close to success," he told me. "I've got it more together than I've ever had in my life. I guess I'm a late bloomer."

ASSIGNMENTS

1) Find out what social services are available for teenage runaways in your area. Interview counselors, social workers, law-enforcement personnel. Try to focus your story, though, on the runaways themselves. Find out what brought them to your area. In your story, try to get at their daily activities, their social order, what makes them tick.

2) Spend several days at a local homeless shelter. Sleep there. Eat there. Interview people who are staying there. Write a first-person piece on what you find, as well as your own reactions.

3) Talk to a local high school principal about spending time with a particular class, club or sport in the school. It could be a drama class, the debating club, the football team. The key is that the group of students you pick are all preparing for a competition or event. The drama class may be rehearsing a high school production, the debate club may be preparing for an upcoming district meet, the football team may be practicing the regional playoff. Write a story, introducing students as real-life characters and the challenges the entire group faces leading up to the big event.

21

FOR MELISSA'S SAKE

When I wrote "For Melissa's Sake", Roe vs. Wade had been the law of the land for a decade. Despite that Supreme Court ruling, though, America's battle lines were clearly drawn between pro-life and pro-choice advocates. Much less clear was a new skirmish on the horizon: the rights of infants born with severe, catastrophic disabilities. Rapid advances in medical technology had created this new frontier. In most large cities, medical centers maintained high-tech neonatal units, where physicians and nurses practiced the new specialty. In the past, such compromised babies would have died in utero or within hours of birth. Parents and physicians privately agreed on medical treatment—if any—to be administered.

That long-term practice, though, was called into public question in April 1982 after an Indiana infant, dubbed "Baby Doe," was born with a severe case of Down's syndrome and a long list of congenital defects. The parents decided to withhold surgery rather than allow the infant to survive disabled. Their action outraged pro-life proponents, resulting in a prosecutor's effort to require the hospital to perform surgery on the infant. Litigation stopped when the baby died six days after birth.

The incident provoked national attention, prompting the Reagan administration to promulgate rules requiring that every newborn, no matter how severely disabled, receive all possible treatment. Hospitals defying the regulation would lose federal funding. To monitor compliance, the Department of Heath and Human Services established a hot line to report possible cases of compromised babies denied medical care.

In the fall of 1982, the federal government raised the stakes. It intervened in the case of a New York infant, known as "Baby Jane Doe," born with spina bifida and hydrocephalus. The parents had rejected life-prolonging surgery. In response, the Justice Department sought the infant's medical files to determine whether her parents had violated the baby's civil rights.

Into this volatile mix of technology, religion, ethics and politics comes "For Melissa's Sake." The story poses thorny questions that are still hotly debated today: What are the rights of such compromised infants? What are the rights of their parents? Who will pay for the cost of prolonging the infants' lives? And most of all: Who should decide whether these babies live or die?

In the case of "For Melissa's Sake," I came up with the idea for the story before I came up with a real-life example. I scanned newspapers daily, searching to find accounts of a compromised infant prematurely born. I called local hospitals. I called physicians and nurses who had been sources for other stories I had written.

My vigilance paid off. In the late spring I read a wire-service piece of a tiny baby born in the small southeast Texas town of Victoria. The attending obstetrician said the infant weighed 13 ounces, and was "so tiny you could put her in the bottom of your hand." Somewhere along the line, someone dubbed the newborn baby, "the world's smallest human being." It was a moniker that would soon catch on.

For Melissa's Sake

18-ounce infant fought for painfully brief life

HOUSTON—The nurse calls Sandy Maurer and tells her to come to the hospital immediately. This time, the doctors have no hope for her infant daughter. They give her six hours to live. Sandy arrives 20 minutes later in a panic. She puts on a surgical gown and hurries into the intensive care unit prepared for the worst.

Melissa, her transparent skin now ashen, lies in her plastic crib struggling for breath. Pain appears to shoot through her body, as though her limbs were attached to an electrical generator. Her stomach is swollen to almost double its normal size.

The rare times she opens her eyes, it is to protest silently against the prick of a needle for yet another blood test. Doctors and nurses watch over her, monitoring her pulse, blood pressure and brain activity.

Among premature infants, Melissa is one of the smallest. One obstetrician says that, at birth, she was "so tiny you could put her in the bottom of your hand." When her weight slipped from 18 to 13 ounces five days after she was born, she was dubbed in news accounts "the world's smallest human being."

Now, 56 days after her birth, Melissa's weight is up to 28 ounces, but she has contracted a virus for which there is no medical cure. Her only weapon is her own antibodies—antibodies that doctors don't expect her to develop.

"If she has to be taken off the machines," the neonatalogist on duty tells the 26-year-old mother, "we will let you hold her before she dies." It would be the first time Sandy would embrace her daughter.

Sandy begins a vigil for Melissa. Six, seven, eight hours pass, and the baby continues to battle. One, then two days pass, and almost "unbelievably," as one doctor says, Melissa develops the antibodies to ward off the infection.

This fragile human being, who looks more like a fetus than a baby, refuses to give up.

●　　●　　●

Melissa was a tenacious fighter; she wasn't a winner, though. Forty-nine days and countless crises later, she died in her mother's arms.

Melissa also was a pioneer. Five years ago, a baby like her would have been dead within hours after birth. Five years from now, medical science will be routinely saving babies like her.

Today, severely premature babies like Melissa survive in a medical netherworld. Their lives are prolonged for weeks or months by a maze of tubes, ultramodern machines and 24-hour medical supervision. Such heroic efforts cost money—in Melissa's case, more than $200,000.

These babies' lives raise uneasy, fundamental questions: To what limits should life be sustained? Should infants be kept alive at all costs?

To the medical personnel who cared for Melissa Maurer, the answer is not easy. Although the doctors and nurses fully protected Melissa's right to life, many of them privately say the money and time could have been better spent on patients whose chances for life were statistically much greater.

To Melissa's mother, there was no other choice but to do everything possible to save her daughter. Sandy's reason was based on the one irrefutable fact: Because Melissa had life, it had to be sustained.

Melissa's birth was completely unexpected. Sandy found out she was pregnant just two days before delivering the baby on June 1, 1983.

Sandy and her husband, Blain, were divorced in November 1982 after five years of marriage. For the next few months, Sandy and her year-old daughter, Brandi, drifted among friends and family in her hometown of Victoria, 84 miles northeast of Corpus Christi.

Sandy's monthly income is an $85 welfare check and $93 in food stamps. Blain has been ordered to send $151 a month in child support, but Sandy says she can't depend on it. In Victoria, she manages to pick up extra cash working as either a cocktail waitress or an operator for a phone answering service.

"When I was young," Sandy says, "I kind of figured I'd have five kids, go to college, get married to a lawyer. Well, I guess it didn't work out like that."

Her father died when Sandy was in fifth grade. She, her mother, brother and three sisters lived off of Social Security benefits. Sandy dropped out of high school at age 15; four years later, she earned a general equivalency diploma. Raised as a Seventh Day Adventist, she was not allowed as a teen-ager to wear makeup or go to dances and movies.

Gradually Sandy broke away from her rigid upbringing. Today, she wears light-blue eye shadow and pink nail polish. She has a flower tattoo on her thigh and usually dresses in bright blouses, blue jeans and rubber thongs. Her chestnut hair is cut in a Farah Fawcett shag.

Last year, she was baptized at a small Baptist church in Victoria. Now she considers herself a "born again" Christian and wears a gold-plated cross around her neck.

Besides her occasional work, she spends her time in Victoria partying with friends, drinking beer, watching soap operas, smoking Marlboro Golden Lights and sometimes marijuana.

On Jan. 12, she was arrested and charged with possession of marijuana. Unable to post the $5,000 bond, she spent a month in Victoria County Jail.

During that time, she underwent two routine pregnancy tests. Both came out negative.

Then early this spring, Sandy missed several menstrual periods. She thought nothing about it until the night of May 30, when she was staying at her mother's one-bedroom apartment.

"I started having real bad cramps," she says, "so I said to Mama, 'This feels like labor pains.'" Her mother, 64-year-old Joyce Mayfield, calls for a taxi. Sandy goes by herself to the emergency room of Citizens Memorial Hospital.

The physician on duty tells Sandy she is pregnant and advises her she probably will miscarry. "I couldn't believe what I was hearing," she says. "It was a double shock."

Sandy is given medication to ease the pain and sent home. The next night, she is back, this time in worse pain. At 2:15 a.m., she is wheeled into the hospital's delivery room. Within 16 minutes, with two nurses present, she gives birth to a baby girl.

Just before Sandy is given a sedative, a doctor tells her the baby won't live more than several hours. At her size—just 18 ounces and 12 inches long—the odds are almost 90 percent against her survival.

The next morning, Sandy is awakened and told the baby is still alive. Sandy is taken to see her daughter in the intensive care unit.

"She looked so tiny and fragile," Sandy recalls.

Dr. Terry Whitehouse, a resident obstetrician-gynecologist, asks Sandy if she has decided on a name yet.

"There isn't any reason to give her a name," she replies. "I was told she's going to die."

"Name her," Whitehouse says gently.

Sandy picks Melissa Michelle.

For the next nine days, the baby is kept in isolation. Sandy, who has since been discharged, comes to visit Melissa every day. Doctors feed the baby intravenously, hoping she eventually will gain enough weight to be transferred to the hospital's nursery.

But instead of gaining, Melissa loses almost a third of her weight. On the tenth day, her color changes from a pale pink to a dusky blue, and she starts gasping for breath.

As Melissa's health deteriorates, she generates more than medical concern. Anti-abortionists attempt to turn her life into a moral issue.

Because of Melissa's size, the Victoria doctors estimate Sandy gave birth when she was only 18 weeks pregnant—when many abortions are performed. If Melissa is that premature, and her life can be sustained, then she could be used as a powerful weapon against abortion.

Melissa catches the attention of right-to-life forces after the *Victoria Advocate* and later, wire services, report her precarious condition. At least once a day, hospital personnel receive anonymous calls concerning the baby. Some of the callers warn, "Don't kill Melissa Maurer," then they hang up.

While the baby's life turns into a hot political issue, doctors in Victoria advise Sandy that Melissa's chances of survival would be greatly increased under the highly specialized care offered at a large city hospital. Sandy readily consents to moving the infant.

Calls are made to several teaching hospitals within a 200-mile radius, but all administrators say their neonatal units are at capacity.

Finally, doctors at Houston's Hermann Hospital agree to take Melissa. Implicitly, the private hospital also agrees to absorb most of the cost of care—about $2,000 a day, not including fees for nurses and other hospital personnel. The complete per diem cost ranges up to $5,000. Because Sandy is on welfare, Medicare will pay for the first month of care. After that, the hospital will assume all costs.

Within 15 minutes of the phone call, Dr. Mac Temple and three associates—two nurses and a pilot—take off from the Hermann Hospital's heliport to transport Melissa the 124 miles northeast to Houston.

The medical team arrives in Victoria at 1:15 p.m. "Her heart rate was dropping so fast," Temple says later, "that my immediate concern was whether she'd make the trip to Houston alive."

To prepare Melissa for the flight, Temple inserts a tube into the baby's trachea to ease her breathing. But the smallest tracheal tube is still too large. Temple resorts to improvising with a tiny plastic pipe he finds in his medical kit. Suddenly, Melissa is no longer gasping for breath. Her heart rate picks up, and within 10 minutes her skin color turns pink.

With Melissa's vital signs reasonably stable, Temple places her incubator on a gurney and rushes her to the waiting helicopter.

A half-hour after takeoff, the tube in Melissa's trachea clogs shut with mucus. She starts to gag and then turns blue.

Temple yells to the pilot to land.

"Where?" the pilot shouts back.

"Anywhere!" Temple snaps.

There aren't many options. The pilot lowers the helicopter onto a bank parking lot in the rural town of Louise. About two dozen residents spot the craft and race to the scene. The town's sheriff is close behind and keeps the crowd from the helicopter.

Temple pulls the tube out of Melissa's throat and covers her face with an oxygen mask. After she receives 15 minutes of pure oxygen, her color returns to pink.

Temple reinserts the tube, the pilot revs the engines and within minutes the team is back in the air. He radios ahead to Hermann, notifying doctors of an arrival time of 4 p.m. The helicopter is met by a crowd of Houston reporters and photographers.

Once in crib No. 6 of the neonatal intensive care unit, Melissa weighs in at 330 grams, a mere 11½ ounces.

Immediately, the doctors—all neonatal specialists—recognize that the baby was not born 18 weeks after conception. She's tiny, Dr. Sharon Crandell says, but her development shows she was born at least five to six weeks later.

But pinpointing when Melissa was born is irrelevant, say right-to-life proponents from anti-abortion groups who began keeping close watch on Melissa's condition through local newspaper and television stories. "Melissa proves to the country that a child is viable at that early age," says Patti Linbeck, a Texas Right to Life spokeswoman who denies her group has participated in any phone campaign. "Through abortion, children like Melissa are routinely destroyed every day."

Crandell is the first of many neonatalogists to attend Melissa. Her initial assessment is not encouraging.

"Melissa is so small, nothing in her body is ready to work yet," she says. "She promises to have problems that form a mile-long list. Her air sacs are beginning to collapse. What she desperately needs is to grow, but she can't handle sugar or any kind of nutrition. She is too tiny and underdeveloped.

The neonatal unit is located deep within Hermann Hospital. To get there, one first must walk through the maternity ward, where pink, robust babies wait to go home. Down the hall and to the left are the ICU babies—gray, sickly and silent. Most have tubes in their throats, which makes crying impossible. The unit is noisy and bright, illuminated 24 hours a day by fluorescent lights. At each crib is a telephone, which parents can call day or night to receive medical updates.

Melissa is one of 15 premature babies in the unit. Most are too small to wear the standard wrist I.D. bracelet for newborns. Instead, their names are taped to each crib, along with slogans and greetings left by parents. "Small but mighty," one sign reads. "Welcome," reads another. On Melissa's bed: "Hi, I flew on the chopper and my name is Melissa Maurer—World's Smallest Baby."

Melissa is tethered to a maze of technological umbilical cords. An endotracheal tube for breathing. A central catheter in a neck vein to administer fluids. A nasal-gastric tube to let her burp. A heat probe to control body temperature. Three wires taped to her chest to monitor heart rate. Three peripheral IVs, stuck into her wrists, feet and scalp to administer medication and chemical nourishment.

Every morning, doctors take students on rounds, usually arriving at Melissa's crib about 11 a.m. One day, a student asks about the baby's temperature gauge. "That's important," the doctor explains. "If she drops even one degree in temperature, she can go like that," and he snaps his fingers.

Melissa is so sick that she seems oblivious to everything around her. When she isn't sleeping, she either yawns or kicks lethargically, her eyelids half-closed over glassy eyes.

All the babies have primary nurses, and Melissa's is Yasmin Walji. Every six hours, nurse Walji vibrates Melissa's chest with the cushioned head of an electric toothbrush to loosen mucus from her lungs. Then she suctions the mucus from her mouth.

Melissa's heel is pricked for blood tests up to six times a day. When the needle goes in, she jerks her leg back and squirms.

"It's the only place we can draw blood," Walji says, almost apologetically. "She really doesn't have enough flesh anywhere else on her body."

A day after Melissa's arrival in Houston, Sandy decides she can't be away from her baby. She packs a suitcase and drives to Houston with 18-month-old Brandi. Sandy has less than $50 and no plans other than to see her baby every day. She stays with friends, who live 15 minutes away from the hospital, and visits Melissa twice a day.

Visitors to the ICU are limited to the immediate family, and all must rigorously scrub their hands and forearms, then don a pea-green surgical smock.

At first, Sandy is overwhelmed by the high-tech medical unit and its gadgetry. She gingerly walks around the equipment, not knowing where to stand or lean.

Sandy dotes on Melissa, stroking her head or holding her hand in between two fingers. She speaks to her daughter in singsong baby talk. "Melissa, your mama is here to see you. You look so pretty, Melissa. You look so sweet today."

Like other parents, Sandy tries to spruce up the baby's hospital home. On one of the machines, she pins up a lengthy prayer handprinted in the shape of a cross. Sandy buys Melissa a "womb bear," a stuffed animal three times the baby's size that emits a wave-like sound.

Sandy is so overwhelmed that Melissa is alive, she doesn't ask the doctors about the baby's future. But they pointedly tell her.

They say the chances are high that Melissa will be blind, mentally retarded and physically handicapped. The low level of oxygen in her blood can cause the blindness. The Houston doctors also discover that soon after birth, Melissa suffered a brain hemorrhage, which could cause neurological disorders.

Sandy shrugs off the prognosis. She says she dreams at night about Melissa. In one dream, she says, "I thought that the hospital wouldn't pay for her anymore, so they had to release her. I took her home and used a light to warm her, and then I stole an oxygen mask from the hospital. She eventually turned out all right."

Were Melissa to be released from the hospital, she would require around-the-clock supervision, as well as elaborate at-home medical equipment.

Such care takes a special kind of financial and emotional commitment from parents, says the ICU's head nurse, Alice Illian. "There is a lot of stress. If you are going to resent the child, it will reflect back on the child. That's a hell of a life for the child.

"If Melissa does live, I think Sandy will wake up one day in a couple of years and feel extremely burdened. I don't think she has the slightest concept of what this baby will mean to her. The media is exciting; this baby is probably the most exciting thing that's happened to her over her entire life. She's going to have to figure it all out sooner or later."

Sandy is told that Melissa has about a 10 percent chance of living past six months. And if she does live that long, she likely would require long-term medical care.

"Oh, all the medical people are doing is just trying to scare me," Sandy says. "God's going to provide for me, Brandi and Melissa. I know Melissa will get well enough to leave the hospital. If something happens—like she's going to be mentally retarded—she's still my baby. I'll care for her no matter what happens. I'll always love her.

"There's just no sense in considering what I'll do if Melissa has problems. What's the use in worrying? I'll take those problems when they come. God gave her to me for a reason, that's all I know."

For the first three weeks Melissa is at Hermann Hospital, her condition is critical but stable. She gains about one-third of an ounce a day.

Then on July 2, her 32nd day of life, she contracts a staph infection, which can lead to damage to her heart lining and valves. The infection also could mean Melissa has meningitis, which can cause brain damage. Doctors change Melissa's condition from critical to extremely critical.

Dr. Margo Cox, the attending neonatalogist, is deeply pessimistic. "All of Melissa's organs are there—but after just 30 weeks, they aren't mature enough for life," she says. "And they can't mature normally if they are infected."

Sandy still steadfastly maintains Melissa will beat the odds, but the stress of daily hospital visits soon begins to wear on her. At one moment, she is laughing; at another, she breaks down and cries.

Money is a constant problem. For food, Sandy and a girlfriend from Victoria hock the friend's engagement ring for $25 at a Houston pawnshop.

Sandy thinks Brandi could earn money by modeling baby clothes. She makes an appointment at a Houston talent agency, but fails to show up.

After Sandy uses up a $25 loan from her mother, she gets a job as a waitress at a topless bar. The owner says she won't have to strip, just serve drinks. But Sandy fails to show up for her first night of work.

On July 3, she stops by the hospital with Brandi. To contain the spread of infection, the pediatrician on duty examines all children who enter the unit. The doctor discovers Brandi's throat is inflamed and advises Sandy that the little girl cannot be allowed into the unit.

Sandy curses loudly enough for everyone in the ward to hear; she says the "infection" is actually red Kool-Aid that Brandi has been drinking.

"I drive all the way here and he won't let me see my baby," she screams as she storms out of the unit.

Walji, Melissa's primary nurse, chases after Sandy and talks her into returning. The nurse takes Brandi in her arms.

"She won't go with anyone else," Sandy says in tears. But Walji is able to soothe the child, and Sandy calms down to visit Melissa.

On July 28, Melissa contracts the infection that doctors are certain will kill her. Sandy calls Blain, her former husband, in Victoria and pleads with him to come see Melissa. He refuses, saying he doesn't want anything to do with the baby.

Sandy's mother, though, decides to make the trip, to see her granddaughter perhaps for the last time. A part-time housekeeper, Mayfield borrows money for the three-hour bus trip.

"I think Melissa has a tremendous will to live," Mayfield says at the hospital. "If God wanted her, he would have taken her already. I know one thing: Melissa is here for a reason."

One purpose of the baby's life, Mayfield says, is to show that abortion is a criminal act. "Someone came up to me and said, 'I want you to thank Melissa for staying alive so long. She is showing everyone that she is human and that killing her would have been murder.'"

Sandy nods her head. "That's just how I feel, Mama," she says. "It really is."

After Melissa develops the antibodies to fight the infection, Cox meets with Sandy in the consultation room adjacent to the ICU. The virus has left Melissa with an enlarged spleen and liver, as well as with an increased need for pure oxygen.

"The longer she has to sit with such high levels of oxygen at such great pressures, the more her lung tissues are damaged," Cox says. "We're caught between a rock and a hard place. The treatment we're giving her to keep her alive is also causing massive amounts of damage to her body. The more we try to save her life, the more we jeopardize her life."

Sandy, though, thinks only in the present. "What's the use of worrying about it, and then nothing happens," she says. "I don't want to think about all the bad things until they happen. A baby that can take as much as Melissa has got to be strong."

The next Monday, Melissa celebrates a birthday of sorts. She is two months old. If she were born that day, she would still be almost two months premature.

In the weeks that follow, Melissa confounds everyone—except her mother and grandmother. She seems to improve. While she still has signs of the debilitating virus, her liver and spleen are back to normal size.

Now that Melissa appears out of imminent danger, Sandy returns occasionally to Victoria. She moves to another apartment in Houston farther away from the hospital and cuts back her visits to once or twice a week, but calls every day to check on Melissa's condition.

Yet even the infrequent visits wear Sandy down. During one visit, doctors say they need to insert a tube in Melissa's throat to ease her breathing. Sandy signs the legal document giving them permission, but she complains about the toll that medical technology is taking on her daughter. She becomes increasingly despondent that she can't take Melissa home.

"She doesn't seem to be going either way," Sandy says. "With all the tests the doctors are doing on her, they can't find any more veins to prick."

Sandy also is tiring of the wet Houston heat, the monotonous trips to the hospital and the doctors, and nurses' guarded prognosis.

"No one really cares about my baby," she says, starting to cry. "I'm the only one in the world who wants her to live."

On Aug. 18, Sandy's problems multiply. Hurricane Alicia sweeps into Houston and destroys her apartment turning the prefabricated building into a wreckage of wood, plaster and glass. She and Brandi narrowly miss being hit by a falling plaster wall.

Mother and daughter move to another building in the apartment complex and salvage what they can of their belongings. High waters also flood Sandy's car—her means of transportation to the hospital.

Because she can't get to see Melissa, Sandy returns briefly to Victoria to stay with her mother. During the visit, she decides to confront Blain about his refusal to see Melissa.

Sandy says he told her, "God is punishing you for getting a divorce from me. That's why Melissa isn't going to make it."

Sandy leaves in a rage. "If he ever shows up at Melissa's funeral, I'll kill him," she says.

Then she realizes what she has said—not about Blain but about Melissa. She rushes to correct herself. "There's not going to be a funeral anyway. Melissa's gonna make it. I know that for sure."

She returns to Houston, still agitated. Her money problems worsen. Her welfare check, which should have arrived on Aug. 3, has not been delivered yet. She has to rely on friends for food.

At the hospital, though, Sandy is greeted with good news. Melissa's weight has increased to 2 pounds 5 ounces, and the doctors decide to allow Sandy to hold the baby.

Sandy dons two sterile smocks and a pair of surgical gloves. Then gingerly, so as not to dislodge any of the tubes and wires, she takes her daughter in her arms and cuddles her against her chest. At one point, Sandy thinks she sees Melissa smile. After almost an hour, Sandy gently places the baby back in her crib and wipes a tear away.

For the next three weeks, Melissa appears to improve slightly. She still has the virus but manages to contain its ill effects. Sandy is content to call the hospital daily and receive reports.

Melissa's last struggle comes suddenly. On the afternoon of Sept. 13, hospital personnel make an urgent call to Sandy. Melissa's heartbeat has dropped to 70 beats per minute, almost half of what is should be. Her color has turned blue-green.

"I don't think she's going to make it," Cox tells Sandy as she walks into the unit. This time after seeing Melissa, Sandy knows she has no choice but to believe the doctor.

At 7:45 p.m., a nun on duty is summoned. She baptizes Melissa, dabbing drops of sterilized water on her head. By 8 p.m., Melissa, her face in anguish, gropes for breath.

Cox injects morphine into Melissa's heel. Her grimace gives way to a blank, almost comatose expression.

By 9 p.m., Dr. John Sloups, another neonatalogist on duty, asks Sandy if she wants to hold her baby. Sandy nods.

Once seated in a rocking chair in the ICU, Sandy cradles Melissa, caressing her head, rocking her gently, softly hugging her daughter through the maze of tubes. Melissa's eyes are closed.

At 10:07, Dr. Sloups puts a stethoscope to Melissa's chest and pronounces her dead. The cause is heart failure.

The doctors take the body from Sandy's arms. Sandy, softly crying, is shown to an adjoining room with low lights and a soft couch. Melissa's body, now dressed in a white gown, is brought to Sandy.

It is the first time Sandy has seen her baby without all the tubes and wires. Sandy lies down on the couch on her right side and places the body next to her. The doctors tell her she can stay with Melissa all night, but within 20 minutes the body grows cold. The eyes will not stay shut. Sandy asks a nurse to take Melissa.

Cox gives her a book about coping with the death of a child. She has inscribed it, "I'm sorry we couldn't do more."

The next day, head nurse Alice Illian reflects on Melissa's life and death. "You know she had her own personality, she really was a lovely baby. The only time she was irritable was when she was feeling pain. Then she'd fuss, but otherwise, she was such a nice baby.

"We noticed she was having more and more pain in the last two weeks. You could tell when you'd touch her. She'd squint, and try to move away from you. You knew she was feeling pain."

By 4 p.m. on Sept. 16, 21 people gather under a dark green tent at Colonial Gardens Cemetery in Victoria. Melissa is to be buried in a section of the grassy, tree-barren cemetery called Babyland.

Sandy has requested the casket be opened. Inside, Melissa's body is dressed in a knitted gown, with matching hat and booties. Although the casket is designed for infants, it dwarfs Melissa's body.

Sandy's brother-in-law Ray Robinson, a Baptist minister, grasps his well-worn Bible and looks down at the body.

"What can you say about a baby this small?" Robinson says, starting his eulogy.

"As I begin to think about this child," he says, "I realize we'll never know how many lives were touched by Melissa. We'll never know how much impact she'll have in the world.

"There are many people who are wrong in their thoughts about a baby this young. She came to this world for a purpose. Try not to look at this as a tragedy, but as a blessing."

On the same afternoon, Hermann Hospital receives an urgent phone call from Beaumont. "Do you have a slot for a premature baby?"

By 5 p.m., crib No. 6 is occupied by another infant.

The Dallas Morning News, November 13, 1983

WRITING THE STORY

I was able to first connect with the mother, Sandy Maurer, by repeatedly calling Citizens Memorial Hospital, talking to the charge nurses and asking them to relay to Sandy my interest in writing a story about her daughter. One of the nurses must have talked to Sandy because within days of Melissa's birth, Sandy called me collect at the newspaper. She seemed open to talking to me, as well as to a story appearing about her and Melissa. She agreed to meet me in Houston, where Melissa was about to be transferred to Hermann Hospital. I hadn't been the only reporter to contact Sandy, but I think I was the only one who had kept calling, pestering the nurses to ask Sandy to get in touch with me. Sandy welcomed my entry into her life, in part, because of the media attention a story in *The Dallas Morning News* would confer.

"Are you gonna make me famous?" Sandy asked me when I first met her in the cafeteria at Hermann Hospital.

"You're already famous," I replied.

"No, I mean *really* famous?"

I moved the conversation from fame to Melissa's prognosis, and immediately sensed a chasm of class difference separating Sandy from the hospital personnel. Sandy said she resented the questions, the looks, the not-so-subtle put-downs she got from the neonatology staff upstairs. Scientists, that's what they were to Sandy. They weren't mothers. How could they be, asking all these questions about what if, or how would she ever be able to care for a baby like Melissa? They certainly weren't the kind of mothers Sandy would be to little Melissa when she got her out of the hospital and the three of them—Sandy, Brandi and Melissa—would return to Victoria. Sandy looked at me kindly. I was a confessor, a comforter, helping her fight off these alien medical forces that had taken over her life.

The medical personnel did not take kindly to my poking my nose into their business, and it took weeks to begin wearing down their apprehension. Before any of the physicians, nurses or technicians would talk to me on the record,

Sandy signed a release that allowed me access to all medical information about Melissa's condition. The hospital staff bristled when they received the document, but they could do nothing to circumvent the waiver.

Reporting and writing "For Melissa's Sake" took three months—daily calls to Sandy, the doctors and nurses, as well as five planes trips to and from Houston to cover the saga of Melissa's short life. I tried to write the piece as flatly as I could. I didn't want to inject more emotion into a story already filled to the brim with emotion. My reporting took up 10 notebooks. Each night, I'd go over my notes, writing out questions for the next day that I hadn't asked Sandy or the medical personnel. Sandy and I were as different as Sandy was from the hospital personnel attending to Melissa. But I had it easy. My job wasn't to save a life. It was to listen.

EPILOGUE

Sandy was the real-life answer to politicians and other preachers of high-minded morality. She was reality. Her story was not remarkable, except for the superlatives Melissa's tiny life unwittingly created. Sandy's story, in fact, was all too common: She didn't suspect she was pregnant until two days before she gave birth to Melissa; she was on welfare; she was a high school dropout; she grew up in a strict religious environment and considered herself a "Christian"; she had a criminal record for drug abuse.

Today, two decades after "For Melissa's Sake" was published, babies Melissa's size are routinely saved. Their lives are severely compromised, and often they must be hospitalized for months and months, but they do live and they do survive. "For Melissa's Sake" exists as a snapshot of an era, much like today, when technology outpaces ethics. The same issues survive Melissa: Do parents have any rights in making life-and-death decisions about their babies; what are the rights of the compromised infant?

As I was finishing writing this section, my curiosity got the better of me. Whatever happened to Sandy?

I did an Internet search, and not surprisingly, wasn't able to come up with Sandy's phone number or e-mail address. I did the same with Brandi Maurer, now 21, and got nothing. I called the Colonial Gardens Cemetery in Victoria, Texas, to find that its name had been changed to Memorial Gardens Cemetery. I asked the attendant whether any contact numbers were in Melissa Maurer's file, and she said no. I asked the attendant if she had any records of visitors to the grave, and she also said no.

I was at a dead end until I did a search for Sandy's brother-in-law, Ray Robinson, the Baptist minister who presided over Melissa's funeral. He was still listed in Victoria. I called him and left a message, asking about Sandy.

The next day, Sandy called my office. Nineteen years had gone by, but Sandy vividly remembered the article I wrote. She sounded exactly the same as I remembered her, as though we hadn't talked for weeks instead of decades. Now 45 and twice-divorced from men she described as "abusive," Sandy today is the mother of three children, a boy, 17, and a girl, 16, and Brandi. She also is a grandmother. Brandi, who works at a pig farm in Oklahoma, had just had a baby boy. Neither of Sandy's children, nor her grandson, had been born prematurely.

Sandy had recently returned to Victoria after years of living in Louisiana, Oklahoma and Washington. She had held a series of jobs—a cashier at a convenience store, an intake clerk at a homeless shelter, and a manager at a Dallas apartment complex.

She remained stoic about Melissa, and said she still believes her baby's purpose on earth was to teach the evils of abortion. Two days before I called, Sandy said she had gone to the cemetery to lay flowers at Melissa's grave. "Melissa's life showed people that abortion is murder. If you don't want a baby, I tell people, give it up for adoption. Melissa came into this world to show what abortion really means." As for why she died, Sandy said, "God took Melissa for a reason. He needed her in heaven."

ASSIGNMENTS

1) Update "For Melissa's Sake." Find an infant born under similar circumstances and track the baby's life, relying on in-depth interviews with family members and medical personnel treating the infant. Contrast the baby's treatment with that of infants like Melissa who routinely died two decades earlier.

2) Talk to the parents and family members of a compromised infant institutionalized with little hope of ever leading a "normal life". Write a story on how the family members' lives have been altered, and the decisions they face daily.

3) Interview a young adult born with a compromised medical condition that could have resulted in death during the time of Melissa. Focus on how such shaky beginnings have affected the person. Ask about whether this has colored his or her outlook on abortion, heroic medical advancements, and carrying on life.

22

THE MAN WITH A HEX

"The Man with a Hex" is one of those stories that started out with a strange telephone call. The man on the other end of the line was blabbering something to me about a curse a Brazilian woman had placed on him.

Say what?

Out of the blue, Keith Johnston, a man as ordinary as his name could imply, said he had tried everything to shake the hex, but nothing had worked. Speaking in a thick Texas-Oklahoma Pannandle accent, he asked whether I would consider writing a story about what he had been through.

Was this guy for real or what?

Despite my initial reservations, the sincerity of Keith's voice made me continue listening. He certainly had a story to tell. Here was a reserved businessman, his entire life governed by fact and reason, sputtering something about a refined middle-aged woman who, before his eyes, had turned into a depraved prostitute, smoking acrid-smelling cigars and talking in tongues. Keith said he had no other recourse but to hire a Brazilian priestess to lift the terrible curse that had been placed on him and his new wife.

Actually, Keith and I were a good match-up. I, too, was familiar with Brazilian voodoo, known as *macumba* or *condomble*. When I lived in Rio de Janeiro and Salvador da Bahia, I attended several voodoo ceremonies. At each, my eyes bugged out as followers would frenetically dance to wild drumbeats. Believers would become so overwrought that they blacked out. When they came to, they would take on the persona of an African saint. I remember seeing mild-mannered women magically transformed before my eyes into hooting, stomping, swearing prostitutes, just as Johnston had described. I used to date a college-educated Brazilian woman who resolutely believed in *condomble* in the same way ardent Catholics believe in the Holy Trinity.

Keith and I met the next day at a smoky barbecued-ribs joint around the corner from the newspaper office. When I first laid eyes on him, Keith looked like the least likely candidate to believe in anything unconventional, least of all Brazilian voodoo. He was as straight-laced as they came—a 52-year-old guy with neatly pressed creases in his brown twill pants, a wide blue necktie that blended in with his polyester shirt. *This* was the guy who believed demonic spirits had taken over his life?

Over brisket sandwiches that day, Keith told his story. It came out slowly, in an unpracticed, rambling manner, which added legitimacy to the tale. Thus began a series of interviews about what we grew to call Keith's "encounter." The story was a grabber, that's for sure, and when I pitched to my editors that I ought to go to Brazil to do additional reporting, they surprised me by saying yes.

The Man with a Hex

She smoked fetid-smelling cigars, stalked around the room, grunting and swearing, speaking in a low, throaty dialect that sounded more like a guttural African than Portuguese. Dona Ivete, a calm and gentle woman, had suddenly turned into the Brazilian voodoo saint Pomba-gira, a vulgar, red-skinned prostitute.

She stood up and looked wildly around her. She puffed on a long cigar. Then she squarely faced the American man and his Brazilian wife. She was specific about how to break the curse that had been placed on them.

A midnight trip to a cemetery was mandatory. A sacrifice of a small animal— a chicken or baby goat—would have to be made. After that, Keith and Sonia Johnston were to go to a waterfall and present offerings.

Johnston recalls, in detail, what followed: Dona Ivete would oversee the midnight cemetery ritual. "It will be too dangerous for you. The chances that an evil spirit will enter your body and never leave are too great," she said.

The following Wednesday morning, the first step completed, the couple met Dona Ivete at a small store specializing in voodoo statues and paraphernalia in Petropolis, 50 miles northwest of Rio de Janeiro. A car, loaded with sacks of food, clay bowls and dozens of cut flowers, was parked on the shady street in front. Dona Ivete and two assistants drove Keith and Sonia to the outskirts of town to reach the waterfall.

They parked, then climbed halfway up a steep, moss-covered mountainside. The morning air was humid and hot; the ground was spongy. The wildflowers that grew between giant palm trees gave off a rich scent. The assistants carried the offerings for the spirits—okra, rice, black beans, pumpkin, hard-boiled eggs, sun-dried meat, beer and a sugar cane liquor known as *cachaça*.

When they arrived at the foot of the waterfall, Dona Ivete, dressed in a white short-sleeved blouse and cotton slacks, started rotating her neck. She took off her sandals and stepped into the clear pool of water surrounded by boulders.

She puffed out her cheeks, then she sucked air in deeply. Suddenly, she whirled around and began speaking in tongues. Dona Ivete had once again received the spirit of the prostitute, Pomba-gira.

She picked up two large rocks, each weighing three or four pounds, and began pelting herself with them on her chest and shoulders over and over. Then she grabbed several waterlogged branches nearby and started lashing herself. She continued to talk in the unintelligible language.

Dona Ivete stopped abruptly. She closed her watery brown eyes. One or two minutes passed. She blinked several times. She had become Dona Ivete again, the kindly, gaunt lady with the mischievous smile.

As the ceremony was drawing to a close, an enormous cobalt blue butterfly appeared. Dona Ivete nodded and said the butterfly was a good sign. The offering to the spirits had worked; the couple was no longer in danger. The butterfly followed the entourage down the mountainside and then disappeared.

• • •

Keith Johnston, a lanky, blanched-skinned, 52-year-old man, now lives in Dallas with his wife and two children. For several years, he says, he lived in fear of something intangible, yet nonetheless real. Johnston's life was controlled by Brazilian voodoo, he says.

The man with the neatly combed hair and bulbous nose does not have the eyes of an adventurer or the appearance of an infidel who once lost his soul. His sideburns creep out toward his cheeks. He shuffles when he walks. He wears open-collar pastel shirts and checked pants. His speech is tentative and soft; the drawl reveals his Texas Panhandle origins.

When Johnston talks about the experience that changed his life, he rambles and pauses. His memory is clear and vivid, yet he talks without emotion about his odyssey into a netherworld of bizarre characters and symbols. An Episcopalian upbringing and a life governed by fact and reason left him unprepared to explain rationally what happened during his years in Brazil.

Johnston graduated from the University of Texas at Austin in 1955 and worked for 16 years in Washington, D.C., as a transportation analyst for the departments of defense and transportation.

After 23 years of marriage, he and his wife were divorced in 1973. By 1975, he had grown tired of life as a Washington bureaucrat. He was looking for a change. "I had always dreamed of Brazil. You know, the Amazon River, the spirit of adventure," he says. "I was ready to move far, far away."

That spring, a colleague told him the World Bank was about to grant a multi-million dollar loan to Brazil for a national transportation study. Johnston booked a seat on a Pan Am flight in July and spent 10 days of his vacation in Rio de Janeiro. There he met with Brazilian officials, who hired him on the spot as a technical consultant. Among the perks of his new job was a chauffeured ride to and from his office.

In September, Johnston moved to Brazil with his 14-year-old daughter, Donna Ruth, leaving his two other daughters with his ex-wife.

Johnston quickly settled in Rio, finding a furnished beachfront apartment on the stretch of land that straddles the established neighborhoods of Botofogo and Copacabana. He enrolled his daughter in the city's American School 40 minutes away.

Johnston marveled at Rio—the raw geographic beauty of the city, the balmy heat, the outdoor cafes, the deeply tanned women at the beach who wore minuscule bikini called tangas.

There was also a down side to the move. As with most expatriates, the first months were difficult. The culture, the language, the traffic and pollution all ground away at the logic of his decision to make a life in Brazil.

On Thanksgiving night, Johnston found himself alone and lonely. He took a bus to Prado Junior, a Copacabana plaza known for its bawdy nightclubs. He walked into a bar called Erotica. Sitting at one of the tables was Sonia, an attractive 29-year-old, olive-skinned woman with long hair the color of mahogany. A former circus ballerina from the interior of Brazil, she had come to Rio in search of work. She had been hired at the bar to flirt with male customers so that they would keep ordering drinks. She had an easy, lilting laugh, and the fact that she spoke halting English was a selling point with homesick Americans.

Johnston asked Sonia for her telephone number and called her the following week. Over the next few months, the two visited Sugar Loaf Mountain, Corcovado, and Ipanema Beach. In February, they spent carnival together, making the circuit of the city's glittery costume balls. Throughout the courtship, Sonia playfully tutored Johnston in Portuguese.

Johnston, who only eight months before was a weary bureaucrat trying to survive alone, enjoyed his new life. "Here I was pushing 50 and falling in love," he says.

The relationship did not sit well with Diva, the woman from whom Johnston had rented his Rio apartment. A blind divorcee in her early 40s, Diva did more than befriend the American, says Johnston. She dropped by uninvited. She spent hours in the apartment. She constantly flirted and teased, Johnston recalls.

It wasn't a relationship he encouraged. Undaunted, Diva persisted. "Forget about Sonia," Johnston recalls her saying. "Marry me. Take me to the U.S." He says his response was to go out of his way to avoid Diva. "She spooked me. There was something going on with her that I never could figure out," he says.

When Sonia came to the apartment for dinner, Diva would suddenly appear from nowhere. She often would take Sonia aside and sternly order her to leave Johnston.

"Diva made Sonia out to be the cause for our never getting married—which was completely out of the question," recalls Johnston. "She never let up. I didn't want to have anything to do with her."

Diva saw things differently. A curvacious woman with an aura of sexuality, she was not to be rebuffed. Johnston says Diva used to let herself into his apartment at all hours. Once she came by and pointedly told him she intended to spend the night with him.

Diva arrived the next evening wearing a flashy, low-cut dress. But when she saw Sonia, she stormed out of the apartment in a rage.

Diva soon changed her tactics. She bought Sonia a bottle of toilet water and when Sonia said she didn't want it, Diva opened the bottle and sprinkled the contents all over her.

If this was the couple's first encounter with voodoo, only Sonia suspected it. She rushed into the bathroom, and just didn't wash off the perfume but scrubbed her skin raw. When she explained her reaction to Johnston, he says he only scoffed.

On several occasions, Sonia received bouquets of wilted red or yellow roses. Johnston frequently would return to the apartment and find rose petals placed between the cushions of his living-room couch. Occasionally, he found burned candle stubs on the floor.

Keith and Sonia tried to ignore Diva, but whenever Sonia mentioned voodoo, Johnston says their conversations were heated. "The only times we ever argued were when we discussed this subject," he told me, avoiding even a mention of "voodoo."

By June 1976, the couple was living together. In January 1978, on vacation in Dallas, they were married by a justice of the peace. Johnny, their first child, was born four months later in Brazil.

Once back in Rio, Johnston began to encounter financial problems. His rent at the beachfront apartment had doubled, and Donna Ruth's tuition at the American school had quadrupled within two years. Keith and Sonia moved to a less expensive apartment in the middle-class neighborhood of Tijuca. Then, in February 1980, Johnston was transferred to the modernistic capital of Brasilia, almost 1,000 miles inland. Donna Ruth moved back to the United States to live with her mother.

Within a year, Brazil had entered a severe depression. Inflation rate was more than 10 percent per month, and unemployment topped 30 percent. The government embarked on a massive campaign of federal cutbacks. By March 1982, Johnston's contract with the Brazilian Department of Transportation had been canceled.

The Johnstons relocated back to the Rio de Janeiro area, this time to the suburb of Petropolis. Sonia soon was pregnant again.

With his government severance pay and pension, the equivalent of about $10,000, Johnston started investing heavily in the Rio de Janeiro stock market. Several times a week, he took the 90-minute bus ride to the city's financial center to buy and sell commodities on the exchange floor. For a while, his investments did well.

But July 7, the day Sonia went into labor, the market dropped more than 30 points. A baby girl, Jennifer, was born just as Johnston lost nearly $10,000 on a stock tip.

By the end of August, the bottom had fallen out of the market, and Johnston had lost everything. "I had enough to pay the rent for a couple of months, and that was it," he says. "One of the rules of the market is that your first losses are your smallest losses. Well, I didn't go by that. I kept waiting and waiting for the market to go up and up, but it never did."

With two children to feed and no money in the bank, Sonia convinced her husband to seek advice from a voodoo priestess, called a *macumbeira* or *mãe do santo*. The couple took the commuter bus to Rio and made an appointment to see Dona Marta, a woman in her late 40s who lived in Copacabana.

But after meeting Dona Marta, they thought she was a fraud. She wanted Johnston to sell his blue Dodge to pay for her services; she told them her husband, a used-car dealer, would give them a good price.

Sonia persisted in seeking the right *macumbeira*. She thought a reputable adviser would at least be able to explain how Keith had gotten into such a financial mess and how he might get out of it. Through friends, they heard about Dona Ivete, a woman who worked out of a religious artifact store named Casa Sete in Petropolis.

Sonia went alone to the first meeting with Dona Ivete. She walked to the back of Casa Sete, past cases displaying hundreds of crudely painted voodoo statues, glass beads and pieces of costume jewelry. She climbed a circular staircase at the rear of the store and entered a small room clouded with the haze of thick, acrid incense.

Sonia explained the couple's dilemma, and then Dona Ivete dealt her tarot cards. After five minutes, she looked up at Sonia and told her a mysterious blond woman was the source of the couple's financial problems. This woman had been responsible for Johnston's losing his job as well as his savings. She had placed a curse on Johnston, who had once lived in the same building with her. For $29, Dona Ivete said, she would remove the curse.

When Sonia told her husband about the meeting, the conservative Episcopalian from the Texas prairie thought back to his first years in Rio. "Blondes are not very common in Brazil. Diva was the only one I knew. I remembered the cheap perfume she poured on Sonia, the rose petals under the sofa cushions, the wilted flowers, the mysterious white candles."

"I didn't know if this business was right or wrong. But by that time, I was desperate," says Johnston. "I was out of work and couldn't get anything. I had two children and a wife to feed. I felt relieved; maybe this would be a way to solve our financial problems. I was willing to try anything."

The Johnstons went together for the next session with Dona Ivete. This time, she did not use cards. She went into a trance and prepared to help the couple neutralize the hex.

●   ●   ●

Sonia Johnston will not talk about her voodoo experiences now, and she wouldn't talk about them when I first met her in Brazil during a trip I made to research this story. She was readying to move to Dallas, where her husband had already settled. Keith had suggested I contact her once I arrived in Rio, telling me she could probably put me in touch with Dona Ivete.

But when I called Sonia, she was nervous, hesitant. When I went to see her in Petropolis, I found her in the midst of packing. The apartment was filled with crates and balls of crumpled paper. Brooms were strewn about. A picture of Sonia as a teenager, wearing a ballerina's tutu, hung on the living-room wall.

I asked about Dona Ivete.

"I don't want to have anything to do with her anymore," Sonia said. "This *macumba* business is evil and dangerous. Leave it alone."

In the center of downtown Petropolis, on the tree-lined street of Imperador, I found Casa Sete.

"Dona Ivete is upstairs and cannot be disturbed," said the sales clerk behind the counter. Five young women sat in a back room, fidgeting, each waiting her turn to climb the circular staircase. "She cannot be disturbed. Go away," the clerk said.

I returned to Rio, but I knew I did not want to leave without meeting the woman who could enter trances and speak in tongues. I went again to Petropolis, and at Casa Sete, the clerk behind the counter was more open this time.

"Go to the chocolate factory at the other end of town," she told me. "Then follow the road till it dead-ends. Take a dirt path, and walk up 200 more meters. Dona Ivete lives in the last house, highest on the hill."

I knocked on doors, asking where Dona Ivete lived. "*Ela mora la encima—* She lives up there," they all said, pointing to the top of the narrow dirt path.

Finally, I reached an exposed brick hut. I knocked on the lavender door. A handsome, middle-aged, dark-haired woman appeared. I had found Dona Ivete.

She invited me inside the tiny compound, with its living quarters and voodoo temple, a square room with a gray cement floor, full of miniature statues of saints, rhinestone jewelry and headdresses.

She apologized for not having cookies; we sat on a wooden bench and drank coffee. She told me how she had become a *mãe do santo*—and how she had tried to help Keith and Sonia Johnston.

"I received the saints 14 years ago," she said in a quiet voice, speaking the deeply accentuated Portuguese of southeastern Brazil. "I remember the day. I was talking to my husband and my daughter in the early evening. All at once, I started to talk in tongues. I didn't know what was happening. I cried, and became a totally different person.

"From that day on, my life changed. My husband still doesn't like what I do, but I have been called, and he has had to accept."

Dona Ivete did remember Keith and Sonia, the time at the cemetery, at the waterfall, the blue butterfly.

"I recall telling the couple about the curse and what would be needed to remove it," she said. "I went to the cemetery, and as soon as I arrived at the gates, I started shaking all over. Then everything went blank. I turned into a puta, ranting and raving. When it was all over and I came out of the trance, I had a throbbing pain in my head and above my heart. I felt like I was going to vomit. It was the worst of sensations."

While Dona Ivete will remove a curse, she refuses to put a hex on anyone. "No hex is good," she told me. "I want to help people with my gift. Once I had a woman who was crippled, and after three visits of intense prayer, she was able to walk."

She was glad to hear that the Johnstons were re-establishing their lives. "They seemed so troubled when they came to see me, so nervous and scared. I was glad to help them. They were such a nice couple," she said.

The last time Johnston saw Diva was in late 1978. Even after being told that a curse had been placed on him, he never confronted Diva. "I didn't want to giver her any satisfaction—whether it was she or not who caused the mess," he says.

He pauses for 10 or 15 seconds to ponder the possibility that perhaps there wasn't any curse, that perhaps his misfortunes were just bad luck, without any intervention of the supernatural.

"I'm not sure if something exercised control over my mind, but there definitely was something that exercised control over my circumstances," he says. "I suppose a pragmatic person could logically explain everything that happened to us. It's impossible to convince someone who hasn't experienced *macumba* that it's real."

Sonia and the children moved to the United States in April to join Johnston in Irving, where they now live in a $440-a-month, two-bedroom apartment just west of Texas Stadium. The place is virtually empty. All their furniture is in storage; Johnston doesn't have enough money to pay the freight bill from Brazil.

He says his career has taken a nosedive as a result of his nine years in Brazil. "If I hadn't gone, I still would be working for the government, and by now I probably would have advanced to G-15, the highest salary level."

On the positive side, he says he never expected to become a father again at his age. "If I hadn't gone to Brazil, I never would have started a family. That in itself has kept me young."

Keith and Sonia have joined the Charismatic movement and attend services at the Word of Faith Outreach Center in Farmer's Branch. Johnston was baptized earlier this year.

"I found out that what I had gone through was the work of Satan, not of God," he says. "I decided to devote myself to the Lord."

For her part, Sonia, who now reads the Bible daily, trembles when talking about Dona Ivete and the time at the waterfall. She still is reluctant to discuss her experiences. "I know that God doesn't like these things," she says. "They are dangerous. I get nervous when I think about those times. I want to follow the right path now. I've had it with the other way."

Without any friends here, Sonia is homesick. She says she can't stomach

American food, and she misses the crowded neighborhoods, the corner grocery stores, the warm ocean breezes at night. "Dallas is a lot like Brasilia, a new city without much feeling," she says.

Her English is still rudimentary; she and her husband converse in Portuguese. The children are just beginning to learn English. During the day, she watches soap operas on Channel 33, the Spanish-language station, and can pick up some of the plot.

Johnston has found part-time work as a salesman at a local department store, but soon plans to operate a franchise selling experimental water filters. He says he might even consider investing in the stock market again.

"From a material standpoint, we are probably worse off than we were in Brazil," he says. "But spiritually, we know that God will provide for us. We have confidence that someone is looking over us."

The Dallas Morning News, Judy 15, 1984

WRITING THE STORY

What is most striking about Brazilian voodoo is the transformation. Seeing a person morph into a different being right before your eyes, that's worth writing about. That's how I start "The Man with a Hex." It's a long beginning, in retrospect probably too long. Its length puts readers at risk. Like all writers, though, I'm banking on the intensity of the scene to pull readers all the way through. I worked on this lede for days, crafting and honing, moving paragraphs, inserting just enough detail to intrigue and welcome readers, not overwhelm them. The words and images are powerful.

Then the cobalt blue butterfly flutters into the story. A sign, says Dona Ivete, an omen of goodness that descends onto Keith and Sonia Johnston to smother the terrible evil that had so consumed their lives.

Phew! That dense, cluttered top requires a rest. The next section of the piece allows readers to put up their feet and take a breath. I set up the ordinary events that, one by one, lead to Keith's transition from Washington bureaucrat to Rio de Janeiro *bon vivant.* The reader follows Keith from meeting the exotic Sonia at the Erotica, their courtship, and ends with a quote designed to connect Keith with every reader: "Here I was pushing 50 and falling in love."

The next section might be entitled "And then the trouble begins." Keith's jealous landlord neighbor, Diva, goes into action, trying to split apart the happy couple. Diva employs all kinds of tactics, but to no avail. Keith and Sonia marry in Dallas. Their first child is born. Keith loses his job. Then he drops $10,000 in the Brazilian stock market just as the couple's second child is born.

The third section connects Dona Ivete with Keith and Sonia by detailing their meeting with the first *mãe do santo*, then Sonia's encounter with Dona Ivete, and finally the full-blown episode I describe in the lede.

The story now changes gears abruptly (too abruptly, I think). I drop in on Sonia in Brazil. I retell my story of finding the elusive Dona Ivete—knocking on doors, being told in no uncertain terms "Go away," walking down dead-end dirt paths until finally, Dona Ivete and the reader are face-to-face.

In my rendition, Dona Ivete bears little resemblance to the evil Pomba-gira prostitute depicted in the story's opener. In fact, the end of the section reminds me of a comment Dr. Ruth might make about two people going through a spate of bad luck. "Such a nice couple," Dona Ivete says as I'm about to leave.

Then it's time for the wrap-up—bringing the reader back to the present. Central to the entire story is Keith and Sonia's newfound connection to a local Charismatic church. They now see the light. Both roundly reject the "work of Satan." The payoff to that message is in the caboose of the story. All of what Keith and Sonia went through was for a purpose, Keith says. God is the answer.

EPILOGUE

On the Monday following publication of "The Man with a Hex," Keith called me. He was not pleased.

"Why didn't you mention our Church more?" Keith asked. *"That's* the word of the Lord. *That's* what people need to know about. By gosh, Stephen, you practically glamorized the voodoo spirits in that story of yours."

I knew that Keith would be disappointed. The reason Keith had pitched his story to me in the first place was to show the evil of Brazilian voodoo, and to demonstrate how with devotion to Christ, such evil could be choked to death. The story Keith wanted me to write was to use his experiences with Dona Ivete as a precursor to his becoming a Christian. The message I got from Keith was that he had hoped my story would help spread the Word—that the Lord is more powerful than the demons of Satan and Brazilian spiritualism. Keith's motive was to announce to the world (at least the world of Dallas, Texas) that he had undergone his terrible ordeal to learn the wonder of God.

Despite my efforts to find Keith or Sonia Johnston these days, they have disappeared, at least from my radar. I tried to track them down in the United States and in Brazil, but came up empty-handed. I tried calling the Charismatic church they had joined, but discovered that the Word of Faith Outreach Center in Farmer's Branch had been shut down by law enforcement authorities. Its leader, televangelist Robert Tilton, had amassed a personal fortune and then disappeared. The Texas attorney general spared no words when he charged Tilton with "raping the most vulnerable segments of our society—the poor, the infirm, the ignorant ... who believe his garbage."

Ultimately, there might not have been too much difference between what Tilton and Dona Ivete preached. Much of Tilton's empire was anchored in mailing to followers a "gift from God"—"miracle" cornmeal packets, holy oil, faith rings, cutout angels. During his revivalist meetings, Tilton, like Dona Ivete, would often mesmerize his following by speaking in tongues.

ASSIGNMENTS

1) Visit an African spiritual supply store in your area. Interview the owner, employees and customers. Write about the services offered at, or through, the store. Probe the community the store serves. Wangle an invitation to a temple of *santeria* or other similar religious affiliation. Write about what you experience.

2) Interview suppliers and manufacturers of products sold in such stores. Find out where the market for such products is growing the strongest. Write about the array of products offered, as well as their intended uses.

3) Interview people in your area who view the existence of African-originated religions to be in direct opposition to Christianity. Find out whether any efforts are being made to curb the popularity of such spiritualistic religions, based on the predominance of Christian theology in America. On another front, pursue whether *santeria* or *macumba* temples and shrines in residential neighborhoods are stirring up opposition, since many are in conflict with zoning ordinances.

23

MAN'S FATE HINGES ON TESTIMONY OF DAUGHTER, 3; CONFUSED PORTRAIT EMERGES OF SUSPECT FREED IN WIFE'S DEATH

While working at *The Los Angeles Times*, my beat was the criminal courts in Van Nuys, the legal epicenter for the sprawling community known as the San Fernando Valley. Then, as now, there was more crime and punishment in the San Fernando Valley than any one journalist could ever hope to write about. A third of Los Angeles lives in the pollution-filled envelope Los Angelinos call "The Valley," and just about all the crime that takes place there is processed in the Van Nuys Courthouse. Every day, when I walked into the 1950s glass-and-steel building, my job was to choose from a vast menu of wrongdoing: homicides, rapes, child molestations, drug deals gone bad.

Homicides, of course, guaranteed the biggest play. Even a patrician paper like the *Times* loved a spectacular murder, especially when it involved money, love, hate or drugs—and most homicides involve three out of the four. There was the story of the teenager who whacked his mother to death with a baseball bat, the elderly real estate agent who loved the color purple (she even drove a purple Buick) bludgeoned by her 22-year-old mariachi-singing lover, and the housewife who shot her husband after he tied her up. (She was acquitted when the jury declared the murder justifiable.) Of the hundreds of bizarre crimes I wrote about, though, one case stands out: the execution-style murder of Darlene Conklin.

The murder seemed spun from the overactive imagination of a TV scriptwriter. Police believed that Darlene was murdered by her husband, Harry J. Conklin, an ex-con-turned Hollywood studio grip. The prosecution had little evidence. Their case rested solely on the testimony of an eyewitness: the couple's three-year-old daughter, Amanda. The girl's testimony was crucial; without it, the district attorney would be forced to let Conklin go free. In a spectacular, emotion-packed hearing, a Superior Court judge ruled that the girl was too young to testify. Faced with freeing Conklin, prosecutors made a last-ditch effort to tie Conklin to the crime by exhuming Darlene Conklin's body. Prosecutors believed that Conklin had secreted the murder weapons in his wife's casket. Conklin had been the last person to see the open casket, and had sealed and locked the casket with a key. But when police examined the unearthed casket, they found no weapons. The district attorney had no choice but to drop all charges against Conklin.

By that time, Conklin had been held in jail without bail for five months. On the morning he was scheduled to go free, I called the jail and asked what time Conklin would be released.

The sheriff's deputy said 12:30 p.m.

I asked from which door of the county lock-up facility Conklin would exit.

At the appointed hour, I positioned myself at the aforementioned door, and met Conklin.

I introduced myself. I had seconds to make my pitch.

"Would you like to give your side of your wife's murder?" I asked.

Conklin looked blank.

"All we've heard is the prosecution's side. If you didn't kill your wife, then publicity may help find the murderer."

"I didn't kill her," Conklin said on no uncertain terms, staring me down.

I pulled from my wallet a business card and asked Conklin to consider talking to me for an interview.

"You gotta be kidding," he replied. Then he reconsidered, "Let me think about it."

"Where're you going now?" I asked.

"To get something to eat. Jail food ain't very tasty."

I'm not sure why I asked what I asked next, but at the time, it seemed only natural.

"Whaddaya gonna eat?"

"A steak and fries," Conklin said, smiling,

Three days later, while working on a takeout on Conklin and the dropped murder charges, my phone rang. It was Conklin.

"I'll talk," he said. "How fast can you get over to my cousin's house?"

Man's Fate Hinges on Testimony of Daughter, 3

On the morning of Aug. 22, Darlene Conklin, a 38-year-old Reseda housewife, was opening her refrigerator door when someone stuck a .38-caliber revolver at the base of her neck and fired a single shot.

The person who led police to the murder suspect—Harry Conklin, Darlene's 39-year-old husband—was the couple's daughter, Amanda. She told detectives and a police-appointed psychologist she was an eyewitness.

The problem was Amanda's age: three.

The question now before Van Nuys Superior Court Judge Melvin B. Grover is whether the testimony of such a witness should be allowed in court.

Legal and medical experts say that if the girl, who was 37 months old at the time of the slaying, is found qualified by Grover to serve as a witness, she will be one of the youngest ever allowed in a California court.

After two days of questioning the child by defense and prosecution attorneys, Grover on Thursday said he will make his decision today.

According to California law, no person can be disqualified from testifying in a court of law unless it can be proven that the person is unable to express himself, or that the person does not understand the duty of a witness to tell the truth.

During more than three hours on the witness stand in qualifying hearings Wednesday and Thursday in Grover's court, Amanda Conklin answered dozens of questions, detailing the day her mother was killed. She occasionally left the chair and crawled on her knees in the witness box.

The unusual case drew not only family members but also dozens of court-watchers and deputy district attorneys.

The questions posed to Amanda this week were aimed solely at establishing her competence, not her father's guilt. The trial jury will not be selected until the issue of her fitness as a witness is resolved.

On the stand, the girl avoided looking at her father, who sat 15 feet in front of her.

Judge Grover asked her why.

"I don't want to look at my daddy because of what he did to my mommy," she said, toying with a plastic cup and spoon.

"What did you see?" Grover asked.

"My mommy on the floor," she said.

When Grover asked her to elaborate, the girl said, "I was in the kitchen when I heard the gun."

If the girl is not allowed to testify, prosecutors say they will be hard-pressed to prove Conklin's guilt.

"She is the only link between the murder and the father," Deputy District Attorney Robert McIntosh said. "That's about all we have to go on."

Deputy District Attorney Gail Tamler, a specialist in the agency's child abuse section, which handles hundreds of cases of children who are called to testify in court, said she had never heard of a younger witness than Amanda.

UCLA child psychiatrist Spencer Eth, the author of a 1984 study about children who witness homicides, said, "If not the youngest, she's got to be one of the very youngest."

Eth said that in a case like the Conklin murder, a child of Amanda's age can be a reliable witness.

He said preschool children cannot recall details and are unaware of time elements when asked to remember specific events, but they usually do not have the sophistication needed to fabricate.

"They may have selective recall, they may embellish stories with elaboration, but they don't intentionally lie," Eth said. Unlike adults, who can block out a catastrophic event through a process known as traumatic amnesia, Eth said children usually can clearly recall central actions of an important event.

"The issue is whether Amanda can perceive, recollect and communicate her recollections about the relevant matters in the case," said prosecutor McIntosh.

"What she saw that day is a snapshot in her mind. All we want is to be allowed to see the content of that snapshot."

When detectives were called to the site of the slaying, which took place on the 17600 block of LeMay Place, they found no murder weapon, nor could they ascertain a motive. The house and all its belongings were intact, and there were no signs of a struggle, they said.

Why would anyone want to kill Darlene Conklin, who from all accounts was a loving and devoted wife and mother?

A week after the murder, Amanda told authorities her father had killed her mother. A month after that, Harry Conklin, a part-time 20th Century Fox Studios grip, was arrested. Unable to post $200,000 bail, he remains in custody at Los Angeles County Jail.

Amanda was found by her aunt, Brenda Barry, at about 1 p.m. on the day of the slaying. She was sitting in her bedroom with the door wedged shut from the outside.

Barry, the sister of the dead woman, testified at a preliminary hearing in November that the girl had "a look on her face I had never seen. She was scared, frightened ... her color was terrible. I had never seen that color skin on her."

When police Detective Patrick Conmay talked to Amanda the next day, she told him, "Daddy knocked my mommy down and put me in my room."

Two pieces of circumstantial evidence were introduced at the preliminary hearing.

A friend of the Conklins, Robert Regalado, testified that the couple's four-year marriage had deteriorated. When asked about the relationship, Regalado said Harry Conklin had told him how unhappy he was. Darlene had been nagging him and breathing down his back. And he said, 'You know, I am going to have to get rid of her.'"

Regalado said he then asked Conklin, "Well, why don't you just divorce her or walk away?"

"No," Regalado recalled Conklin's saying. "I will figure something out."

But perhaps the most curious evidence introduced at the preliminary hearing was a book entitled "Death Dealer's Manual," written by Bradley J. Steiner. According to a stamp inside the book, it was purchased at a North Hollywood survivalist store.

The book, found inside the headboard in the couple's bedroom, is a step-by-step guide to murder.

Detectives at the hearing said the methods listed in the book nearly match those used to kill Darlene Conklin.

"The book indicated that the primary place to shoot a person would be at the base of the brain, and the other place would be the spinal cord," Detective Joseph Diglio testified. "The book also indicated to destroy and get rid of the weapon, because without the weapon, the police couldn't put a case together."

One week after the slaying, police took Amanda to child psychologist Joy Graves, who interviewed the girl over 14 sessions.

Reading her notes aloud Thursday in court, Graves testified that at the first session, Amanda was asked to act out the day of the slaying by using dolls.

"She threw the father doll away and looked anxious, her eyes becoming wide. She froze and her eyes were wide open. She stated her daddy hit her mommy in the kitchen."

But Conklin's attorney, Deputy Public Defender Barry Taylor, argued Thursday that such testimony from the girl could be a fabrication.

"She doesn't have a sufficient capacity to recollect what happened on the day of the slaying, as opposed to what she's been told happened," Taylor said in an interview.

He pointed to the fact that since Aug. 22, Amanda has been staying with her aunt, Barry, who he says maybe influenced the girl and colored her recollection.

"She has been programmed by several people," Taylor said. "The question is at what point does she tell us what she actually remembers, as opposed to what other people have told her what they think happened?"

Los Angeles Times, February 1, 1985

Confused Portrait Emerges of Suspect Freed in Wife's Death

Harry J. Conklin, a 39-year-old Reseda man with a penchant for hunting knives, pet leopards and swastika tattoos, works as a studio grip. His credits include "Hill Street Blues," "Remington Steele" and "Cover Up."

Now Conklin finds himself starring in a real-life drama. He is playing a man who says he was falsely charged with shooting to death his 38-year-old wife in front of their 3-year-old daughter last year.

The case against Conklin hinged on testimony from daughter Amanda, who told police that she had witnessed the slaying. But after a judge refused to allow the girl to testify in court because of her age—stripping the prosecution of its only firsthand evidence—charges against Conklin were dropped two weeks ago.

Both the police detective and the deputy district attorney who investigated the case say they remain "absolutely convinced" that Conklin killed his wife.

Conklin answers: "I know my conscience and my heart are clear. I can go up to Forest Lawn and kneel next to my wife's grave and speak my sentiments and have no guilt."

Released after five months in jail, Conklin says he doesn't know who killed his wife or for what reason.

To police he was a logical suspect. Sent to a series of reformatories before he reached his 15th birthday, Conklin went on to serve terms for two burglaries, a prison escape and assaulting a police office, court records show.

"I know it looks bad for me, but they've closed the case," he said. "They think I did it. If you've done something wrong and you've paid your dues, it should be over and done with."

Because there is no statute of limitations in murder cases, prosecutors can reopen their case against Conklin whenever they want—in one year or in 20 years. Prosecutors say they may wait until Amanda, ruled by a judge to be an unreliable witness last month, can be certified at an older age.

"This will always hang over my head," Conklin said. "It's like living in the shadow of a guillotine—you can have the blade fall on your head at any minute."

Interviews with friends and relatives draw a contrasting portrait of Conklin.

On the surface, Darlene and Harry Conklin appeared to be a happy couple with a four-year marriage, lovingly raising their only daughter. Darlene's brother, Lewis Cohen, said the couple "never argued, and looked lovey-dovey all the time."

But others described Darlene Conklin as a woman in constant fear of a sadistic man with a violent temper who habitually terrorized her. One former neighbor recalled a pregnant Darlene hysterically saying that Harry had stuck a loaded gun into her stomach and threatened to shoot.

Wearing a plaid cowboy shirt with snaps at the pockets, faded jeans and scuffed white tennis shoes, Conklin this week talked about the case against him. He is a compact, muscular man with a wide, toothy smile.

His arms, wrists and legs are covered with tattoos. On his right biceps he has a tattoo of a growling black panther; on his stomach is a skull-and-crossbones tattoo in the shape of a swastika. The stomach tattoo is merely "a war and peace sign," he said. "It has nothing to do with anything. Its significance is the turmoil I've been through."

On this day, staying at a relative's home in the San Fernando Valley, he was preparing to leave for work at a motion picture shoot in Moorpark.

Conklin calls himself a patriot, a survivalist, a man ready to defend his family with a home arsenal of knives and guns. When police searched his Reseda home after the slaying, they found a photograph of Conklin dressed in army fatigues, a camouflage-colored headband and an orange T-shirt with the emblazoned slogan: "I'd Rather Be Killing Communists."

At age 18 he was convicted of commercial burglary in Kentucky. While on parole, he was convicted of grand theft auto. In 1968, he was sentenced to the California Institution for Men at Chino for residential burglary. While he was assigned to the fire-patrol detail at Chino, he escaped.

Three weeks later, as he sat in a Long Beach bar, police made a routine identification check of patrons. Lined up and about to be frisked, Conklin said, he pulled a gun on the officer, who returned with five shots that missed him. This time he wound up in San Quentin.

Released in 1973, Conklin resettled in Los Angeles. He resumed his hobbies of collecting motorcycles, rifles, shotguns, pistols and vintage hunting knives. He bought a pet leopard that he said he eventually had to shoot after it mauled a neighborhood child.

He returned to the vocation he had entered in 1969, working as a grip, a handyman on motion picture and television sets. He married in 1974, but after six months, he and his wife filed for divorce. He remarried in 1976, and that marriage ended after two years because of irreconcilable differences.

In October 1979, Conklin married Darlene Cohen, whom he met when he was doing carpentry on her house.

"It was like we had known each other our whole lives," Conklin said in a dreamy reverie. "There were a lot of people who were jealous of the life Darlene and I had together. We lived, we enjoyed."

They would often take off on Conklin's powerful motorcycle, driving 800 miles on a single weekend. "We'd just pick a direction and go," he said.

With their daughter, Amanda, born in the summer of 1981, the three became a family, first living in Panorama City and eventually moving to Reseda. He doted on his wife and daughter, he said. Whenever he was working on a movie set, he said, he would call home two or three times to check on them.

However, two former neighbors—a husband and wife who spoke on the condition that their names not be used, explaining that they fear Conklin—described the relationship differently.

One neighbor said Darlene told her that Harry often held a gun to Darlene's head.

"Darlene said to me if she ever told her sister and brother anything about" their private life, "he would kill her," the neighbor said.

The other neighbor said Conklin boasted that he "kept his wife pregnant and her mouth shut."

The neighbors and Darlene's brother said Harry often taunted his wife about the fact that she was Jewish. He would point out to friends that she had a hooknose, they said. One of the neighbors said Harry told him that he hated Jews, and flaunted the four-inch-wide Nazi tattoo as proof.

"She was scared since the day she married him," said one of the neighbors.

Conklin responded: "I never had occasion to ever get angry with Darlene. There's no one who can look me in the eye and can say they have ever seen me get angry with my wife."

Bob Anger, who was Conklin's boss on the television show "Cover Up" last summer, recalled Conklin as "a macho sort of man, into bikes and knives, who was a loudmouth."

When Conklin wasn't working, he indulged in what was becoming his consuming hobby: survivalism. On at least one occasion, he stopped by a North Hollywood store called The Larder, which stocks items ranging from knives and compasses to manuals on the use of submachine guns. It was sometime in 1983 that he went there and bought a step-by-step guide to murder called "The Death Dealer's Manual," whose author was listed as Bradley J. Steiner.

Conklin said that when he returned home with the book, he read it aloud to his wife. "It was strictly a curiosity item. We got a good laugh over it; it was a joke, that's all."

But after Darlene Conklin's nightgown-clad body was found with two bullet holes—one in her back, the other at the base of her neck—police did not share that view.

They found the 100-page paperback in the headboard of the couple's bed, and the method described in the manual fit the pattern in which Darlene Conklin was killed.

By 1:15 p.m. on the day Darlene Conklin was killed, her younger sister, Brenda Barry, arrived at the Conklin house at the 17600 block of LeMay Place to baby-sit Amanda while Darlene was to have her hair cut. When Barry walked into the kitchen, she found Darlene's body lying on the floor in front of an open refrigerator.

Amanda Conklin was shut in her bedroom, the door wedged closed from the outside. She was playing on her bed with a toy kitten stuffed with straw.

Police say they did not suspect Conklin as the murderer until Amanda told a police psychologist one week after the slaying that she had seen her father hit her mother in the kitchen on the morning of the killing. The child, who was three years, one month old at the time, said she then heard a gun fire.

That, along with evidence that Conklin had bought the murder manual and complained to a family friend that he wanted to "get rid" of his wife, persuaded police to arrest Conklin.

He was taken into custody in late September, five weeks after his wife's death. When questioned, Conklin denied that he was home when the incident took place. He told police that he had left for work early that morning. Police checked with studio personnel, who verified that Conklin had been on location by 6 a.m. However, testimony by a coroner's examiner at Conklin's preliminary hearing indicated that the killing could have taken place before Conklin left the house.

Anger says he doesn't believe that Conklin killed his wife.

On the afternoon of the slaying, Conklin called Anger and told him about Darlene's death.

"He's either a great actor or expressing the anguish anyone would feel when his wife gets killed," Anger said. "He was sobbing; he was full of sorrow. Based on that, I don't think he killed his wife. His voice conveyed complete surprise. He was completely blown away."

Conklin dismisses the circumstantial evidence against him.

"The police think I'd leave that book around if I'd followed the instructions?" he asked rhetorically.

"That doesn't make any sense. You look at any movie about crime these days, you read any cheap paperback, and it lists how to kill someone. If I'm being held because of that book, then you'd have to hold several million other people who read best sellers."

He contends that his daughter, Amanda, has been coached by zealous prosecutors and by Barry, her maternal aunt, with whom she has been living since his arrest.

Conklin doesn't deny that his daughter saw the murder.

"I feel that Amanda probably did see something," he said. "But I don't think she was sufficiently awake to understand what she saw. I think her mind was in a confused state, and now she's been tutored about what she thinks she saw."

Brenda Barry was given temporary custody of Amanda on Oct. 15. Conklin said he wants his daughter back, and on March 15, when Barry's custody order expires, he will seek return of her.

"If I have to, I'll spend every single penny I have to get her back," he said. "Nobody else is going to care for my daughter and rear her."

Not allowed to talk to her because of a court order, he said, "The hardest thing

I've ever done in my life was having to sit in a courtroom looking at her, and not being able to touch her or talk to her," referring to the witness qualification hearings held in Superior Court last month in Van Nuys.

Conklin said his parents intend to relocate from New Jersey to California to help care for the girl. Because she "has been conditioned into thinking that I killed her mother," he said, both he and his daughter will seek the help of a therapist.

Unable to raise bail, Conklin remained in jail from the time of his arrest until the district attorney dropped charges.

No physical evidence, not even the weapon, has ever been recovered. There was no apparent motive for the murder, nothing was found missing at the house, the house showed no signs of forced entry and there was no evidence that Darlene Conklin had been sexually molested.

If Harry Conklin didn't kill Darlene Conklin, who did?

"It could have been someone who went to the wrong house," Conklin suggested, "or someone reaching out to try to hurt me from my past." He declined to go into specifics.

Conklin and Darlene's family members said they miss Darlene. Curiously, her brother, Lewis Cohen, recalled that the night before the murder, Darlene told him she had a dream that a man had come in to the Reseda house and had taken a gun, pointed it to her head and shot her.

Conklin has heard the story from Cohen. He says he doesn't know what to make of it. He shakes his head, is silent, and then looks down at his knees.

"As long as whoever did it is out there, I'll never feel free," he said.

Los Angeles Times, February 22, 1985

WRITING THE STORY

The Harry Conklin story had all the elements of a blockbuster story. Everywhere I turned, there was something in the story that grabbed the reader's lapel and said, "You're not going to believe this, but ... ." The crime itself was lurid, then came the startling news that the couple's daughter was an eyewitness. Then, when Superior Court Judge Melvin B. Grover played the role of the spoiler, ruling that Amanda Conklin was too young to testify, the story got hotter. The plot, though, took the most bizarre turn when police dug up Darlene's body in the hope of finding the murder weapons.

"Man's Fate Hinges on Testimony of Daughter, 3" is a straightforward daily about Amanda Conklin's day on the stand to determine her eligibility as a witness. There is no reason to hype the story; the sensational facts speak for themselves. Short paragraphs sell the story, particularly the third graf in which I place the "nut" of the piece. As always, detail is important. So is observation. Writing that Amanda left the chair and crawled on her hands and knees in the witness box is essential to creating the scene of this extraordinary day in court. So is writing that during the entire court proceeding, Amanda avoided looking at her father, who sat only 15 feet away from her.

The use of dialogue is essential, since it helps convey suspense. It also takes the reader by the hand inside the forbidding courtroom of officialdom.

When asked why Amanda didn't want to look at her father, I quote Amanda as saying, "'I don't want to look at my daddy because of what he did to my mommy,' she said, toying with a plastic cup and spoon."

This is material no writer could ruin.

Because of my enterprise at the door of the county lockup facility, I was rewarded with the interview with Conklin. But even if Conklin hadn't called me, I was preparing to write about him. There was too much to ignore. Going through voluminous court documents, I discovered a dark shadow of Conklin's past—his multiple prison terms, his love of guns, motorcycles, knives and pet leopards. I wove segments of the interview throughout the piece. I went out to the neighborhood where the Conklins had lived, and knocked on neighbors' doors. One neighbor told me to call someone who used to live next to the couple. I was able to get alarming information about Harry Conklin, but off the record. Next, I talked to Darlene's siblings about their sister's murder, and they gave me an earful. I talked to Conklin's boss, as well as employees at a local survivalist store where Conklin had bought *The Death Dealer's Manual*, the book police found in the headboard of the couple's bed.

At one point, I asked Conklin to show me his stomach. I wanted to verify what the neighbors had told me about the Nazi tattoo. This was significant because Darlene was Jewish; her maiden name Cohen.

Conklin gave me a hateful stare. I persisted. There was a standoff of sorts, until Conklin lifted his shirt, and then sneered at me, bare chested.

Everything I had discovered about Conklin pointed to his involvement in his wife's murder. But there was no hard evidence to prove any connection, and that's why the story was so compelling. As I peppered Conklin with question after question, I kept asking myself whether Conklin was a murderer—or a grieving widow whose wife had been killed by someone out to settle an old score. That a man who may have gotten away with murder was sitting across from me, just the two of us in a private house, was an eerie sensation. I felt a sense of relief when I finished the interview, shook Conklin's hand, and walked out the door.

EPILOGUE

While preparing this book, I sent letters to Darlene Conklin's brother and sister, who both still live in the San Fernando Valley, yet received no responses. I was able, though, to contact Robert McIntosh, the prosecutor in the case.

McIntosh said that for the last decade and a half Amanda had been brought up by Brenda Barry, Darlene's sister. Conklin had never contested custody after the murder, and had had no contact with his daughter since the slaying. Almost 20 years after the murder, McIntosh insisted that Conklin was the killer.

Amanda was the key to the case, McIntosh said. "She heard them argue. She saw him hit her. He put her in her room, then she heard the gun go off. She saw him standing over her dead mother. When the judge disallowed her testimony, I knew that this guy had gotten away with murder. There is absolutely no doubt about it in my mind."

For McIntosh, no longer a deputy district attorney but since 1987 a court commissioner in Van Nuys, the Conklin murder has stayed with him. "I still dream about the case often. I think over and over, what else could I have done?"

Through an Internet search, I discovered that Harry Conklin still lives in the Los Angeles area, but my attempts to reach him were fruitless. I contacted Local 80 of the Motion Picture Studio Grips Union in Burbank, and was told that Conklin no longer was a member and had dropped out of the business. The last film Conklin had worked on was a horror movie entitled *Halloween 4,* released in 1988.

ASSIGNMENTS

1) Locate a person who was tried for a crime and found not guilty. The case doesn't have to be a homicide, but any felony. Interview the former defendant. Allow him or her to air gripes and grievances about the legal system. Interview victims, family members, and the defendant's attorney, as well as the presiding judge and prosecutor in the case.

2) Talk to adults who have suffered severe trauma as children. Often there are support groups for such persons. With permission, attend such group meetings. Write about the lasting effects childhood trauma can have. Use specific examples from victims you interview.

3) Interview a retiring prosecutor or police officer, and write about the cases that got away—unsolved crimes. Find out whether your local, regional or state law-enforcement agency has a cold-case division, a department specifically designed to pursue investigations of unsolved felonies. What was the last case solved, and how?

ORDINARY CIRCUMSTANCES

24

A CANNERY CONNECTION

Two months after I graduated from the University of California, I showed up one morning at the Del Monte Cannery in nearby Emeryville, looking for a job. With 40 or so other unemployed men, I sat for eight hours on a straight-back, wooden bench in the cannery's Worker Applicants Room. Every hour or two, a square-shouldered man wearing a clip-on tie, short-sleeved white shirt, and white hard-hat would open up a side door to the Bullpen, as the men around me called it, and with his right hand, hold up one to five fingers, indicating how many new men he needed. A snarly woman with auburn-colored hair twisted in a tight bun would point to one of us. "You!" she'd snap, and off the man would go with the foreman.

That first day, the Pit Boss, as we called her, ignored me, but my patience paid off the next day. After two hours, she pointed her index finger my way. Through the side door, I followed the foreman, who issued me a hardhat and earplugs. Inside the plant, the noise was deafening; the foreman motioned me to insert my earplugs immediately. I had to walk fast to keep up as we passed scores of conveyor belts carrying tens of thousands of sliding, clanking cans of fruit cocktail. The sickening sweet smell of syrup pervaded the plant. The sugary scent clung to the insides of my nostrils long after I left the cannery each day. As "A Cannery Connection" details, my job was to be a "depalletizer."

A Cannery Connection

BERKELEY, Calif.—The pungent smell of peaches and pears being canned and the constant droning of cans clanking and machinery buzzing are enough to make any newcomer sick.

Under the nonstop motion of Del Monte's cannery in Emeryville, Calif., lies an eternal monotony. Time and space are unknown to employees. Severed from outside, they are wedged into a self-contained world, witnessing one rung of a giant ladder spanning from nature's product to man's convenience.

When I first started with Del Monte I was assigned—apparently by luck—to one of the more exciting jobs. I was a "depalletizer," which meant my job for eight hours a day, 56 hours a week (cannery employees work every day) was to push a button, which lowered 144 cans of fruit cocktail onto a wooden tray. The initial excitement died after 10 minutes; the boredom began after 15. I had a partner whose name I never knew. He was big, muscular—he did 100 pushups once a day between pushes of his button—and had his hair tied in a yellow satin bandana.

His greeting when I first began to work startled me: "Hey man, whatsyagot to get loaded on?"

I laughed, "Hey what do you mean? This stuff looks so easy. All you have to do is just look busy."

My co-worker gave no reply, only a look of disgust that remained with him for the six days of my job. We never talked again.

Soon I, like my partner, became sophisticated. Getting high, I discovered, was the only thing to do. It was the only alternative to watching thousands of fruit cocktails continually sliding down from a conveyor belt, perfectly fitting into molded slots, and perfectly filling up the wooden pallets. Every eight minutes the same process was repeated.

I quickly learned vicious little games workers played on each other. One that drew my attention took place along the endless conveyor belts, lined with crews of workers each doing anything from sorting peaches to loading cans in shipping cartons. A testy worker would hold up several cans from continuing down the conveyor belt and, when he had enough of them, suddenly send them down, bombarding the next worker with an overload of cans and jamming up the assembly line, causing the second worker anguish (He could lose his job.) and, in some instances, physical harm.

Excitement for cannery workers meant something unexpected happening: a can lodged sideways, stopping up the conveyor belt, or a machinery failure. But even those small joys would last only three or four minutes. Everything—workers included—had to run smoothly. And if it didn't, it was quickly repaired or replaced.

So for the most part, workers got loaded on either alcohol or drugs. Every

Thursday—we were paid on Wednesday—my partner would come to work happy, relieved and loaded on LSD. Marijuana was passed around freely in the locker room among men in their forties and fifties.

And who could blame them, having to spend a third of their day under such conditions? I soon joined their ranks. There was no social pressure to join them; it was the only alternative to the din of cans and the monotony of work.

During the two, 12-minute breaks workers were allowed each eight-hour day, I usually went to the cafeteria, where employees could find quiet. Most would close their eyes and nibble on a candy bar or sip cheap whiskey.

After six straight days, I quit. I had made $200 and was sick of the new experience. Most workers continued to endure, hoping to make enough money to buy liquor or drugs so they could stay high enough to work another week. There really was not too much else to do, or even think about.

The New York Times, September 20, 1973

WRITING THE STORY

This short piece was no ordinary fare for the staid op-ed page of *The New York Times,* and I wanted to alert readers to that fact fast. I opted for a one-two-three punch in the lede: the sights, sounds and smell inside a west-coast cannery, as well as my own assessment of such sensory overload. In the second and third grafs, I pull back my focus. I identify where the action is taking place and how long I worked at the cannery. I sum up the essence of the job: transforming "nature's product" to "man's convenience." I let the reader know my specific job, the hours I worked weekly, and my relationship with my co-worker.

The description of my partner—that he does 100 pushups a day on the job, that he wears a satin bandana, and that his first words to me were an inquiry (really a plea) about drug availability—are essential details the reader must get as quickly as possible. When I respond to my partner that the job appears easy, he greets me with scorn. I find out that it's the simplicity of the job that motivates him and almost everyone else at the cannery to take drugs as often as possible. Thus the headline: "A Cannery Connection."

During my breaks, I watched how workers sabotaged each other along the assembly line for short-lived moments of pleasure. But what I noticed most was how widespread drug use was. After my shift ended each day, I recorded my observations in a spiral-bound reporter's notebook in my car.

Soon, I realized why management required such a ready supply of labor in the Bullpen. Employee turnover was constant. Workers quit not just every day, but every hour. For the minimum wage earned, some workers chose not to endure the noise, stink and monotony any longer than absolutely necessary. For those who stayed, the only solace seemed to be drugs. When the foreman caught workers smoking marijuana or taking drugs, he would fire them on the spot. Alcohol, at least back then, seemed to be tolerated by management unless it interfered with productivity.

On the evening I quit, I went home, reviewed each day's account in my notebook, and worked the story top to bottom. The next day, I sent the completed piece to the *The New York Times,* never really expecting the newspaper to publish it.

EPILOGUE

The original version of "A Cannery Connection" sent to *The Times* was three times as long as what the newspaper published. After a month of hearing nothing from *The Times,* I assumed the piece had been summarily rejected. Six weeks later, at 7 a.m., an attorney who represented the canners' union called me to say how much he liked the article.

"What article?" I asked groggily.

"Why, the story in today's *New York Times.*"

Besides shortening the piece, *The Times'* editors sanitized it considerably. In my version, the last word in the lede was not "sick," but "vomit." I wrote much more about the monotony of the job and introduced three workers I had met. But all that was too much detail for a 500-word glimpse into the world of a California cannery.

I probably surprised not just a few readers by my admission of marijuana use. In addition to being true, the confession helps sell the story to readers. Even for the short time I spent at the cannery, I became a part of its subterranean environment. I didn't indulge to join the cannery's subculture. I partook for the same reason as the others: to make the job tolerable. Drugs were so pervasive they became as much a part of the fruit cocktail we canned every day as did the peaches and pears.

The ending of the piece, even after three decades, remains one of my favorite closings. "Most workers continued to endure, hoping to make enough money to buy liquor or drugs so they could stay high enough to work another week. There really was not too much else to do, or even think about." These guys were not working for sustenance, to buy a TV or to send their kids to college. They worked only to get enough anesthetic to numb themselves to work another week.

The job had been story material for me, and I got out after six days. My co-workers shared no such luxury. The cannery defined their lives. Each day they continued to work, the cannery carved out larger and larger slices of their dignity and self-esteem.

ASSIGNMENTS

1) Write a lively account of a menial job you've held. Make sure you take the reader from the beginning of the experience to the end. Focus on the aspect of the work that required the most patience and tolerance. Write about going from outsider- to insider-status with other co-workers on the job.

2) Find several blue-collar workers (preferably of varying ages) in your community who recently have been laid off. Hang out with them. If they are looking for work, accompany them to employment agencies, drive with them to job interviews, and discuss their prospects of work and strategies to find jobs. Explore the mental and financial toll the workers' unemployed status has taken on their self-esteem, as well as on their families. Write a powerful story based on your reporting.

3) To learn about workplace drug and alcohol abuse, interview workers at a local plant. By necessity, this story will have to start with an informant, i.e., someone you already know who may be willing to talk off the record about such volatile issues. Look in your local paper for reports of such abuse. Talk to area drug- or alcohol-abuse counselors to find out if particular factories have more serious problems than others. Call personnel offices at various plants to find out about required drug or alcohol testing of workers.

4) Interview an industrial psychologist about workplace monotony. Call a local university and find an expert on the issue of blue-collar job satisfaction. What innovative practices are in place to make menial jobs more meaningful?

25

MIKEY'S CLOSE CALL

We had a routine. Every morning at 8:20, my son and I would walk the four blocks to his elementary school. Hannah, our dog, would tag along, and the three of us would amble toward the school. On this particular fall morning, dogs being dogs, Hannah starting sniffing at a telephone pole somewhere along the way. I stopped. Mikey kept going. When Mikey saw a friend walking his way, he hollered hello and started to cross Clark Street. From my vantage point a half block away, I saw Mikey step into the street, but out of the corner of my eye I also saw a Volvo tearing down the same street. The driver seemed oblivious to everything except the Styrofoam cup of coffee in his right hand. Mikey and the car were about to collide in less than three seconds.

Mikey's Close Call

So the three of us are walking to school, Mikey, Hannah the dog, and me, and just as we're coming up to Clark Street, Mikey, who's nine, sees a friend coming his way, and suddenly, he does something he's never done. At least, never done in the last five years.

HE CROSSES THE STREET WITHOUT LOOKING BOTH WAYS.

And, just as he steps off the curb, it's like the evil demon of death has descended. One of those new turbo Volvos comes screeching around the corner, and tears down Clark Street. I see Mikey merrily walking across the street. I see the Volvo careening toward him. Within a matter of a second or two, Mikey is about to be hit.

Instantly, everything goes slow motion. The driver of the Volvo HAS to see Mikey. He has to notice the blue GAP backpack Mikey is swinging from his right arm. How can he not notice the red sweatshirt Mikey is wearing?

But the Volvo driver must be daydreaming, speeding 30 mph, oblivious to everything, and heading directly for little Mikey.

The live scene unfolding in front of me kicks into an even slower slow motion. I see each scene in freeze frames, a sort of New Age Zapruder film. Mikey will surely turn his head to the right. He will see the car roaring toward him. He will stop, brushed back by the ominous sight of this silver Volvo about to whiz by.

But Mikey continues to spring ahead, innocent and carefree, not in the least figuring that the two-ton tank barreling toward him is now only 15 feet away.

I imagine hearing a thump, Mikey's muted screams, and then seeing his limp, 60-pound body flying through the air, coming down with a dead plop on the Clark Street blacktop.

This is a simple issue of physics. A body at rest tends to stay at rest. A body in motion tends to stay in motion. The body in motion would soon be my little boy.

"MIKEY!!!!! WATCH IT!!!!!"

I scream this as loudly as I can from the hollow of my stomach, my voice piercing the robin's-egg sky on this otherwise ordinary, run-of-the-mill fall morning.

And at this point, everything does stop. The asshole driver of the Volvo, his windows up, doesn't hear me. He continues driving very much unlike Volvo drivers are supposed to drive, speeding down Clark Street as though he is on lap 499 at Indianapolis.

But Mikey does hear me. He suddenly stops in his tracks, smack in the middle of the street, more scared, I think, by the ferocity and pitch of my voice than anything else.

The Volvo misses him by less than six inches.

Mikey is shaking, literally shaking. "Dad," he says, looking back at me, still in the middle of the street. "I saw that car. I did. I really did."

But both Mikey and I know he didn't see the car. We both know, too, that the car was going so fast that if Mikey didn't stop, if he had gone along his merry way, he would have been creamed. "No, you did not see the car!" I yell at my only son, our only child. "You almost got run over! Because you didn't look both ways! How many times have Mom and I told you to look both ways when you cross the street? Even a kindergartener knows that! For God's sakes, Mikey!"

I am steaming mad. Mikey is so nervous that all he can say is that he really saw the car coming and he was going to stop. "I saw it, Dad. I saw the car. I did."

Which is a total fabrication. Mikey continues shaking, and even does something I have never seen him do before. He starts stuttering—so close a call it had been.

But how can I continue being angry? At this point, I also feel a sense of sublime grace showering Mikey and me. If Hannah had sniffed at another hydrant, if I had stopped to admire the newly painted house at the corner or the blue jay fluttering on the corner hickory tree, I might have never seen the Volvo. I might not have screamed.

It's been two weeks since the near-accident. Every day, I play the scene over in my mind. When I am lying awake at night, I think about it. And sometimes, I think that maybe Mikey really wasn't that close to the Volvo. Maybe it wasn't as perilous a scene as I thought it had been. Maybe Mikey had been right. Maybe all along, Mikey had seen the car racing toward him and was about to halt in his tracks. Could I have projected and perverted this whole scenario, turning a close call into some sort of omen of doom?

Last night over pizza, I brought up the incident again. Sounding way too much like my own father, I said, "You know you almost got run over by that car. Do you realize how lucky you were?"

I fully expected Mikey to shrug off the whole thing with cocksure bravado. But he didn't.

"I know, Dad," Mikey said, looking up, totally earnest, totally there. "That really *was* a close call."

The Cake, June 1, 2000

WRITING THE STORY

The opener for the piece is about as idyllic as it gets: father, son and dog walking to school on a fall morning. I wanted to create a pastoral mood of simpler times. I also wanted to make the story accessible, and because of that, I chose to write the piece in the present tense, as well as to use a colloquial tone throughout. This explains the extreme informality, which I signaled to the reader with the first word of the piece, "So."

The next paragraph—an eight-word sentence—is in all uppercase, something I don't think I'd ever done before or since this story.

The third paragraph connected the simplicity described in paragraph 1 with every parent's nightmare. In this case, it's technology (a supercharged turbo Volvo) about to slam into a nine-year-old boy.

I was banking that this setup would hook the reader. Who's going to flip the page with such a life-and-death scenario? Does the car slam into Mikey, or does Mikey make it out alive? Knowing that the reader would be going nowhere, I slowed the cadence of the piece. I invited the reader into my own mind. I shared with the reader my own thoughts one by one. In my reverie, I projected the image of a little boy swinging his backpack back and forth. That image crashed with the realization that unless I snapped out of my morning meditation, Mikey would soon be flying through the air. In the nanoseconds that followed, I summoned forth an instant call to action. Again, I chose to make that paragraph ("MIKEY!!!!! WATCH IT!!!!!") all uppercase, just three words.

Now it's time to slow down even more—at the point of would-be impact. I tracked my own thoughts and actions. As the car continues down the street, a sublime cocoon of protection descended upon Mikey. How can I *possibly* be angry? The boy, who seconds before was headed for doom, is alive, well—and nervous as he sputters excuses to allay my fright and anger.

Two more paragraphs and it's time to wrap up. I wanted a caboose here that would make the entire train memorable. And it came when Mikey dropped pretense and gave it up. I wanted him to realize how serious the incident could have been. He 'fessed up in the last paragraph, in a payoff for Mikey and for me, but also for the reader.

EPILOGUE

The piece touches on the innocent actions of children—and jolts the reader by deliberately slowing down a chain of events that, unless stopped, could have turned deadly.

Every day we face similar events, so-called near misses. Such "tragedy averted" stories seldom show up in the news. They aren't conventional news, after all, because no one dies or is injured. But each such incident speaks to the precarious nature of life. If written with the right touch, these no-news stories pack more emotion than almost any other story of the day.

ASSIGNMENTS

1) Write your own story about a "close call," when the safety of your life or that of another person could have been compromised.

2) Hang out for a day with the Safety Patrol of a local elementary school. Ask questions. Observe. Find out which corner is the busiest, and which corner is the most coveted by Safety Patrol guards and why. Write a narrative piece on what you see, hear and learn.

3) Experiment by writing about an event in your life with the same kind of transactional introspection that this story uses. Slow the action and dissect your own emotions as they unfold.

26

I SHALL RETURN, SCOUT'S HONOR

What better place to find material than to go back to that strange, impressionable time called childhood? Be cautious, though. The material has to be ordered and doled out sparingly. There's got to be a protagonist to pull the reader all the way through the story. Details are essential, but they can't be random; they must work together to create a mood as well as to tell (and sell) the story to the reader. Watch out for cloying anecdotes, generalities, imprecise detail. Memory pieces ought to have a turn to them, and that turn ought to be something fresh and contemporary. Surprise works well, whether it plays on the storyteller (as in the plot of "I Shall Return, Scout's Honor") or on the reader. Above all, the reader has to leave the story affected and moved. If the story works, it ought to result in the reader's desire to recall details of his or her own childhood, however different those details may be from the writer's.

I Shall Return, Scout's Honor

Camp Kenetiwapec, a Boy Scout camp near Newton, N.J., was hidden within 140 acres of dense forest. At its center was a lake so clean that generations of campers drank from it. By today's standards, the camp was spartan. No tennis courts, horses, water skiing, or cabins. The bathrooms, which we grandly called "louies," were outhouses. The only girl who set foot in Kenetiwapec when it wasn't visitors' day was the nurse's daughter. Judy Simpson was fifteen, with blonde hair and blue eyes. She walked with a wiggle. We talked about her constantly, but were too scared to say a word to her.

Camp was at once a terrifying and enchanting thought for a kid: to be away from your parents for four weeks. I was twelve, both a tentative teenager and tentative camper, more accustomed to city life than to owls, raccoons, deer—not to mention pink bellies and camp legends like the Purple Bishop. I have nearly forgotten the starchy meals, the taste of frozen Three Musketeer bars, dripping Creamsicles, chipped beef in cream sauce (SOS).

For three decades, I have blocked out of my mind the still nights lying atop my flannel sleeping bag when I thought every rustle in the forest was a supernatural predator about to leap on my bunk and suck my blood. I haven't thought about pink bellies—the summer-camp ritual of older boys, all with wide smiles, pouncing on terrified younger campers, holding their ankles and wrists, slapping their stomachs until the taut skin turned the color of ripe plum flesh. I used to get goose bumps thinking of the Purple Bishop, a renegade priest wearing a purple robe and hood, pounding away like a crazy man on a church organ at midnight.

But I never forgot the flagpole. Thirty years ago, 15 boys set out one clear summer morning into the northern New Jersey forest to fell a towering oak tree. Once we sighted it, we went to work; we chopped it down, and as the sun was high in the sky, scraped off every shred of the tree's bark. We removed all branches and nubs of limbs. We sanded the trunk, 30 hands honing and polishing the wood like it was sculpture. The smell was fresh, green, clean. After five hours of work, we took turns rubbing our hands over the trunk, now smooth. It felt like baby skin.

We dragged our prize back to camp, and over the next week, smeared four coats of sticky brown creosote over it. Then, using an elaborate system of ropes and pulleys, we set the pole into a wet concrete base and hoisted it up. The pole was as straight as a ship's mast. We argued whether each of us should dip a finger into the wet concrete to sign our name.

No, we decided. We were to leave something that would stand forever. Let us sign as one: "Lenape Unit—Summer of 1964."

It was to be our legacy. Our counselor, Ken York, tall and straight like the tree we had felled, told us in the most solemn of tones that once we were men, married, with jobs, homes, children of our own, we could return to this camp and find what we had accomplished. Illness, bad fortune, death might strike us, but the flagpole would still be there.

Decades later, I decided to see if Ken York was right.

One early spring day, my wife and I left the commotion of New York City, speeding past general stores and antique shops, driving fast in anticipation. In April, the northern New Jersey green is so deep that it seems to reflect blue on the rolling hills. We stopped for gas, and were immediately rewarded. No fancy electronic pumps with flashing orange numbers. As I pumped gas, the antiquated pumps totted up dollars and pennies on a metal dial that click-clacked as the sweet smell of gasoline clung to my nostrils. And there were no modern pop machines, either. On the curb were refrigerated metal boxes stocked with rows of red cream soda. The stuff looked like pressed maraschino cherries and tasted as sweet.

But just past Newton, and right before the double hairpin turn that my father's 1959 Impala station wagon used to huff and puff to conquer, the road was blocked, closed to cars. Camp Kenetiwapec had been converted into a federal recreational area. We were informed by a sign to park and hike up the steep, macadam road.

The humidity was still heavy, just as I remembered. The mosquitoes buzzed next to our ears. The deer were as frightening and as curious as I recalled—seen off in the distance, still and quiet, staring face-to-face with a trespasser, both man and animal unable to move for fear the other would bolt.

Atop the hill, there was no sign of the camp, only a ramshackle guard station that had once housed a solitary camper whose official duty was to direct parents where to park on visitors' day.

Camp Kenetiwapec had been abandoned, closed more than two decades ago. Now all that was left, it seemed, were dilapidated buildings with rickety doors that banged when gusts of wind swept off the lake.

My wife Iris and I walked past the Iroquois unit, a campsite reserved for older boys; no one from outside the unit was ever allowed inside. We honored that tradition, hurrying along the road toward the main parking lot. The blacktop, which used to be rough and uneven, full of tire imprints stamped into the hot tar from parents' cars, now was smooth.

Up a half mile, past a bend, was the lake, still clean, but not pristine. No beer cans, but menacing dragonflies. The wood-slat dock and the platform raft 50 yards from the shore were no longer there. And the lake looked surprisingly small. Had the lake once been breathtaking because it belonged to me and my friends and no else? It was the lake we drank from, dove and belly-flopped in. We used it as a measuring stick for those who could swim across and those who could not.

The parking lot—where there once had been a clearing the size of three football fields, where we assembled every morning upon hearing scratchy reveille on a loud speaker—was now overgrown with weeds. There was not a trace of the campfire area, a clearing among oak groves, where at twilight we gathered for Movie Night every week to boo when the projector seemed to break down on cue. The well-worn paths we followed from campsite to campsite after Taps, with flashlights shut off, chasing fireflies, were no more. The same paths Bobby Lippman and I used to follow, giggling about girls who had just started to wear bras, had been subsumed into the forest.

Iris and I stood in front of what had once been the dining hall and faced north from the lake. We began walking east. This was the direction to Lenape unit, to the flagpole. Walking past a runty-looking building with red paint peeling 50 years away, I recognized the Arts and Crafts Center where I had once made a green-and-yellow lanyard for my father. Lenape was up and over a slight crest from here, past Cayuga, past the obstacle course, past a stand of white birches. Inside the grove, Bobby Lippman, while casually leaning against one of the birches, had patiently explained to me girl hygiene, the difference between Kotex and Tampax. Amazing! Bobby and I walked to the dining hall that evening, laughing, taking pods from the birches, peeling them apart on one end, and sticking them to the tips of our noses.

I sensed we were getting close. There were no longer any wooden platforms, but the concrete foundations that once supported heavy canvas tents were still in the ground, now overgrown with weeds—and my nemesis, poison ivy. The gray slabs, barely visible, were all in the same semicircle pattern.

This was Lenape! The pathway, once lined with rocks we chose so they fit together *exactly*, had given way to a haphazard forest of wispy maples and gnarled scrub brush. I looked left and right, trying to push my bearings back 30 years. I concentrated, visualizing how it used to be.

And then I spotted it. The flagpole was straight ahead, 15 feet away. Its skin was no longer clean. The color had aged into a rich brownish-gray. But the pole was still tall and straight, taller than the other trees that had grown up around it in a circle.

"That's it!" I shouted to Iris.

I dropped my knapsack and ran to the base of the pole, clomping over twigs and saplings and bushes. I knelt down to look at the concrete foundation, covered with leaves and dirt. I brushed away layers of soot, and with my right forefinger, traced the same letters: "Lenape Unit—Summer of 1964." I felt like Indiana Jones discovering the Holy Grail.

Iris took some photos of me as I knelt by the pole. We pulled out a bottle of wine, and spread a red-checked tablecloth on the bumpy, scratchy ground for a picnic. I took out a Swiss Army knife my parents certainly never would have bought me, and sliced into a baguette and shaved pieces off a triangle of hard jack cheese.

There were more memories. In the middle of the night when I was too scared to go to the louie 25 yards up a spooky hill, I used to open the tent flap and sprinkle the tentside foliage. When my dog was run over by a taxicab back in South Orange, my mother told me the devastating news one Sunday morning right here, at the base of the flagpole. When I was hiking with a dozen other boys, we came upon a couple necking in a meadow of tall grass; they seemed much less shocked than we were, and waved merrily as we hurried by.

But there was something profoundly sad about finding the flagpole. It blended in with all the other trees. Like the lake, the flagpole didn't seem very big anymore. I had idealized its geography and its place in time. I had envisioned generations of campers standing in its shadow, our glory. But now, 30 years later, the pole means nothing to anyone but to me—and maybe 14 other men spread throughout the world. Nature hadn't so much regained the camp, it had obliterated it. There was nothing left to commemorate the past. The camp's surroundings, the people that had once given the place so much meaning, were gone.

No more groaning over reveille, no more furtive whispering after Taps. No smelly sneakers, merit badges, Order-of-the-Arrow secret oaths. No more squeaky metal bedsprings and lumpy, mildewy mattresses. No more clothing lists that mandated our mothers sew name tags on each and every garment. No more campfire stories about the maniacal Purple Bishop pounding on a church organ at the stroke of midnight. Nary a belly turned pink.

Three decades later, I've lost touch with every one of my fellow foresters. High school brought inevitable cliques; the Boy Scouts promptly fell out of favor. My family moved. I went to college in California. Eventually, I married and now have a four-year-old son. I work as a college professor. In fact, as I wrote this memory piece, my wife called me at my office and asked me to stop at the grocery store to pick up a box of Tampax—the same miracle contraption Bobby Lippman first informed me about. Outside of my memories, the only thing that remains the same seems to be the flagpole.

Wherever you are, Ken York, you were right.

Iowa City Magazine, July 1993

WRITING THE STORY

The structural centerpiece of the story, of course, is the flagpole. The first three grafs of "I Shall Return, Scout's Honor" are lead-ins to that main character. For those opening paragraphs, I tried to suck the reader into the story. I ended the first paragraf with the paradox of the camp nurse's 15-year-old daughter: "We talked about her constantly, but were too scared to say a word to her."

The next graf opens with the same kind of opposition: "Camp was at once a *terrifying* and *enchanting* thought for a kid: to be away from your parents for four weeks." I'm banking on drawing in the reader to the drama I announce in the fourth graf—going back to find the flagpole. That's the gambit, the treasure I set out as the rationale for the story. Before we get there, though, I try to tempt the reader with other camp images stuck in my (and, I hope, in the reader's) memory: frozen candy bars, Creamsicles, SOS, imaginary nocturnal predators.

With the trap set, grafs four through eight set up the premise of the story: Would the flagpole still be around 31 years later? With the question posed, the reader hops in for a literal ride. More images—red cream soda in metal boxes, buzzing mosquitoes, deer. We arrive at our destination, and the first turn of the piece is out: the camp is no longer.

I weave memories with visual clues, then we go on the treasure hunt, searching for the flagpole. When I finally find it, I try to share my sense of discovery—and disappointment. That's the payoff to the story, the morale to a larger tale, triggered by the memory of a solitary tree lost in the piney woods of northern New Jersey.

EPILOGUE

Wherever the almost mythical Ken York is today (indeed, if he is still alive), I wanted him to pick up and read "I Shall Return, Scout's Honor." I also wanted the 14 other boys in the story, now middle-aged men, to read the story. The piece reached out to all of them. But none responded—hardly a surprise. Instead, I received letters from plenty of other grown-up Boy Scouts and ersatz campers across the nation. One sent me an album of photos chronicling *his* return to his boyhood camp. Still, no one from Camp Kenetiwapec.

As I wrote in the ending to the piece, there was something poignant about the obliteration of the camp. Upon my return, I fully expected the place to be humming. The louies by now certainly would have been replaced by plumbing, the tents by cabins. But nowhere while preparing to return, did I ever entertain any thoughts that the camp would have vanished. Perhaps that was as much a tribute to the etched nature of my Kenetiwapec memories as it was to the idealized permanency of childhood institutions. After all, the camp had predated me and my stay by decades; why shouldn't it be around for my own son, perhaps his son? That there was no longer a camp was the first shock. The next shock was how the scrub forest had erased the setting of so many events still vivid in my memory. There was a disconnect between knowing where these events took place—and 30 years later, seeing hardly anything left to mark those memories any longer.

Outside of my own mind, the only other proof to that past were 14 other men who may or may not still be out there.

ASSIGNMENTS

1) Return to a place of your childhood. Record how the place has changed and how the change jars your sense of a personal historical record.

2) Conduct a series of oral-history interviews with former workers of a shutdown local factory. Write a story that illustrates the plant's impact on the lives of the workers, as well as on the surrounding community.

3) Go to your high school reunion. Write a story about your expectations matched with the reality of the event. Pay special attention to detail. Include in your piece a sense of the significance of the changes you observe.

27

SLANG LEADS TO MISCUES

As a newcomer struggling with a foreign language, I ran into wonderful—and unconventional—stories every day when I lived in Brazil. Even though I spoke Spanish fluently, Portuguese was a difficult language to master. Where I lived, Rio de Janeiro, residents seemed to speak in a chamois-soft cadence, ticked with a natural whooshing accent that made speakers sound as though they were gargling. The first several months in Brazil, every time I opened my mouth, someone seemed to laugh. This short piece looks at the humorous side of language acquisition.

Slang Leads to Miscues

RIO DE JANEIRO, Brazil—Language barriers are often as impenetrable as physical barriers—and sometimes can be downright hilarious. Take, for example, what happened to me last month at a local supermarket.

At the checkout counter, the bagger asked me if I wanted my groceries put in a paper sack. I said, "Sure, I can carry the bag home with me." This was enough to put everyone in the local Food Fair in stitches, including the cashier who thought it was so funny she had a hard time punching out the next shopper's prices. Why? I had inadvertently confused the Portuguese word for bag with slang for testicles.

But that was nothing compared to what happened to a friend of mine when she first arrived here five years ago.

"I had my groceries delivered by a teenage boy, and after he had put everything on my kitchen table, I looked around for my pocketbook, and realized I had left it in my car. I said, 'I'm sorry, I can't give you a tip because I don't have my purse with me.' The only thing was I had mixed up the word purse with the Portuguese slang for vagina. It turned out I didn't have to give the boy a tip. He was ready to run out of the apartment and tell all his friends about the horny foreign lady."

The peculiarities of language can reach million-dollar proportions. Several years ago, General Motors introduced a Chevrolet model called Nova to Argentina. The car, GM executives thought, would be ideal for Argentina—small, zippy and inexpensive. But it sold miserably. The reason, it was soon discovered, had nothing to do with multinational politics, lack of accessories or corporate mismanagement. "No va" in Spanish means "won't go," and, after all, who wants to buy a car with the name, "Won't Go"? GM changed the model's name, and now it is one of Argentina's most popular cars.

Ten years ago, I was in Chile, and after a full dinner with bottle after bottle of rich red wine, I thought of a slightly risqué joke, started it, and then reached the point where I realized it just wouldn't be proper for the setting. I said, "I can't go on because I think I'm going to be embarrassed." That was enough of a joke. The word "embarazada" in Spanish means pregnant.

It's not just words that can be confusing. Gestures can too. Last year I saw the Woody Allen movie, "Bananas." Midway through it, Allen says to a friend, "Great, the plan's all set," and then puts his thumb and index finger together as though to say, "Okay." Everyone in the audience broke out in laughter. Ask any Brazilian and he'll say why: The U.S. "okay" sign here means something akin to "you——,——,——jerk."

An American newcomer to Brazil recently was lost in a maze of streets in downtown São Paulo, trying to find a particular address on a street called Benjamin Constant. Whenever he asked passersby, they'd laugh and walk away. It wasn't until he explained his predicament to a Brazilian that he figured out why: Instead of asking where Benjamin Constant Street was, he was saying in Portuguese, "Kiss me constantly."

You don't have to go to Latin America to see how the language barrier works. A couple of years ago in a small cafe in Jasper, Alberta, I asked a waitress for "a good, homemade crumpet, hot and with melted butter, please." Any western Canadian will tell you that crumpet is slang for a pleasantly shaped girl.

October 15, 1980

WRITING THE STORY

This piece is what editors refer to as "a bright"—a short, curious story that illuminates. Good brights leave the reader smiling. Great brights are "didja stories," i.e., they prompt readers to say to each other, "didja read that one?" In the first paragraph of "Slang Leads to Miscues" the reader is immediately pulled into the piece with the construction, "Take, for example, what happened to me last month... ."

That's a cheat to get the reader to a longer second paragraph where the first anecdote gets told. Depending on the reader, the punch line is either going to propel him or her to the next paragraph, or I'm dead in the water. I decide to take the chance.

The next paragraph sets up the second anecdote, another off-color story told in a long (and risky) direct quote. By now, the reader is either totally mine, or gone.

At this point, I serve up a taste of the larger issue of translation confusion and what it can mean for unsuspecting multinational corporations. Then I go back to a personal anecdote, confusing the Spanish word for "pregnant" with the English word for "embarrassed." I follow up with another south-of-the-border tale and get out of the piece by bringing the issue of language peculiarities home, so that the reader understands the universality of the issue.

EPILOGUE

This piece was easy to write. I did my research in a bar, trading stories with other English speakers about the nightmare of learning a foreign language on the spot. Everyone I met had his or her own story, and as the beers flowed, the stories got more outrageous. If there was a problem with the piece, it was in sanitizing the copy so that American newspapers would print it. The topic of this story was far from the usual fodder U.S. newspapers were (and still are) comfortable running.

I paid a price for going too far. My employer, the Field News Service, wouldn't touch the piece, and it was never published.

ASSIGNMENTS

1) Interview non-native English speakers in your community and ask about their experiences confusing American idioms. Write about the problems their linguistic faux pas created.

2) Talk to students who have returned from semesters or summers abroad and find out about embarrassing moments that happened because of the vagaries of language.

3) Interview international business and marketing executives, and ask what steps their companies have taken to ensure that the names or jingles of products introduced into foreign markets are free of double entendres. Find out how the name of an established product is created for a foreign market.

28

THE DOG'S HOUR

"The Dog's Hour" is another "you won't believe this" story. As the events unfolded, I knew this story absolutely had to be chronicled. It was too surrealistic to let go for banter at parties or bars. I wrote the piece in an hour-long sitting. It came out of my head and onto my computer screen almost as fast as I could type.

The Dog's Hour

Here's the story of how a nine-pound, 12-week-old yellow Labrador narrowly escaped lethal injection.

The day of "the incident" was like any other day. My son, Mikey, and I walked Hannah to school four blocks away. When we arrived, three or four children petted Hannah. As the 8:25 a.m. bell rang, Mikey marched into school with his second-grade class. Hannah and I went home.

Two hours later, an Animal Control officer called to inform me that Hannah had savagely bitten a student at the playground that morning. The student had a deep puncture wound in her right hand.

"That's impossible," I said. "I was with Hannah at all times. The dog hardly has any teeth!"

No matter, the Animal Control people told me. Hannah had to be quarantined for two weeks. She was under house arrest. Another incident like this and Hannah would get destroyed.

But Hannah didn't do anything, I insisted.

That didn't make any difference. The AC people faxed me a dog-bite report. I had to sign it—or Hannah would be removed from our house that day. Hannah was being railroaded, and there was nothing I could do about it.

The plot thickened. After dinner that night, Mikey and I went to a Cub Scout meeting at his school. Sitting across the aisle, Mikey pointed to the alleged dog-bite victim.

Between popcorn sales and knots, I walked over to the girl and took a look at her right hand. I was shocked. She *did* have a deep puncture wound.

"How'd you get that?" I asked in the sweetest tone I could muster.

The girl fidgeted.

"I dunno," she said, doodling on the back of a Kit-Kat wrapper.

Hannah's future rested with this eight-year-old's answer. She was holding four aces to Hannah's nothing.

"C'mon. Please tell me. How'd you get that cut on your hand?" I felt like a fly talking to a spider..

The girl put down her crayon and stared ahead for a few seconds.

"O.K.," she started tentatively. "If you really *must* know."

But then she paused. "But I don't know if I *want* to tell you." She was teasing me and she knew it.

"It's important that you tell me what happened," I said with feeling. What this little girl really needed was a good smack on her *toochis*.

"O.K.," she said. "My dog at home bit me."

I was steamed, but needed to keep my cool.

"Then why'd you say that Hannah bit you?"

"I dunno."

Didn't all this sound vaguely familiar?

The whole scenario was spun out of *The Children's Hour,* the Lillian Hellman play about a schoolgirl who starts a rumor that steamrolls everything in its wake. In this real-life version, Hannah plays the double role of the two unmarried teachers, acted by Audrey Hepburn and Shirley MacLaine, and the I-dunno-girl is slander-spreading Veronica Cartwright.

Who knew why the girl did it—maybe she wanted to visit the school nurse, maybe she didn't want to tell her parents that her own dog had bitten her, maybe she hated—or had a crush on—Mikey. Whatever. The girl was setting Hannah up to take the fall for her own dog. For an eight-year-old, it was pretty crafty. Imagine when she's 40.

The next day, armed with the truth, Mikey and I marched into the principal's office. We wanted to clear Hannah's name. We wanted an apology.

Instead, all we got was a bureaucratic runaround. "Our hands are tied," the principal said unapologetically. "When we learn of a dog bite, we have to report it. It's a mandatory reportable."

"But you never determined which dog did the biting."

"The girl said she was bitten by your dog. The nurse examined her hand. It definitely was a dog bite," the principal said, nodding his head and smiling like Mr. Whipple in the toilet-paper commercials.

I talked to the school nurse. "The girl's hand was bitten. She said your dog bit her. It's not our job to investigate which dog did the biting. It's a mandatory reportable."

I talked to the Animal Control people, who said they had no choice once they received the report. The only way to clear Hannah's record, they said, would be to call the parents of the bitten girl.

At which point, I was certain the parents would deny that their dog had done the damage.

Fortunately, though, the mother of the girl confessed, but it was a confession that dropped my jaw. The mother said that two years earlier, another neighborhood dog had bitten the girl, and the family received a settlement from an insurance company. Ever since, the girl had gone out of her way to approach dogs of all sizes and varieties. The mother told the AC people that she thought her daughter associated dogs with lots of money.

This was getting freakier and freakier.

That should be the end to the sorry story, and it is—except for one thing.

Mikey and I marched back to the principal's office. I asked him what if this incident hadn't involved a dog at all, but instead, was about a student who had accused an adult of child abuse.

"Oh, we would follow the same procedures. Absolutely. It's *never* up to us to investigate. That's a mandatory reportable."

"You'd report the adult to the police even when you could determine that the accusation was false?"

"Absolutely," the principal said solemnly.

I needed to make peace with Mr. Whipple. Mikey would be at this school till 2003. All I really wanted was for the principal to allow that perhaps he and his staff of robots had rushed to judgment.

"Well, at least we got to the bottom of this," I said, trying for a sliver of vindication. "At least we found out the truth."

The principal smiled again in that tight-ass Mr. Whipple way, and looked me straight in the eye. "I'm glad you have closure to an event that no doubt caused you some anxiety," he said.

That's when *I* wanted to bite him.

July 19, 2002

WRITING THE STORY

The piece is literally framed as a story, with the third word in the lede ("story") explicitly saying to readers that "The Dog's Hour" will follow standard convention, i.e., it will be told chronologically with a beginning, middle and end. "The Dog's Hour" is, in part, a whodunit, but in this story the victim is dog and the assailant an eight-year-old girl. That makes the piece a parody of the classic definition of news: News isn't when dog bites man, it's when man bites dog.

To be successful, the story has to move fast, in part because it shares the detective-story genre, but also because the subject matter, when you get down to it, isn't the stuff that shakes worlds and topples governments. The paragraphs are exceedingly short. I don't want to give readers cause for abandoning the piece with too-large blocks of type. I need to hook readers early, and once the readers are mine, I pull them through a slalom course of plot twists. And that's done in a relatively short amount of space (fewer than 1,000 words). I want to get in and out as fast as I can.

EPILOGUE

While "The Dog's Hour" was a detective story, I wanted it to be something more. That's why I introduced the Lillian Hellman play (and William Wyler film), *The Children's Hour,* midway through the piece. I realized that I was running a risk by citing the play since few readers would be familiar with a 40-year-old work of drama, but that's what gave this story bite (sorry for the pun). A simple story about a dog became a parable about what happens when rumors get spread and no one has the ability to stop them from steamrolling over everyone. What would have happened if false charges were leveled against a person? What would have happened if the accused were charged with a serious crime, such as child abuse? When I presented that hypothetical to Principal Whipple, the reader was rewarded with that amazing phrase, "mandatory reportable." Those two words seemed to embody everything ridiculous and, at the same time, perfectly essential and logical about administrators and bureaucracies.

ASSIGNMENTS

1) Pay a visit to the local animal shelter. Find out which animals in the shelter that day are the most/least popular for adoption and why. How long must an animal remain unclaimed before it is euthanized? Talk to shelter workers about their attachment to animals that must be euthanized. Alternatively, how does the shelter investigate reports of biting animals, and what are the penalties for such incidents? Talk to the dog owner and the victim of a recent attack.

2) Talk to local owners of pit bulls and rottweilers about the public perception of these dogs. Interview national breed organizations to see what they are doing to address such negative publicity. Interview officials in nearby cities where such dogs are illegal to own as house pets. Does such an ordinance exist in your community, or might one be introduced?

3) Follow the case of a person charged with child or sexual abuse. Present the story as a "tick-tock," allowing the reader to follow the entire case from allegation to trial, from the point of view of the defendant—instead of the more conventional story angle as seen from the alleged victim's point of view. An alternative story is to profile local attorneys who specialize in representing defendants charged in such cases.

29

WHAT'S THAT IN YOUR MOUTH?

While living in Brazil, I noticed that everyone seemed to use toothpicks. It made no difference whether you were dining at a five-star restaurant, chewing on a hard-boiled egg in a dingy bar, or sitting in your pajamas at a friend's breakfast table. The toothpick assumed tremendous utility in all of Brazil. Brazilians were as serious about toothpicks as they were about coffee and soccer. Was there a story in this national affection for the lowly toothpick? Granted, toothpicks aren't nuclear weapons, but their everyday, nonstop use underscored for me a small cultural phenomenon. I figured my readers in the United States had read enough trenchant political analysis on the comings and going in Brasilia, so why not animate their information overload and give them a tongue-in-cheek piece on something that no proper Brazilian could live without?

What's That in Your Mouth?

SÃO PAULO, Brazil—The scenario at one of Brazil's most elegant restaurants could go something like this: After the rich chocolate mousse, after the espresso coffee, the waiter puts down on the dinner table a canister that resembles a salt shaker with just one hole.

Each member of the dinner party passes the small receptacle around the table, and over candlelight, the lingering guests extract toothpicks and discreetly pick at their teeth.

Even in the fanciest of Brazilian restaurants, the *palito,* or toothpick, is more than used—it is expected, just like the check at the end of a meal or, to a lesser degree, like an after-dinner mint.

"The moment when you finish dinner, when you lean back in your chair, put your hands on your stomach, and think, 'My, that was a good meal,' that's the time to reach for the toothpick," says Moyra Ashford, an English journalist who has lived here for four years. "Besides, it's much more satisfying than smoking a big cigar."

Brazil probably has more toothpick consumers than any other country in the world. Its 125 million residents are frequent habitués of cafes, outdoor bistros, bars and restaurants—none of which would ever serve a meal or snack without the finishing touch of a toothpick. Even the dingiest bar in a run-down workers' area may not offer its patrons napkins, but serves a toothpick along with either a drink or light sandwich.

Do they help prevent tooth decay? In Brazil, where medical treatment is out of the economic reach of most residents, could the toothpick mean fewer visits to the dentist?

Dr. David K. Kramer, a Baltimore, Md., dentist who has practiced here for 10 years, says no. "As far as dental value is concerned, toothpicks have little, if any, value."

And if they could prevent tooth decay, says Dr. Kramer, "I doubt if there'd be many dentists left practicing in Brazil."

Marceilo Augusto, a Brazilian graphic artist, says toothpicks are as Brazilian as Carnivale. Finishing a meal without the satisfying feeling of a toothpick, would be "like taking a bath without soap," he says with a shrug of his shoulders.

Not everyone is sold on toothpicks—or can get used to the custom. Alva Rubini, a native of the Falkland Islands who has lived in Brazil for six years, says using a toothpick is like "taking a toothbrush to the table. I'm still not used to it, but you know, when in Rome, do what the Romans do."

The humble toothpick is here to stay. At one of São Paulo's most exclusive restaurants, Vila Roma, in the city's posh Higenopolis section, the management decided not to offer them to their patrons. "How crude," complained a new maître d' from Rome. But after a night with request after request, the management relented. Now, at least, the restaurant offers its diners individually wrapped toothpicks.

The Field News Service, November 2, 1979

WRITING THE STORY

I led the piece the only way I knew how: creating within the reader's mind a cinematic vision of gastronomic gratification. In a few words, I sought to paint the scene of diners at their supreme moment of satisfaction. I also sought to tease the reader. What exactly is in this strange object—a canister with one hole—passed from one diner to the next?

The punch line can't be delayed too long or I'll lose the reader. So, I settle for the end of the second graf, with a glaring disconnect: 1) elegant restaurant and 2) picking your teeth. I follow with a fuller explanation and then go to my killer quote, which puts the toothpick phenomenon in context. The quote compares the oral satisfaction of a toothpick to that of a big fat cigar, which is exactly the kind of visual cue I want to stick in the reader's mind. The fifth graf broadens the piece and puts Brazil's toothpick fascination in a larger context.

The next graf comes from a question I anticipate readers posing: So, if Brazilians are so involved with beloved toothpicks, do they have less tooth decay? I found an American dentist who debunked my assumption about Brazilian tooth decay. Dr. Kramer, though, does it with panache, which pushes further the thesis of the piece that toothpicks are wildly popular among Brazilians.

I get out of the story with an observation I made while dining at Vila Roma, a restaurant so expensive that each time I ate there, I could only afford a cup of soup.

EPILOGUE

Writing never needs to be drudgery, and this piece is a case in point. "What's That in Your Mouth?" was a blast to write, and that's because the topic—

toothpicks—is so off-the-wall. Topics for stories are everywhere. Open your eyes. Think. Anything goes. Good stories are about events, yes, but they also are about trends. Imaginative stories cover sentiment, too—what people are talking and thinking about. Such stories used to be called "watercooler" pieces—topics that people would talk about around the watercooler at work. Now that the office water cooler has been replaced by personal water bottles, I'm not sure what these stories are called any longer. Still, such stories are often the most visceral; they're the ones readers talk about most.

ASSIGNMENTS

1) Interview international students and find out what they find most interesting and/or peculiar about American customs.

2) Go to a football game with international students in your community and write a piece on their reactions.

3) Dentists: Who would want to look into people's mouths all day long? What kind of person gravitates to dentistry? The burnout rate for dentists is among the highest of all professions. Interview dentists who have left the profession and find out why.

30

YO!

One of the joys of being a writer is that almost anything that gets you to scratch your head can be turned into a story. That's the case of *Yo!*

Many moons ago, when my junior high school gym teacher would take roll, some guys in class would respond with a booming "Yo!" Frankly, I never could figure out why. I knew from Spanish class that *"Yo"* meant "I," but "Yo!" had to be an awfully strange way to announce your presence, particularly north of the border, where I grew up.

"Yo!"—and the mystery surrounding it—was one of those unanswered questions that kept ricocheting inside my brain for years. Then in the mid-1980's "Yo!" started popping up all over in films, TV, slang. In my adult incarnation as a writer, I finally had license to find out where "Yo!" came from and what it really meant.

Yo!

"Yo!"

Eddie Murphy yells it in *Beverly Hills Cop*. Whoopi Goldberg writes it in *Jumpin' Jack Flash*. Ed McMahon booms it on "The Tonight Show."

A sweat-soaked Sylvester Stallone ends *Rocky II* with it, shouting, "Yo, Adrienne, I did it!"

On a Taco Bell TV commercial, a hip warrior strides up to a long-haired man holding up pillars to a temple and says, "Yo, Samson!"

What's going on here? Isn't "yo" the Spanish word for "I"?

Sure it is, but "yo" means a lot more these days.

It has suddenly become slang for "hello," "howdy," "what's going on?" or "hey!" It even has crossover appeal, becoming popular among both blue-collar and young urban professionals.

Example: "Yo, Vinnie, I got da stuff. C'mere!" Or, "Yo, Jennifer, let's do brunch."

"Yo" can also turn into a threat, meaning, "Wait a minute!" as in "Yo! What you want, mister?"

Where did "yo" come from?

The "yo" capital of the world happpens to be Stallone's hometown, Philadelphia, says Dennis Lebofsky, associate professor of English at Temple University, who wrote his doctoral thesis on Pennsylvania expressions.

"It started here, but I don't know why," he says.

"Yo is part of our culture," reports Clark DeLeon, a Philadelphia native and yeoman columnist for *The Philadelphia Inquirer*.

"It's part of our everyday speech. It's a way of saying, 'How you doin'? or 'Get off my car!' You even hear yo at city council meetings."

DeLeon says a Philadelphia rabbi not long ago misspoke the 23rd Psalm: "Yo, though I walk through the valley of the shadow of death... ."

A disk jockey who distributes a Philadelphia Trivial Pursuit-type game says the expression started with a milkman in the late 1800s who for some reason favored the word over "giddyap" to spur his delivery horses. Like chicken pox, "yo" spread.

Most etymologists, though, say "yo" pre-dates Philadelphia milkmen. The Oxford English Dictionary says it dates to 1420, when a European hunter was heard shouting, "Yo!" as an exclamation of excitement. (Why he said it is unclear.)

In 1859, Charles Dickens employed the word in one of its current meanings—"hey, you!"—when he included it in *A Tale of Two Cities*. ("Yo there! Stand! I shall fire!") It also made it into Robert Louis Stevenson's *Treasure*

Island, published in 1883, in the pirate lyric, "Fifteen men on a dead man's chest. Yo-ho-ho and a bottle of rum."

But J.L. Dillard, author of *Black English,* says "yo" is straight from the black ghetto. "Yo really comes from the word, 'here,' which pronounced like 'hee-yuh,' gradually evolved to 'hee-yo,' then to 'hyo,' and finally just to 'yo.'"

There is corroboration for the yo-here theory. Military men and high school gym students for years have responded during roll calls with "yo" instead of "here."

To make matters more complicated, Allan Metcalf, president of the American Dialect Society, has a whole different theory. "Yo is a very simple exclamation. It's almost a grunt. I would think it's evolved from 'yea,' to 'yeah,' to 'yo,'" he says.

San Jose Mercury News, October 9, 1986

WRITING THE STORY

For decades, I had been waiting to ask all sorts of questions to satisfy my "Yo!" obsession. First, I did a database search and came up with examples of usage. One of the most common was from "The Lone Ranger," whose trademark command to his trusty companion and horse was "Hi Yo Silver, Away!" I also found references to "Yo!" in *Treasure Island.* But these tantalizing usages were red herrings, throwing me off the contemporary slang track.

Ultimately, I contacted Dennis Lebofsky, the professor whose scholarly reputation was, in part, built on "Yo!" Despite his academic pedigree, Lebofsky was no help—except to refer me to Clark DeLeon, a *Philadelphia Inquirer* columnist who waxed rhapsodic about "Yo!" although whether a rabbi actually said, "Yo, lo I walk through the valley of the shadow of death" is up for grabs.

Next, I went to the traditional source of all English etymology, the *Oxford English Dictionary* (the OED to regulars). Then it was to J.L. Dillard, a linguist who had just published a book on Black English. Dillard had studied the origins of "Yo" and shared his research with me.

Wanting to corroborate Dillard's findings, I called on another linguist, Professor Metcalf, who wasn't interested in "Yo!" at all, but volunteered that he could tell within 10 seconds where a person had been raised, based on the speaker's pronunciation of three words (nice white rice). Give him one minute, and he said he could pinpoint the speaker's hometown within 50 miles. Metcalf was right on the money with me. Having dispensed with "Yo!" our conversation led to another story I wrote soon thereafter on Metcalf's special talent.

EPILOGUE

Now, 16 years after I wrote "Yo!," the word has become as American as tacos, egg foo yung and baked zitti. "Yo!" is truly everywhere these days. It can be an abbreviation for the word "your," as in the popular rap songs, "Put Yo Hood Up," by Lil' John and the East Side Boyz, or "Do Yo Thang Girl," by D.J. Jubilee. Or it surfaces in such expressions as "Shut yo' mouth, mutha!" Black slang has expropriated "Yo!" as a salutation or an interjection: "Yo, check it out, dog!"; "Yo, mama, lemme see you wobble!"; "Yo, ma mahn, gimme five!"; or the ubiquitous, "Yo, wassup?" "Yo!" continues to have crossover power. As I pointed out in the original piece, "Yo!" is still used by whites as well as blacks across the economic spectrum. Buttoned-down businessmen have been known to greet each other with "Yo!" Whether its usage is a put-on is for another story to sort out.

"Yo!" has also become popular in Australia these days, and many Australians are lamenting the demise of "G'day mate" in favor of "Yo bro!" says Roly Sussex, a linguistics professor at the University of Queensland.

In the wake of September 11, 2001, the expression "Osama Yo Mama!" has become a popular putdown, and in fact there is an Internet site with the same name (osamayomama.com). The site is not to be confused with Yo.net, the homepage for a Canadian software company.

Last year, Jamaican-American artist Renee Cox caused a stir at the Brooklyn Museum of Art with her reinterpretation of Leonardo da Vinci's "The Last Supper," when she depicted Christ as a nude, black woman in a photograph. The title of the artwork: "Yo Mama's Last Supper."

The San Francisco-based wire service, Pacific News Service, publishes a widely syndicated newspaper and Internet column pitched to young people, called "YO!—Youth Outlook."

The Spanish meaning of "*yo*" has not been forgotten in all this Yo-mania. When the chatty Taco Bell Chihuahua told the TV world, "*Yo quiero Taco Bell*," the dog was speaking both Spanish *and* English.

ASSIGNMENTS

1) Pick out a dozen contemporary slang words. Define them using sources such as high school and college students, linguists and other specialists in current

language usage. Write about the derivations of such words, and how the mass media have (or not) populated their uses.

2) Identify local, regional or national politicians known for fracturing the English language. Talk to experts about the reasons for the malapropisms, as well as what such speech says about the politician. Cite examples throughout your story.

3) Track the popular usages of words once thought to be profane, as well as words currently considered profane but that are reaching greater levels of acceptance in conventional speech. Depending on which publication you hope to have the piece published in, be prepared to defend your story and urge skittish editors to publish it.

4) Write a story about Tourette's syndrome, which often manifests itself in sufferers shouting out words involuntarily. Talk to sufferers as well as physicians and therapists who treat the disease. Find out when the disease was first diagnosed, its history, and current treatment strategies.

LaVergne, TN USA
19 November 2010
205519LV00004B/2/P